PROFIT HUNGRY

PROFIT HUNGRY
The Food Industry in Canada

John W. Warnock

New Star Books • Vancouver

New Star Books
2504 York Avenue
Vancouver, B.C. V6K 1E3
Canada

Canadian Cataloguing in Publication Data

Warnock John W., 1933-
  Profit hungry

  Bibliography:
  Includes index
  ISBN 0-919888-86-0
  ISBN 0-919888-85-2 pa.
  1. Food industry and trade - Canada
I. Title
HD 9014.C32W35   338.4'7'641300971   C78-002145-2

For Betty

LIST OF TABLES

CONTENTS

PREFACE

My research for this book began in 1972 while I was still teaching in the Department of Economics and Political Science at the University of Saskatchewan in Saskatoon. It began as a study of the structure of agribusiness in Canada. As it developed, it grew in length. For the purposes of publication, I have limited the subject matter of the book to the structure of the food industry in Canada. The research and writing I have done on the role of the underdeveloped countries in the world food system, and an analysis of the structure of the farm supply industry in Canada, will have to wait for a later effort.

In 1974 I decided to resign my teaching position at the University of Saskatchewan. The protracted conflict in the department there was giving me a stomach ulcer. But I have also had many different jobs in my life, and I was beginning to feel that it was time, once again, to try something new. So in April of that year our family chose to begin a new career as commercial tree fruit growers in the Okanagan Valley in British Columbia.

Our new occupation has been rewarding in many ways. It is nice once again to be a producer. It has also provided me with a second perspective on the food industry in Canada. I learned about the cost-price squeeze first hand, as we took a rather substantial cut in our income. While I was familiar with credit unions and consumer co-operatives from our years in Saskatchewan, I could now add the experience of being an active member of a producer co-operative. We also sold our produce through a marketing board, and it didn't take long to learn just how weak they are in the highly concentrated wholesale market and to appreciate the difficulties they have when facing an open border. As the growing of apricots is most important to our survival on the farm, and as most of these are now processed,

9

we have first hand evidence of the effects of imports of processed fruits from low-wage countries. We came to understand the plight of the small Canadian fruit and vegetable processors. Our membership in the B.C. Fruit Growers Association, with its links to the Federation of Agriculture, helped me to learn more about the problems of farm organizations.

In 1977 and 1978 I participated as a resource person in the Ten Days study program of the B.C. Inter-Church Committee for World Development Education. This educational effort is sponsored by the Anglican, Roman Catholic, Lutheran, Presbyterian and United churches. I very much enjoyed visiting the different communities in British Columbia and meeting many people with widely varying backgrounds, interests, and views on the problems of the food industry and consumers. But these people also greatly helped me to understand the problems of food in the underdeveloped countries. As a result of participating in this programme, I was forced to look beyond North America and to discover how Canada and its food system fits into the world situation.

When I began this research I chose to use 1971 as a base line for all data, as this was the latest year for which Census figures were available. It took me an entire year of work (outside of my teaching) just to identify the firms in each area of food and beverage manufacturing and to dig out figures on their sales for 1971. This was made most difficult by the fact that so many of the major firms in the field are American branch plants, wholly owned by their parent firms, who publish no figures on their Canadian operations. The fact that Canadians cannot find out how foreign firms operate in this country is an indication of the colonial mentality which prevails in Ottawa and the extent to which the Liberal Party in particular, appropriately referred to as "The Governing Party," is subservient to the interests of foreign corporations.

Due to other pressures on my time, the manuscript of the book has been delayed beyond what I had originally hoped. Therefore, the reader may feel that the 1971 figures in the tables are a bit out of date. They are. It would take a great deal of time to go back now and update them to 1976. But more current figures would not be that important. All they would reveal is a greater domination by the same large firms. They would not show any major change in the structure of any of the individual food industries covered in this book.

Another fact which might be noticed by readers is the reference to American studies of the food industry. I have often had to cite U.S. studies simply because comparable work on the situation in Canada has not been done. We live in a continental food market, and the food industry assumes that Canadian consumers behave in the same manner as Americans. The North American food industry does not feel that it is necessary to do any separate studies of the Canadian situation. Canada is seen as a northern region of the American food market. Canadian academics seem to share this opinion.

The book as it now stands concentrates on the food and beverage manufacturing industries. In that respect it is different from and tends to complement Don Mitchell's *The Politics of Food*, which emphasizes problems at the farm and marketing board level. It is also different from Walter Stewart's *Hard To Swallow*, a journalistic effort which places most of its emphasis on retailing food and the problems caused here for consumers. These are the only two popular studies of the food industry in Canada. I feel that *Profit Hungry* fills a needed gap in this area.

One of the major problems I faced was whether or not to use footnotes. As a former academic, I was quite prepared to use them, as I have in my previous writings. But for two reasons I decided not to.

First, I have not written this book for academics. It is a trade book, oriented to the general reader who is interested in the question. The sources at the end of each chapter can lead to further reading. I also felt that endless footnotes tend to break the reading of an already complicated and detailed book.

The second reason has to do with sources. There is precious little written on the food industry in Canada. Aside from government studies and statistics, a great deal of the factual material on various industries and firms has been taken from trade publications such as *Canadian Grocer* and *Food in Canada,* and the financial press, in particular *The Financial Post, The Financial Times,* and the Toronto *Globe & Mail's* Report on Business. In the nineteen-page article I wrote on this subject for *Our Generation,* I used 71 footnotes. If I had tried to put in all the footnotes that one normally uses, it would have made the length of the manuscript unmanageable.

I would like to thank the Canada Council for providing me with a research grant that made possible my trip to Toronto and Ottawa to gather data on individual corporations. I appreciate the effort by the staff of the Analysis and Development Section, Manufacturing and Primary Industries Division, Statistics Canada for sending me material that had not yet appeared in printed form.

The staff in the Corporate Affairs section of the Department of Consumer and Corporate Affairs in Hull, Quebec was most co-operative and sympathetic to my efforts to obtain information on the wholly-owned branch plants of foreign corporations. The business libraries of the Toronto and Vancouver public libraries are excellent sources of information, and their staff members were very helpful.

The same can be said for the staff members in the government publications departments of the University of Saskatchewan and the University of British Columbia libraries.

Nadia Greschuk did statistical research and analysis for me, particularly in the area of wages in the food industry. Unfortunately, most of that material shall have to wait for a subsequent publication.

The original draft of the manuscript was greatly improved by the critical comments of those who read all or part of it. They include Harold Bronson, Cy Gonick, Fred Gudmundson, Pat Munro, Gary Teeple, Mel Watkins and Janet Stephens. Of course, I am completely responsible for the text as it now appears.

I would also like to thank the many people I have come to know over the years who are connected with the National Farmers Union. My comprehension of the position of the farmer in the food industry in Canada grew out of long talks with Roy Atkinson, Stuart Thiessen and many other active NFU members. I would also like to mention my particular association with the members of the NFU locals around North Battleford, Saskatchewan; the winter study programme with which I was associated was intended to increase their understanding of the Canadian economic system, but I am sure I learned more from them than they did from me.

All the people at New Star Books who have read and worked on my manuscript deserve special praise, and in particular, Stan Persky, Lanny Beckman, Lynda Yanz, David Smith and Joe Dougherty. They are certainly publishers with a difference.

Last but certainly not least, commendation must go to my wife Betty. Without her support this manuscript would never have reached the publication stage. She didn't type my manuscript; she did much of my orchard work so I could sit in my study. She has also had to put up with my frustrations and complaining over the past six years. I also regret the fact that this project has taken so much time away from Delia, Robert, and Duff. I only hope I can now find the time to make it up to them.

John W. Warnock
Naramata, B.C.
June 30, 1978

1. THE GROWTH OF OLIGOPOLY AND FOREIGN DOMINATION

Everyone has a direct personal interest in the food industry. For every society, the production of food is the most essential activity. It is the basis for all other economic activity. Most Canadians take the existence of food for granted. We expect that it will always be there and that we will be able to buy what we need. We never worry about food shortages, let alone famines.

As is the case in most advanced capitalist countries, there is only a small percentage of the work force actually producing food, and the number declines every year. In 1971 only 6% of the labour force was working in the primary production of food. Nevertheless, this is obviously a very important sector of the overall Canadian economy.

Each year Canadian farmers spend several billion dollars purchasing necessary inputs for their operation. Farm purchases are very important to the machinery, motor vehicles, fertilizer, pesticide, feed, and construction industries. Modern farming also requires large loans from the financial sector. Between 1969 and 1976, bank loans alone to farmers rose from $1 billion to $3.2 billion.

The food and beverage industry is the most important manufacturing industry in Canada. In 1971 the value of shipment of goods of this industry totalled over $9 billion, representing 18% of all manufacturing. It employed more people than any other sector in manufacturing: 218,313, or 13.4% of all manufacturing.

At the retail store level, food sales in 1971 totalled $7.9 billion, or 25.8% of all retail sales in Canada. The wholesaling of food and beverage items in that year totalled $6.2 billion, representing 24.6% of all wholesaling of consumer goods.

Added to this is the growing industry of providing food out of the home, through institutions and various kinds of restaurants. One out of every three meals is now eaten out in Canada.

Finally, there is a large sector of the provincial and federal governments that is directly involved in the agricultural and food support areas. It is an important source of employment.

The Major Questions

We live in a competitive capitalist society. Everyone is supposed to pursue his/her own self-interest. The production, distribution, and consumption of food is determined by our basic economic system. At every level, these practices are governed by the profit motive. Within such a system it is inevitable that conflicts emerge between different sectors of the total food industry, not excluding those who are only consumers. It is an adversary rather than a co-operative system.

In view of this, how can we judge whether or not the Canadian system of food production and distribution is doing a good, efficient job? Can we expect that the present system will provide everyone with an adequate income, security, health and well-being? Will it provide satisfaction for those who work in the food area?

For the market system to work, liberal economists insist that competition must exist. The alternative is a monopolistic system, with higher than necessary prices and misallocation of resources. How does the Canadian system, as it actually functions, measure up to the standards set for a competitive capitalist system?

In the area of production and distribution of food, we will see that Canada is in reality part of the American market. The large American food corporations are major factors in the food industry in Canada. We know that through our own experience.

But what effect does this have on the structure of the food industry in Canada? How does the American presence influence individual Canadian food firms? What is the effect of having very low tariffs and quotas on imports of foods from other countries?

We have heard a great deal about the rise of the multinational corporations and their key role in Canadian industry. As we will see, the food industry is not to be exempted from this development. What is the effect of the multinational corporation on the industry in Canada? Can or should we try to control those corporations which import foods from the underdeveloped countries? What is the effect of the corporate model of food production on the quality of food? These are the important questions that are the keys to understanding what is happening to farming, food production and distribution, and consumption in Canada.

14

THE GROWTH OF CONCENTRATION

It is common knowledge that throughout the Western capitalist world there is a steady trend towards the concentration of economic power in the hands of a small number of corporations operating on an international level. If capitalism is a competitive system, then weaker firms fall by the wayside, and the stronger prevail. This basic liberal theory operates largely according to plan in this case.

In theory, in any industry a monopoly will eventually emerge, if competition is carried to its logical conclusion. However, we know from historical reality that there comes a point in this process when the large firms stop competing against each other in this sense. We have seen the creation of combines and cartel agreements which divided up markets, set prices, and allowed the key dominant firms to survive.

Today, however, the formal combine or cartel is unusual. Instead, there is a general understanding among the major firms that they will allow each other to exist and to share the market. This is the basic characteristic of all advanced capitalist countries: the domination and control of all major industries by relatively few firms. This situation has traditionally been described by economists as *oligopoly*.

When firms operate on an international level, similar conditions occur. By the time a corporation moves into the international market, it is generally a large firm, dominant in its domestic industry. In most cases the multinational firm operates out of an oligopolistic situation in the home country.

At least since the time of the first international capitalist depression, we have witnessed the creation of international cartels. The fertilizer and petroleum industries offer classic examples of such cartels. The Economic Council of Canada defines a cartel as an "arrangement whereby independent business enterprises enter into agreements that have the purpose of restricting competition among them."

However, since World War II formal international cartels have declined in importance, primarily due to the domination of the United States and its business interests in the international market. While American firms have often participated in formal cartels, the U.S. government has on occasion taken action against them.

As a result, informal cartels are more prevalent today. These are arrangements by corporations through "gentlemen's agreements," tacit agreements, or simply the process of recognizing a price leader. Such a situation exists in the international farm machinery industry, as was documented by the Royal Commission on Farm Machinery.

Other existing cartels have had open government support. This has

15

been the tradition in Europe and Japan. But it is also true in Canada, though to a far lesser degree.

A perfect example would be the potash sharing agreement established by the Government of Saskatchewan. It established a system of allocation of market shares, a central selling agency for the private firms, and a government-enforced floor price.

Most recently it has been revealed that the Trudeau Government established a uranium cartel in 1972 covering the production of the five corporations in Canada; it also extended to South Africa, France, and Australia. The federal government in this case guaranteed Rio Algom Mines, Gulf Minerals Canada, and Denison Mines that they would not be charged with contravening the Combines Investigation Act.

But in today's business world, power is not simply measured by horizontal control of a single industry. This is the era of the conglomerate firm, where a corporation is active in several different industries.

Secondly, there is the fact of vertical integration. The power of a firm can be greatly increased if it is integrated backward into its source of basic supplies, and if it is integrated forward into the area where it markets its products.

In the real world of the present, this is the normal pattern of business operation in the advanced capitalist countries. The large modern corporation is a conglomerate, vertically integrated, and operating on a trans-national basis. The markets in which it operates are definitely not characterized by a high degree of price competition. As a result, these corporations, as we shall see in the food industry, are capable of earning profits that are higher than the average for the industry in which they operate, or are higher than the national average. They are certainly higher than the average for the smaller and medium sized firms.

Measuring Industry Concentration

The degree of monopoly control of an economy or of one of its industrial sectors has most often been judged according to the degree of concentration of sales, assets, profits and/or employees in the hands of the largest corporations. Concentration in manufacturing, as a whole, reveals the extent to which this basic sector of any advanced economy is controlled by a few corporations. If the *trend* in any market is towards a higher degree of concentration, this reveals the degree to which the larger corporations have economic and financial power as compared to the smaller firms.

16

Traditionally in Canada and the United States the standard of judgment used to measure the degree of oligopoly (control of a market by a few firms) has been that set forth by Joe S. Bain, one of the leading liberal business economists in the United States. Under Bain's system, an industry is judged by the percentage of sales, assets, profits, or employees held by the four largest firms. His classification is as follows:

1. 75% to 100% — very highly concentrated oligopoly
2. 65% to 75% — highly concentrated oligopoly
3. 50% to 65% — high-moderate oligopoly
4. 35% to 50% — low-grade oligopoly
5. under 35% — unconcentrated

For this study, the only available criterion for judging the share of market held in the food and beverage industry is sales. This is due to the fact that there are a large number of wholly-owned subsidiaries of foreign corporations operating in Canada which do not publish or make available statistics on assets, profits, or employees. While the federal government has these statistics, it does not make them public.

In contrast to the United States, there has been precious little data available on the degree of concentration in Canada. In 1971 the Combines Commissioner issued his report for the Department of Consumer and Corporate Affairs, using data for 1965. Prior to this, the only substantial published study was that done by Gideon Rosenbluth, published in 1957, using 1948 data.

The study for 1965 covered about 170,000 corporations doing business in Canada. In that year, 174 corporations (.1%) had about 50% of the total assets of all corporate enterprises. Of the non-financial corporations, the largest ninety-four had 38% of all assets in this area. The fifty largest manufacturing corporations had 40% of the assets in that sector. In 1965, the 100 largest manufacturing corporations had 42% of all manufacturing shipments; by 1970, Statistics Canada reported that their share had risen to 47%.

Every year the federal government issues a report on corporations under the Corporations and Labour Unions Returns Act (CALURA). The latest report at this writing was for 1975, and covered about 206,000 non-financial companies operating in Canada.

The top 500 corporations, representing less than one-quarter of one per cent of all non-financial enterprises, accounted for 51.2% of all sales and 63.4% of all profits earned in Canada in 1975. They also accounted for 59.2% of all assets and 65.4% of the equity in such enterprises in that year.

The top 100 corporations accounted for 34.3% of sales, 39.2% of

17

assets, 40.9% of profits, and 44.9% of equity. This data reveals the very high degree of concentration of power in the Canadian economy.

Exact comparisons between Canada and the United States simply do not exist, but enough data is available to make general conclusions. In 1963, the fifty largest corporations in the United States accounted for 25% of the value added by manufacturing. In 1965 in Canada, the top fifty corporations in manufacturing accounted for 36% of the total value added by manufacturing. In 1963 the top 100 U.S. corporations accounted for 33% of all value added; in 1965 the top 100 Canadian corporations accounted for 46%.

When a breakdown of manufacturing is done by individual industries, the study of the Combines Commissioner found that of 116 Canadian industries surveyed, ninety-eight were "significantly more concentrated than their U.S. counterparts." This conclusion was the same as that reached by Professor Gideon Rosenbluth in his study for 1948.

Furthermore, the classification of industries by the two governments differ significantly. Had the study by the Combines Investigator been able to use the more detailed U.S. classifications, Canadian concentration levels would have been even higher in comparison. The conclusion of the study by the Combines Commissioner was that "concentration in manufacturing as a whole would appear to be considerably higher in Canada than in the United States."

The Food and Beverage Industry in the United States

In both countries, the concentration level in the food and beverage industry is very high. In the U.S. in 1963 there were about 31,000 manufacturers of food, of which 20,000 were corporations. The 100 largest firms accounted for 45.8% of the value added to manufacturing, 58% of the total assets, and 71.1% of the total profits. Concentration has been increasing over the years. There has been a steady decline in the non-corporate sector of food manufacturing, reflecting the demise of the independent proprietor.

The study by the U.S. Federal Trade Commission for the National Commission on Food Marketing (1966) found that the largest firms had the highest profits. In each of the different industries in the food and beverage area the leading firms enjoyed a rate of return on investment that was 25% above the industry average as a whole. Their general conclusions were as follows:

In most industries: (1) gross profit margins of larger firms have grown more rapidly than those of smaller firms; (2) profit rates of larger firms are considerably higher than those of other industry members and the industry average; (3) the larger firms exhibit greater stability in rate of profit than do firms in other asset-size groups; and (4) these trends seem to be most pronounced in areas of higher concentration and increasing product differentiation.

These conclusions are supported by other independent U.S. studies of the relation between high levels of concentration and high profits. The most widely cited is that of Norman R. Collins and Lee E. Preston, covering the period from 1935-1955, but there are others as well.

The Food and Beverage Industry in Canada

The degree of concentration in the food and beverage manufacturing industry in Canada is demonstrated in Table Ia. Of the sixteen industries surveyed, total shipments by 4,638 firms in 1970 were $8,283.8 million. This represents about 95% of the shipments (sales) of the food and beverage industry as a whole in that year.

Between 1965 and 1970 the number of enterprises (firms) which either went bankrupt or were absorbed by other enterprises totalled 1,373, for a decline of 22.8%. The number of establishments (plants) that were shut down totalled 1,338, a decline of 19.8%. While the value of total shipments for the sixteen industries covered increased by 34.9% between 1965 and 1970, the number of total employees increased by only 1.4%.

The share of the national market controlled by the top four firms varies from 29% for the dairy products industry to over 80% for the flour and breakfast cereal industry, vegetable oil mills, sugar refineries, distilleries and breweries. The tobacco industry is also very highly concentrated, with the four largest firms having over 90% of the national market. In recent year this industry has moved into the food and beverage area as well.

But as both the U.S. Federal Trade Commission and the Director of Investigation and Research for the Combines Act are quick to point out, national concentration figures can be very misleading. In many industries there is simply no national market. For most consumers, they must buy in a much more restricted local market.

In the food and beverage industry, there are no national markets for some products due to perishability, weight, or industry practices. These include poultry, dairy products, feed manufacturers, bakeries, soft drinks, and to some extent meat packing. A survey of these

TABLE Ia

Concentration in the Food and Beverage Industry, 1965 & 1970

Industry	Firms		Plants		Percent Top 4		Shipments Top 8	
	1965	1970	1965	1970	1965	1970	1965	1970
Slaughtering and Meat Proc.	365	407	399	453	58	53	68	62
Poultry Processors	137	86	150	102	24	37	38	53
Dairy Factories and Cheese	1165	643	1421	880	25	29	35	42
Fruit & Vegetable Canners	266	187	313	238	39	42	52	58
Feed Manufacturers	739	647	855	789	28	29	38	39
Flour Mills & Breakfast Cereals	36	32	51	51	80	70	90	88
Biscuit Manufacturers	36	34	44	42	67	68	84	84
Bakeries	2376	1857	2465	1921	32	31	44	45
Confectionery Manu.	173	132	180	139	47	53	65	72
Sugar Refineries	8	7	13	14	95	95	100	100
Vegetable Oil Mills	10	10	12	10	81	78	100	100
Miscellaneous Food Manu.	240	228	272	275	33	34	48	50
Soft Drink Manu.	410	333	470	395	41	46	48	54
Distilleries	13	12	22	27	84	86	96	98
Breweries	11	9	52	42	95	94	99	100
Wineries	13	14	19	22	71	64	95	95
Totals/Averages	5996	4638	6738	5400	56	57	69	71

NOTE: Statistics Canada does not provide figures for top 4 and top 8 firms for Breakfast Cereal Manufacturers, Sugar Refineries, and Vegetable Oil Mills. Estimates are from industry sources.

The franchise system, as exists in the soft drink industry, grossly misrepresents the degree of concentration and foreign ownership.

SOURCE: Department of Consumer and Corporate Affairs, *Concentration in the Manufacturing Industries in Canada*. Ottawa: The Queen's Printer, 1971. Appendix, Table A-1; Statistics Canada, *Industrial Organization and Concentration in the Manufacturing, Mining, and Logging Industries*, 1970. Cat. 31-402. Ottawa: Information Canada, December 1975.

industries in the United States by Frank J. Kottke, presented to the U.S. Senate Subcommittee on Antitrust and Monopoly, revealed that regional concentration ratios were, on the average, 50% higher than national concentration ratios.

The study published by the Department of Consumer and Corporate Affairs for 1965 shows the share of the market of the top four and eight firms for some industries on a regional basis. In the ten food and beverage industries included (see Table Ib), the regional concentration was much higher than the national concentration.

TABLE Ib

Regional Concentration in the Food and Beverage Industry, 1965

Industry	(Shipments) Share of Top 4	Share of Top 8
Slaughtering and Meat Processors	76	96
Poultry Processors	60	80
Dairy Factories and Cheese Manufacturers	67	81
Fruit and Vegetable Canners and Preservers	53	73
Flour Mills	83	99
Bakeries	46	55
Confectionery Manufacturers	66	82
Miscellaneous Food Manufacturers	52	72
Soft Drink Manufacturers	53	75
Breweries	93	100
Industry Averages	65	81

NOTE: These are the only food and beverage industries covered by the study.

SOURCE: Department of Consumer and Corporate Affairs, *Concentration in the Manufacturing Industries of Canada*. Ottawa: The Queen's Printer, 1971, Appendix, Table A-7.

Tables Ic and Id reveal the extent to which the large corporations dominate the food and beverage industry in Canada. The Census year 1971 was chosen as the base used in this study. The seventy-two firms listed here are all of those in the food manufacturing industry in 1971 whose sales were over $10 million, with the exception of co-operatives and food manufacturers who are subsidiaries of chain supermarkets.

These last two categories were omitted because of the inability to obtain relevant data from the firms.

After discounting the non-food sales of a few of the large conglomerates, we can estimate that this handful of corporations (roughly 1.5% of the total in the food and beverage manufacturing industry) accounted for over 75% of total sales in 1971. Clearly, there is a very high degree of concentration in the food and beverage industry.

Thus, it is apparent that statistics showing the share of *each individual industry* by the top four firms does not present a true picture of economic concentration. This is due to the fact that the large firms are diversified and operate in several different food and non-food industries. The growth of the conglomerate firm in the food and beverage industry has been the single most important industry development in the past twenty years. And with it has come the expansion of vertical integration. A large firm which can integrate back to the source of its inputs, and can expand into the area of distribution of food, has a tremendous advantage in terms of market power over the small firm, operating in one industry, which must buy and sell in oligopolized markets. The growth of the conglomerate firm certainly deserves special attention.

THE DEVELOPMENT OF THE CONGLOMERATE FIRM

Both the study by the U.S. Federal Trade Commission (1966) and the Combines Commissioner (1971) reveal that there has been a very significant growth in conglomerate mergers in manufacturing, and in particular in the food and beverage industry. The large firms in the field have branched out into other industries (food and non-food) and now normally operate in many different areas.

In the United States, the FTC found that the 200 largest firms in the food and beverage industry in 1963 were, on the average, manufacturing in more than six different food areas. This was a 50% increase in diversification in just a ten year period. Large non-food manufacturers (particularly tobacco and soap corporations) were entering the food business. This diversification had been achieved primarily by the merger (takeover) of existing firms in the food area.

The same trend has been occurring in Canada. Statistics Canada did a special tabulation of all manufacturing industries for the 1965 study on concentration. Of the 30,348 business enterprises in manufacturing in that year, 29,895 (or 98.6%) were operating in only one industry.

TABLE Ic

Canadian Controlled Food and Beverage Corporations
1971 Sales of Over $10 Million

Company	Ownership and/or Control	Sales
Canada Packers	W.F. McLean	$937,720,000
Seagrams Co. Ltd.	Bronfman family	687,000,000
John Labatt Ltd.	Brascan	426,757,000
Burns Foods	R.H. Webster	359,301,000
Hiram Walker Gooderham & Worts	Hatch family	345,000,000
Molson Industries	Molson family	314,700,000
Silverwood Industries	Silverwood family	118,043,000
Intercontinental Packers	Mendel family	95,720,000
J.M. Schneider Ltd.	Schneider family	84,163,000
B.C. Sugar Refinery	Rogers family	71,408,000
Jannock Corporation	Glengair-Tannenbaum	67,750,000
McCain's Foods	McCain family	60,000,000
Becker Milk Co.	Euclid Securities/Lowe family	56,956,000
General Bakeries	Dominion Stores/Argus	36,225,000
Crush International	McConnell Trust	35,909,000
Vachon Inc.	Societe de Fiducie	34,500,000
Essex Packers	McPharlin family	33,620,000
Sucronel	McConnell family	25,000,000
F.G. Bradley Co.	Bradley family	21,000,000
Agra Industries	Torchinsky family	20,946,000
Moosehead Breweries	Oland family	19,200,000
Dover Industries	M.M. Campbell	17,793,000
Canadian Food Products Ltd.	Del Zotto family	16,419,000
Old Dutch Foods	Winnipeg interests	13,816,000
T.G. Bright & Co.	Hatch Estate	10,474,000

SOURCES: Financial Post, *Survey of Industrials,* 1974; Annual Reports of the public corporations; Dun & Bradstreet (Canada) Ltd., *Canadian Key Business Directory,* 1972, for private firms which publish no records of their financial operations.

TABLE Id

Foreign Controlled Food and Beverage Corporations
1971 Sales of Over $10 Million

Company	Ownership and/or Control	Sales
IMASCO	U.K.—Imperial Tobacco	$569,629,000
Canadian Breweries	S.A.—Rembrandt Industries	396,210,000
Swift Canadian Co. Ltd.	U.S.—Swift & Co.	280,440,000
Maple Leaf Mills Ltd.	U.S.—Norris Grain Co.	202,154,000
General Foods Ltd.	U.S.—General Foods Corp.	181,816,000
Kraft Foods Ltd.	U.S.—Kraftco	161,443,000
Standard Brands Ltd.	U.S.—Standard Brands Co.	148,541,000
Beatrice Foods (Canada) Ltd.	U.S.—Beatrice Foods Inc.	135,000,000
Lever Brothers Ltd.	U.K.—Unilever	114,428,000
Coca Cola Ltd.	U.S.—Coca Cola Co.	110,213,000
Procter & Gamble (Canada) Ltd.	U.S.—Procter & Gamble Co.	108,704,000
Robin Hood Multifoods Ltd.	U.S.—International Multifoods	104,881,000
Redpath Industries Ltd.	U.K.—Tate & Lyle Ltd.	86,341,000
Ralston Purina (Canada) Ltd.	U.S.—Ralston Purina Co.	82,896,000
Nabisco Ltd.	U.S.—National Biscuit Co.	74,023,000
Campbell Soup Co. Ltd.	U.S.—Campbell Soup Co.	70,505,000
Borden Co. Ltd.	U.S.—Borden Inc.	66,903,000
H.J. Heinz Co. of Canada Ltd.	U.S.—H.J. Heinz Co.	66,205,000
Brooke Bond Foods Ltd.	U.S.—Brooke Bond Liebig Ltd.	59,681,000
Canadian Canners Ltd.	U.S.—California Packing Corp.	50,582,000
Pepsi-Cola Canada Ltd.	U.S.—PepsiCo Inc.	50,167,000
Nestle (Canada) Ltd.	Switz.—Nestle Alimentana Co.	48,844,000
Consolidated Foods Canada Ltd.	U.S.—Consolidated Foods Corp.	46,800,000
Cadbury, Schweppes & Powell Ltd.	U.S.—Cadbury, Schweppes Ltd.	46,500,000
Quaker Oats Co. (Canada) Ltd.	U.S.—Quaker Oats Co.	45,680,000
General Mills Canada Ltd.	U.S.—General Mills Co.	44,000,000
Carnation Company Ltd.	U.S.—Carnation Co.	40,969,000
Distillers Co. (Canada) Ltd.	U.K.—Distillers Co.	40,500,000
Hershey Chocolate of Canada Ltd.	U.S.—Hershey Foods Corp.	40,000,000
Canada Starch Co.	U.S.—CPC International	36,000,000
National Agri-Services Ltd.	U.S.—Cargill Inc.	32,623,000

24

Green Giant of Canada	U.S.—Green Giant Co.	31,000,000
Kellogg Co. (Canada) Ltd.	U.S.—Kellogg Co.	30,000,000
Libby-McNeil & Libby of Canada	Switz.—Nestle Alimentana Co.	30,000,000
Canadian Salt Co. Ltd.	U.S.—Morton Industries	26,523,000
Adams Brands Ltd.	U.S.—Warner-Lambert Inc.	25,000,000
Humpty-Dumpty/Mott	U.S.—American Brands	25,000,000
Canadian Schenley Distillers	U.S.—D.W.S. Corporation	22,000,000
Rowntree MacKintosh Canada Ltd.	U.K.—Rowntree MacKintosh Ltd.	20,376,000
Alberta Distilleries Ltd.	U.S.—National Distillers Inc.	18,584,000
Gilbey Canada	U.K.—International Distillers	17,898,000
Canada Dry/Hunt Industries	U.S.—Norton-Simon Inc.	15,000,000
Dominion Seven-Up Co. Ltd.	U.S.—Seven-Up Co.	13,653,000
Dole of Canada Ltd.	U.S.—Castle & Cooke Inc.	13,500,000
Associated Biscuits of Canada	U.K.—Assoc. Biscuit Manu. Ltd.	13,137,000
Chiquita Brands (Canada) Ltd.	U.S.—United Brands	12,742,000
Cott Beverages Ltd.	U.S.—National Industries Inc.	11,131,000

NOTE: A number of wholly-owned foreign corporations do not publish any figures on their Canadian operations. Dun & Bradstreet (Canada) Ltd. estimates sales figures for some of these. The remainder are at best guestimates from figures in *Moody's Industrials.*

SOURCES: Financial Post, *Survey of Industrials, 1974.* Annual Reports of the Corporations filings of federally incorporated corporations, Department of Consumer and Corporate Affairs. Dun & Bradstreet (Canada) Ltd., *Canadian Key Business Directory,* 1972. *Moody's Industrials.*

There were only 453 firms operating in two or more industries, *yet they accounted for 52% of all factory shipments.* In manufacturing as a whole, the domination by a few large conglomerate firms is very pronounced.

This carries over to the food and beverage industry as well. The foreign-owned firms (see Table Id) are all large conglomerate firms operating in many food and beverage areas. The few large Canadian food corporations (with sales over $100 million) are also conglomerate operations (see Table Ic).

Canada Packers not only dominates the meat packing industry, but is also a prominent firm in the following industries: poultry, dairy, fruit and vegetable canning, edible oils, feed, hatcheries, leather tanneries, and soap. Burns Foods operates a large string of dairies and a large grocery wholesale operation in addition to packing meat. John Labatt has branched out of the brewing area into wine, canned and frozen foods, dairies, food services, confectionery, flour mills, bakeries, feed, hatcheries, and poultry processing. While Molson

Industries still obtains a majority of its revenues from brewing, it has decided to diversify in non-food areas: hardware and lumber retailing, office equipment and furniture, petroleum marketing equipment, and construction products.

Hiram-Walker and Seagrams have remained primarily distilling firms. But they have grown large through expansion abroad, mainly in the United States. For both firms, about 80% of their sales are outside Canada. In recent years, Seagrams has been diversifying at a noticeable rate.

Vertical Integration

Related to the growth of horizontal conglomerate growth has been vertical integration, both back into basic sources and forward into the marketing areas. This has been most visible in the grocery retailing area, where the large chains in both Canada and the United States have integrated back into food manufacturing and wholesale distribution. In 1963, the U.S. Federal Trade Commission found that the largest retail chains accounted for eleven of the top 200 food and beverage manufacturers.

In Canada, the empire created by George Weston is perhaps the best example of vertical integration in the Western capitalist world. There is hardly a single area of food manufacturing and distribution that has escaped the corporation's takeover policy. The other national chains are also significantly integrated back into food production and wholesaling.

Many of the large food manufacturers are also integrated back into the area of food production at the primary level. In the 1960s, there was a significant move by the larger conglomerate corporations into direct production of food at the farm level. To some degree this has levelled off. As *Fortune Magazine* pointed out in 1972, the corporations found that farming was not profitable (aside from land speculation), as they had to provide the capital, hire the managers, and pay for farm labour. The growth of the United Farm Workers Union in California was also a deterrent to profitable farming at the corporate level. Instead, the large corporations have shifted to contract farming, where the independent farmer has to provide the capital, his own labour, and pay for seasonal help.

In Canada, the vertical integration of the food corporations into direct ownership of farm land has never advanced to the same degree as in the United States. The main reason for this seems to be the existence of marketing boards, and the fact that on the whole farming is organized more on a small family basis in Canada than in the United

States. Nevertheless, there is some direct ownership of farms in eggs and poultry production, fruit and vegetable growing, and in feed lot animal production.

Of more significance is the movement of the food and beverage corporations into the area of packaging: production of metal cans, glass containers, wooden containers, paper boxes, paper bags, and commercial printing. A study by the U.S. Federal Trade Commission in 1963 found that fourteen of the fifteen largest canners in the United States had integrated into can making. They concluded that this was not only due to their desire for increased market power, but because the industry was "highly oligopolistic"; the returns on equity were 20% per year, higher than the 14% average return in the canning industry itself.

The other major area of integration by the food and beverage conglomerates has been in the area of food distribution through institutional food services, restaurants, and fast food operations. All the large conglomerates in Canada are moving in this direction, and in this case they are following behind developments in the United States.

For example, Jim Hightower lists thirty-four of the largest American food corporations; all of them are in conglomerate food and beverage manufacturing, and all of them are operating chains of restaurants or fast food outlets. This includes such familiar names as Borden, Campbell Soup, Carnation, CPC International, General Foods, Green Giant, H.J. Heinz, Kraftco, Nestle, Pet, Pillsbury, Quaker Oats, Ralston Purina, and United Brands. All of these corporations are among the largest food and beverage firms operating in Canada.

Vertical integration is a characteristic of the large food conglomerates. Control over supply and markets gives these corporations a distinct advantage over the single-industry food manufacturer. Some economists have argued that the control that derives from vertical integration is more significant than that which comes from strictly horizontal concentration. The main text will give a number of examples of the market power which stems from this type of corporate organization.

Advantages of Conglomerate Structure

There are a number of advantages that a conglomerate firm has over a firm that operates in only one industry. In summary, they are as follows:

1. *Subsidization*—transferring economic support from one

27

     market to another to overcome short-run difficulties, and to break into new markets;

2. *Full-line selling*—the economic power which comes from having a long line of products to sell;
3. *Greater brand recognition*—by having products in a number of different industries and wider advertising;
4. *Reciprocity*—the economic power which comes from being in the business of both manufacturing and marketing;
5. *Forbearance*—the "live-and-let-live" atmosphere which prevails between the large conglomerate firms, respecting each other's share of the market and the avoidance of active price competition;
6. *Higher profits*—this appears to be a by-product of conglomerate food corporations, as their profit rates are close to double the industry average.

In the food and beverage industry, conglomerate firms have a special advantage which derives from the fact that the industry is characterized by a very high degree of product differentiation, brand name identification, and advertising. These are the major factors contributing to the development of a monopolized industry and therefore warrant further examination.

THE POWER OF MARKETING

Since the end of World War II, we have witnessed the rapid proliferation of items carried by the average-sized supermarket, from around 3,000 items to over 8,000. Furthermore, most shopping today is done in the large supermarkets. Jennifer Cross cites three separate studies done in the United States which found that the food shopper spends on the average 27-29 minutes in the store selecting merchandise. This means that the buyer passes, on the average, 300 items per minute. Under such circumstances, *brand identification is essential*, as price-comparison shopping is nearly impossible.

The *Progressive Grocer* found that 60% of U.S. shoppers no longer made shopping lists before they went to the supermarket. A survey done by David T. Kollatt for the American Marketing Association found that 50.5% of all food purchases made by the customer were on impulse. Other studies for the Grocery Manufacturers Association of America revealed that customers with a relatively good knowledge of prices could at best remember only within 5% the prices from their last trip to the supermarket—even for staple items.

In 1977 a survey of shopping behaviour was conducted by Dupont Corporation and the Point of Advertising Institute in the United States. This was the most complete study of consumer behavior since 1965, carried out in 200 supermarkets.

It found that the average shopper spent 24.9 minutes in the store and spent on the average $17.68. While many shoppers made lists ahead of time, 46.8% of all purchases were still not planned. Two-thirds of all decisions on which brand to choose were made on the spot in the store and not ahead of time.

The study also found that the longer a shopper could be kept in the store, the more money he or she would spend. An extra ten minutes would, on the average, add $9 to the cash register.

Developing "New" Products

In spite of the existing proliferation of similar items in the food stores, the food and beverage manufacturers continue to turn out more and more "new" products every year. The most thorough study of this aspect of the industry was made by Robert D. Buzzell and Robert E. M Nourse of Harvard Business School. They concluded that in the period between 1946 and 1964 there were only eighteen items introduced which could be considered "innovative": representing an "entirely new process." A second category of food items were those which were "distinctly new": new enough that "the manufacturer had to put in the basic work of research and development and test marketing."

However, Buzzell and Nourse concluded that at least 80% of the "new" products that appeared on the market were simply minor modifications (if that) of existing products. They described these as "me too" products.

The number of "new" items being introduced by the industry each year is almost beyond belief. A survey done by A.C. Nielsen for *Supermarket News* found that in the United States in 1966 there were 7,300 "new" items and in 1967, 8,000. This included items ranging from the idea stage to market introduction. Another survey done by Nielsen for the Grocery Manufacturers of America found that in 1967 the average supermarket in the United States was offered seventy-nine new items per week, and accepted, on the average, eighteen. A spokesman for Loblaws told the House of Commons Special Committee on Trends in Food Prices in 1973 that "new" products come to them on the average of fifty-four items per week, or 2,808 per year.

The costs involved in developing and introducing "new" products in an already grossly over-developed market are, of course, quite high. The survey done by A.C. Nielsen (and supported by Buzzell and Nourse) found that 80%-85% of the "new" food items will fail before they reach the marketing state. Buzzell and Nourse found that the average firm spent (in 1965) about $345,000 just to bring a "new" product into the *idea* stage.

For a "distinctly new product," Buzzell and Nourse found that it cost the firm about $1.8 million to carry it through one year of advertising. For an "innovative product," they found that the firm spent on the average $750,000 to introduce it and about $5.7 million for the first year for marketing. What this means is that the introduction of "new" products is limited to the large corporations; all the small manufacturer can do, in reality, is copy an existing product and hope to gain a small share of the market.

The high degree of product differentiation in a glutted market, plus the high costs of introducing "new" products, means that it is cheaper for a corporation to buy out existing companies and their established brand names than to develop "new" ones on their own. For example, Crush International, a Canadian-controlled beverage firm, was able to succeed in a highly oligopolized market (soft drinks) by buying established American brand names: Orange Crush, Hires Root Beer, and Royal Crown Cola. On the other side of the problem, Granby Co-op in Quebec produces about 30% of the cheese manufactured in Canada and sells it to Kraft Foods. The manager of the co-op feels that they have no alternative. They know that there is no way that they could sell that much cheese in the Canadian market under their own brand name. Kraft Foods has about 80% of the cheese market in Canada, a highly developed brand identification, a vast advertising programme, and tremendous corporate power behind it.

The Role of Advertising and Promotion

In a market which is characterized by a high degree of product differentiation, and where price competition has generally been ruled out by the dominant firms, there can only be conditions leading to monopolistic practices. As the specific studies of individual manufacturing industries have shown, in such markets advertising is a major barrier to entry by new firms.

A firm trying to break into such a market must spend very large amounts on advertising and promotion. As a general rule, they must also have sufficient economic backing to be able to sell their product at a price lower than those of the established national brands. In addition, they face the fact that the well-established large firms usually have advantages of scale of production.

The food and beverage industry is by far the largest advertiser in both Canada and the United States. The high degree of advertising and brand promotion is a major factor in the growing monopoly concentration in the industry. The oligopolistic markets, characterized by a high degree of product differentiation, also provide a major stimulus to the rise of the conglomerate firm, for with the volume of advertising comes very substantial discounts.

Advertising in the United States

The study by the U.S. Federal Trade Commission found that between 1950 and 1964 advertising in the food and beverage industry in the United States increased 300% to $1,400 million. This spending is highly concentrated in the dominant firms. In 1963, there were about 31,000 firms in the U.S. food and beverage industry. Yet in that year a total of only 337 corporations bought *all* network advertising, and seventy-two of these were in the food and beverage field.

In 1965, the twenty largest food firms spent 44% of the total of all spending by food and beverage firms on advertising; the fifty largest spent 80% of the total. In 1964 the twenty largest food firms accounted for 71% of network television advertising and 60% of magazine advertising by all food firms. Furthermore, the degree of concentration in advertising spending is steadily increasing.

Testimony before the U.S. Senate Antitrust and Monopoly Subcommittee revealed that volume discounts available to national television advertisers ranged between 40% and 60%. Smaller advertisers have to pay much more for similar time exposure. Very large advertisers, like General Foods, can obtain even larger discounts.

Similar discounts are available from magazines and newspapers, where food and beverage firms usually spend the balance of their advertising budget. The U.S. Federal Trade Commission found that in 1965 the large national magazines gave between 12% and 17% discounts to firms which spent over $2 million per year. Newspapers gave discounts of between 20% and 40% to firms which ran full-page or large advertisements on a weekly basis, over an entire year.

Advertising in Canada

A similar situation exists in Canada. A small number of large corporations account for most national advertising. Table Ie lists the twenty-two food and beverage firms in the top fifty national advertisers in 1970. These food and beverage firms accounted for about 47% of the advertising by the top fifty corporations in Canada.

TABLE Ie

Largest Food and Beverage Advertisers in Canada, 1970

Rank	Company	Ownership/Control	Spending
2.	Procter & Gamble Co. of Canada	U.S.	$6,198,203
3.	General Foods Ltd.	U.S.	5,686,946
4.	Canadian Breweries	U.K./S.A.	5,655,014
5.	IMASCO Ltd.	U.K.	4,984,007
6.	Warner-Lambert Canada Ltd.	U.S.	4,623,898
7.	Molson Industries Ltd.	Canada	4,362,022
10.	Kraft Foods Ltd.	U.S.	3,862,013
16.	Benson & Hedges Canada Ltd.	U.S.	3,312,541
18.	Lever Brothers Ltd.	U.K.	3,031,671
22.	Kellogg Co. of Canada	U.S.	2,855,227
26.	Nestle Canada Ltd.	Switzerland	2,441,254
27.	Coca Cola Ltd.	U.S.	2,414,472
28.	Standard Brands Ltd.	U.S.	2,356,370
33.	Labatt Breweries of Canada	Canada	2,184,057
35.	Seagrams Co. Ltd.	Canada	2,129,524
36.	Campbell Soup Co.	U.S.	1,937,270
37.	Dominion Stores Ltd.	Canada	1,842,280
39.	Quaker Oats Co. of Canada Ltd.	U.S.	1,790,170
42.	Salada Foods Ltd.	U.S.	1,593,684
45.	Wm. Wrigley Jr. Co. Ltd.	U.S.	1,480,845
46.	Hiram Walker-Gooderham & Worts	Canada	1,476,319
50.	Nabisco Ltd.	U.S.	1,367,340

SOURCE: Elliott Research Corporation, Toronto. Reprinted in *The Financial Post*, May 8, 1971, A-5.

NOTE: Total spending reported by the top fifty corporations was $142.9 million. Of this, the twenty-two firms in the food and beverage field accounted for $67 million, or around 47%. The five Canadian-controlled firms accounted for only 18% of spending by the food and beverage firms listed above.

The Food Prices Review Board did a survey in 1974 of the advertising expenditures by sixty-two major food corporations in Canada. In that year, the sales of this group were about $8,000 million and covered over 60% of total sales in the industry in that year. They spent over $100 million on advertising. While the Board did not estimate the share of the total advertising held by these firms, they published a chart by the Elliott Research Corporation for 1974 which listed total advertising expenditures in the "food and food products" industry at $85.9 million (the discrepancy is accounted for by the fact that the survey did not include local press, radio and television advertising). It is surprising that the Board did not make any comparisons between spending by large and small food corporations. In any case, it is quite clear that a very few number of firms account for a very high percentage of total advertising in the food and beverage industry in Canada.

Discounts are also available to large advertisers in Canada. In 1975, for prime-time television hours, CTV offered discounts of between 3% and 15% for network programmes; CBC offered discounts of between 3% and 21%. *Maclean's* discounts ranged between 3% and 17%, depending on volume and regularity. The Toronto *Globe and Mail* offered a 22% discount for a full page advertisement; the *Toronto Star*, 17%. All of the above give larger discounts to regular volume advertisers.

Other Promotional Activities

The large corporations also spend significant amounts on other forms of product promotion. The following were cited in the hearings of the House of Commons Special Committee on Trends in Food Prices in 1973:

1. *Buying shelf space*. Most of the large supermarkets sell shelf space in the store. As detailed studies have shown, items sell much better when raised from the floor, to waist, and to eye level. In Canada, this is a $300 million business.
2. *Special Displays*. Food manufacturers pay amounts for the end-of-aisle displays and special individual displays placed throughout the store. In 1973, Dominion Stores charged $9,000 for an end-of-aisle display for one item, for one week. The smaller corporate chain, A & P, charged $3,500 for the same space.
3. *Co-operative advertising*. The food and beverage manufacturer pays a fee to a supermarket to cover space in weekly newspaper advertisements. Very often this helps the manufacturer clear out a backlog of certain items through special sales.
4. *Volume discounts*. All the large food and beverage manufacturers offer discounts (usually between 5% and 15%)

33

for buyers who purchase in large amounts, usually by the railroad carload.

5. *Cash discounts*. Buyers who pay cash for their orders, or pay within a short period of time, are also offered (as a general rule) an additional discount.

6. *Kickbacks*. While the chain stores deny this practice exists, it is well-known in the industry that salesmen from the food and beverage distributors offer kickbacks to individuals working in stores to see that their products are displayed.

For the large chain stores, promotional advertising is an important source of revenues. Walter Stewart found that in 1972 Steinberg's received $3.6 million in volume discounts, $4 million in cash discounts, and $5.2 million in "product promotion allowances." The total, $12.7 million, was more than the profits for the Steinberg chain in that year.

Advertising and Conglomerate Mergers

The development of the conglomerate firm in the food and beverage field has been one of its most significant characteristics. In a market which is characterized by a very high degree of product differentiation, the takeover of other established firms is the normal way in which an existing firm enters a new industry. This is true of both horizontal and vertical expansion.

The advantages in advertising discounts and the high cost of developing and marketing a "new" food product seem to be the major factors involved in conglomerate expansion. The 1966 study by the U.S. Federal Trade Commission found that the greater profitability of many of the acquiring corporations was simply a result of larger advertising discounts due to economics which resulted from the addition of new brands to advertise.

The big food and beverage manufacturers generally spend most of their sales promotion budget on advertising. Some, however, like the breweries, split the budget. A minority of the large firms spend more on sales promotion. Standard Brands and General Foods spend large amounts on various promotional gimmicks.

It is important to remember that these sales promotion efforts are in reality only available to the dominant firms. Small firms simply do not have the resources to compete in this type of promotion. Furthermore, the "benefits" of this spending fall to the large chain stores, and to a lesser degree to the large voluntary chains (like IGA Canada Ltd.) who are captives of large wholesalers. As Walter Stewart points out, the sales promotion system is a form of income-distribution: "It takes money from the smaller store and gives it to the bigger one."

Within the food and beverage industry, there is a very wide range of spending on advertising between industries. In those with a high degree of product differentiation (like soft drinks, candy, miscellaneous food products, and breakfast cereals) there is very high spending on advertising, between 8% and 12% of sales. In the industries where there is a low degree of product differentiation (like sugar, meat, and milk) advertising is generally less than 2% of sales.

The various studies by the staff of the U.S. Federal Trade Commission have found that the "high product differentiation industries were the only ones to experience increasing profit as a percentage of sales since 1947." In 1947, the big corporations spent less on advertising than the small corporations; this has changed dramatically. In the United States, between 1947 and 1965 the profits of the small manufacturers declined, while those of the large manufacturers rose. It is unfortunate that the Food Prices Review Board did not see the need to compare the profit rates in Canada between the large and small food manufacturers. But then the Board spent most of its time attacking farmers and marketing boards; it did not seem to be concerned about the corporate sector of the food industry.

The 1966 study by the U.S. Federal Trade Commission found that in 1962 those food and beverage firms with assets of over $50 million (.4% of the total) received 62.1% of all profits. The leading firms averaged a return on equity that was 25% above the industry average.

Between 1947 and 1962 average gross profit margins rose 5.5%, from 15.9% to 21.4%. This varied from the low product differentiation industries, like meat packing, with a 10% margin, to the miscellaneous food manufacturers, where the gross margin was 50%. Thus, the overall pattern is quite clear: there is a strong correlation between high and rising gross margins, high advertising expenditures, high product differentiation, high profits, and the growth of conglomerate firms.

U.S. DOMINATION OF THE INDUSTRY IN CANADA

It is widely known that the manufacturing sector of the Canadian economy is characterized by a high degree of foreign ownership and control. In the area of consumer goods it is particularly pronounced. Furthermore, the rate of expansion is continuing, as the Foreign

Investment Review Agency, created in 1973, has proven to be a bad joke foisted on the Canadian public. In 1973, total foreign investment in Canada stood at $33 billion; by the end of 1975, it had risen to $41.7 billion.

Of the 500 largest companies surveyed in the CALURA report covering 1975, 280 were foreign-controlled. These 280 corporations, representing only .135% of the 206,000 non-financial enterprises in Canada, accounted for 30% of sales, 28.7% of all assets, 39.2% of the profits, and 34.3% of equity.

The federal government's study, *Foreign Direct Investment in Canada*, popularly known as the "Gray Report," found that in 1968 non-resident ownership for all manufacturing was as follows: 54% of sales, 58% of assets, 62% of taxable income, and 63% of profits. For the food and beverage industry, foreign-owned firms held 27% of sales, 31% of assets, 33% of taxable income, and 30% of profits.

By 1970, according to Statistics Canada, foreign-owned interests in the food and beverage industry accounted for 33.2% of sales, 34% of all employees, and 39.9% of total value added. These figures tend to underestimate foreign control, for the rule of thumb used to determine control is 51% ownership of voting stock. Control often exists at a much lower percentage of ownership. Nevertheless, on the surface it appears that this is one sector of manufacturing where Canadian ownership is dominant. I will argue that these figures present a greatly distorted view of the food and beverage industry as it now exists. Furthermore, the dominant trend is to increased foreign ownership and control.

The Situation in 1971

In 1971 there were about 4,500 firms in the food and beverage field in Canada. Those with sales of over $10 million in that year are listed in Tables Ic and Id. These seventy-two firms accounted for about 75% of the total sales in the industry in that year. Of the total sales of these seventy-two firms, the forty-seven foreign-controlled firms accounted for about 50%. (The non-food sales by IMASCO, Lever Brothers, and Procter & Gamble tend to be offset by the non-food sales of Molson Industries and by the fact that about 80% of the sales listed for Seagrams and Hiram-Walker are outside of Canada). Thus in terms of who dominates the industry, the foreign-controlled firms have a much bigger share of the market than revealed by the 1968 figures cited in the Gray Report.

But this is only part of the true picture. All of the forty-seven foreign-controlled firms are branch plants of huge foreign conglomerates enjoying all the economic advantages that this brings. They all market their products on a national level. All engage in extensive national advertising. This is not true of the Canadian firms in the industry. Only a handful operate on a national scale and advertise on a national level.

Canada: The Northen Region of the American Market

For the food and beverage industry, Canada is seen simply as part of the larger American market. At least, that is how it is viewed south of the border. How Canada produces and distributes food is in reality dictated by contemporary American practices. This is simply a reflection of the overall American domination of Canada.

The consumer goods industry in the U.S. has always viewed Canada simply as an extension of the American market. In the food area, this is even more pronounced. The American food and beverage firms which operate in Canada are almost always wholly-owned subsidiaries of the parent. The parent corporation plans on a continental basis.

The integration of the Canadian and American food markets is made easier by the fact that there are very few instances of quotas on imported fresh or processed foods. The tariffs on processed foods set in the 1930s, and only slightly revised in the 1940s, are not on an *ad valorem* basis (percentage of value) but are set according to weight. They are so low as to be meaningless. This situation encourages integration and the importation of fresh and processed foods by the multinational corporations.

Food retailing in Canada clearly follows American practices. Traditionally, Canadian businessmen have felt that the U.S. system was best and should be imitated. Furthermore, there is the tremendous U.S. cultural and ideological impact on Canada as a whole, which has created our dependency mentality. Even the early volunteer food retailing chains established in Canada (e.g., IGA, Red & White, and Clover Farm Stores) were originally American operations, invited in by Canadians.

This continental fact is illustrated by the role of research and development in the food and beverage industry in Canada. In 1965, research and development expenditures by manufacturing as a whole in Canada averaged 1.3% of sales, far lower than that in the U.S. But in the food and beverage industry in Canada, expenditures were only .2% of sales.

While the industry is the largest in manufacturing in total number of employees, it is the second lowest in proportion of employees who are scientists or engineers. A study by A.G. Meiering of Guelph University found that in 1971 of all the establishments in Canada in the food and beverage industry, only 3% had "technical laboratories" capable of research and development. We know that the costs today of introducing a "new" product are very high. While most of the true innovations in the food industry in the U.S. originated with smaller firms, the innovations were soon taken over by the larger corporations. Given the structure of the industry, and the continental market, there really is no justification for research and development operations in Canada.

Is There a Miniature Replica Problem?

For many manufacturing industries in Canada, there is a "miniature replica" problem caused by the branch plant economy. As economist H. E. English demonstrated in the case of the appliance industry, this occurs when there are too many firms producing the same product, resulting in high unit costs and higher-than-necessary costs to consumers. Ed Safarian concluded in his study of foreign ownership in Canada that the great majority of the branch plants in Canada "are a small fraction of the parent in size, yet they are producing almost the full range of the identical or slightly modified products of the parent." Kari Levitt has argued that foreign-owned branch plants do not necessarily have a technical superiority over Canadian firms; they enjoy *a marketing advantage* due to overflow advertising in product differentiated markets.

This issue appeared as a key one in the hearings before the Bryce Royal Commission on Corporate Concentration. Many spokesmen for business interests claimed that there is *not enough* industry concentration in the smaller Canadian market to provide consumers with the efficiencies of larger economies of scale. Is this true of the food and beverage industry?

The bankruptcy rate in Canada has been increasing very rapidly in the past few years. In 1976 there were 3,233 failures, which set the Canadian record at that time. Dun and Bradstreet Canada Ltd. reported that in 1977 there were 4,316 business failures, an increase of 33% from the previous year. Some of the big losers included important food and beverage firms: Melchers Distilleries; Martin, Robertson and Bain; Delta Food Processors; and Marche Union.

The trend in the food and beverage industry in both Canada and the United States is towards concentration of market power in the hands of a few large corporations operating as conglomerates in several (or many) different areas. Between 1961 and 1971, over 2,000 food and beverage plants in Canada were shut down, a decline of about 28%. Most of these business failures were small private or co-operative firms, unable to compete with the larger firms. Preponderantly, these failures have been of Canadian-owned firms.

For example, between 1951 and 1974 the number of milk processing plants in Quebec declined from 1,080 to 160. These were almost all Canadian-owned, many co-operatives. In British Columbia in the mid-1960s there were fifteen plants which processed local fruit; by 1976, this number had dropped to five, and it was widely reported that they were having economic difficulties due to cheap imports from the United States, Australia and South Africa.

In the United States between 1954 and 1963 there was an absolute decline in plants of 4,600—a drop of about 13%. Only in meat packing and animal feeds was there an increase in the number of plants. This was attributed to the regional nature of these two industries, and more importantly to the lack of product differentiation and advertising, a fact which permitted the entry of new firms.

While there has been a decline in plants in both countries, there is also an increase in multi-plant operations by the large firms. In its major study of the food industry, the U.S. Federal Trade Commission concluded that "economies of scale, except for advertising and promotional activities, are generally insignificant . . ." Large plants are not necessarily required for efficient operations. The largest corporations did not operate the largest plants; there was, in each industry market, a minimum and maximum efficiency size for a plant depending on factors associated with that particular product. Middle-sized plants were able to exist side-by-side with the larger plants. The large corporations absorbed plants in mergers, and as a norm continued to operate them.

The evidence does not suggest that further concentration is necessary to provide more efficient scale of plant manufacturing in the food and beverage industry. Marketing, however, is the key question. With all the major retail food chains in Canada expanding their own private brand products, and with available shelf space disappearing with the onslaught of "new" products, only the major food producers have been able to protect the position of their advertised brands. Most of the smaller companies, like the seven vegetable processors in the Fraser Valley, have been reduced to packaging for the chain store private labels. Now, with these stores increasingly putting their labels on products manufactured in other countries, many small firms are facing possible bankruptcy.

The Advantages of the U.S. Branch Plant

The food and beverage industry in Canada is one manufacturing area where the trend is definitely towards increased foreign ownership

39

and control. Canadian capital was at one time in a strong, dominant position. It is only in recent years that several of the major Canadian firms have been taken over by foreign corporations: for example, Canadian Canners (by Del Monte), Clark Soups (by Green Giant), Redpath Industries (by Tate and Lyle), Canadian Breweries (by Rothmans of Pall Mall), Maple Leaf Mills (by Norris Grain), and Christie Brown (by Nabisco).

The Labatt family and board of directors sold controlling interest to the U.S. brewing firm, Joseph M. Schlitz Co., but this was voided by the U.S. Justice Department and a supporting decision by the U.S. Supreme Court. Today, Labatt's is controlled by Brascan. When the U.S. Federal Trade Commission ordered Beatrice Foods not to expand further, the company moved quickly into Canada, taking over many dairies; in a few years they emerged as a dominant dairy firm in Ontario, and the market leader in Manitoba. In July 1976, the Weston Empire sold their food processor, Nabob Foods, to a Swiss firm, Jacobs AG of Zurich. Nabob Foods was (by sales) one of the largest Canadian-owned fruit and vegetable processors in Canada; but the Foreign Investment Review Board did not hesitate to declare the sale to be in the "Canadian national interest."

In the long run, the American firms have a decided advantage over the Canadian firms and other foreign-owned corporations. Because of the high degree of product differentiation, advertising is most important, and the American firms have the advantage of overflow advertising. It is estimated that 70% of Canadians now have access to cable television and thus watch American programmes sponsored by American food corporations which also sell in Canada. The other major area of food and beverage advertising is in commerical magazines. Again, the American firms benefit from the fact that our newsstands are flooded with American magazines, all carrying advertisements by the large American food corporations.

The Food Prices Review Board, in a 1976 publication on advertising by food processors in Canada, was grossly misleading. They ignored the fact that the large American corporations (a majority of the firms in their survey) treat Canada as part of a North American market.

The Food Prices Review Board reported that advertising and promotion by the sixty-two firms surveyed amounted to only 1.7% of sales, which is far less than the U.S. average. They reported that miscellaneous food manufacturers in Canada spent only 3.4% of sales on advertising in Canada. In contrast, U.S. firms in the same area spent 8.3% of sales in 1961. This discrepancy can only be accounted for by the overflow advertising and the fact that the large firms in this field in Canada are American-owned.

The amount spent on advertising by the American food giants is rapidly increasing. As noted before, in 1947 the smaller firms actually spent more on advertising than the large firms; by 1961, the large firms (corporations with over $50 million in annual sales) were spending four times as much as the smaller firms. Some examples are presented in Table If.

In the long run, the average Canadian firm in the food and beverage industry faces a bleak prospect. The few large Canadian firms which have expanded in a conglomerate manner will undoubtedly survive. But in the highly differentiated market, even they are at a disadvantage vis-a-vis the branch plant of the large American corporation. For the small corporation, with sales less than $50 million per year, the future promises lower profits, increased threat of bankruptcy, and a takeover by a larger conglomerate.

TABLE If

Advertising Expenditures of Some U.S. Corporations, 1973

Food Corporation	Expenditures	As a % of Total Sales
General Foods	$180,000,000	8.1
Heublein	77,800,000	5.9
Coca Cola	76,000,000	3.5
General Mills	74,200,000	3.7
Kraftco	74,000,000	2.4
Nabisco	69,050,000	6.8
Hunt-Wesson	61,700,000	5.1
PepsiCo	58,000,000	4.4
Pillsbury	50,000,000	5.0
Standard Brands	50,000,000	4.5

SOURCE: *Advertising Age,* August 26, 1974. Cited in Jim Hightower, *Eat Your Heart Out.* N.Y.: Crown Publishers, 1975, Table V-1, p. 116.

SOURCES

Bain, Joe S. *Barriers to New Competition.* Boston: Harvard University Press, 1956.
Blair, John M. *Economic Concentration.* N.Y.: Harcourt, Brace, Jovanovich, Inc., 1972.

Block, Harry. "Prices, Costs and Profits in Canadian Manufacturing: The Influence of Tariffs and Concentration," *Canadian Journal of Economics*, VII, November 1974, pp. 594-610.

Buzzell, Robert D., and Robert E.M. Nourse. *Product Innovation in Food Processing*. Boston: Harvard University Press, 1967.

Collins, Norman R., and Lee E. Preston. *Concentration and Price-Cost Margins in Manufacturing Industries*. Berkeley: University of California Press, 1968.

Corporations and Labour Unions Returns Act. *Annual Report, 1971*. Ottawa: Statistics Canada, Cat. No. 61-210, March 1974.

Cross, Jennifer. *The Supermarket Trap*. Blomington, Ind.: Indiana University Press, 1970.

Director of Investigation and Research. Combines Investigation Act. *Concentration in the Manufacturing Industries of Canada*. Ottawa: Department of Consumer and Corporate Affairs, 1971.

Economic Council of Canada, *Interim Report on Competition Policy*. Ottawa: Information Canada, July 1969.

English, H.E. *Industrial Structure in Canada's International Competitive Position*. Montreal: The Canadian Trade Committee, June 1964.

Epps, A. *Co-operation Among Capitalists: The Canadian Merger Movement, 1909-1913*. Unpublished Dissertation, Johns Hopkins University, 1973.

Food Prices Review Board. *Advertising Expenditures and Food Prices*. Ottawa: Food Prices Review Board, February 1976.

Galbraith, J.K. *The New Industrial State*. Boston: Houghton Mifflin, 1967.

House of Commons. Special Committee on Trends in Food Prices. *Minutes of Proceedings*, 1973.

Jones, J.C., L. Laudaclio, and M. Percy. "Market Structure and Profitability in Canadian Manufacturing Industry: Some Cross Section Results," *Canadian Journal of Economics*, VI, August 1973, pp. 356-368.

Levitt, Kari. *Silent Surrender; The Multinational Corporation in Canada*. Toronto: MacMillan of Canada, 1970.

McFetridge, D.G. "Market Structure and Price-Cost Margins: An analysis of the Canadian Manufacturing Sector," *Canadian Journal of Economics*, VI, August 1973, pp. 344-355.

Naylor, Tom. *The History of Canadian Business, 1867-1914*. Two Volumes. Toronto: James Lorimer & Co. 1975.

Orr, Dale. "The Determinant of Entry: A Study of the Canadian Manufacturing Industries," *The Review of Economics and Statistics*, LVI, February 1974.

Reynolds, Lloyd G. *The Control of Competition in Canada*. Cambridge, Mass.: Harvard University Press, 1940.

Rosenbluth, Gideon. *Concentration in Canadian Manufacturing Industries*. Princeton, N.J.: Princeton University, National Bureau of Economic Research, 1957.

Rosenbluth, Gideon, and Hugh G. Thorburn. *Canadian Anti-Combines Administration, 1952-1960*. Toronto: University of Toronto Press, 1963.

Safarian, A.E. *Foreign Ownership of Canadian Industry*. Toronto: McGraw-Hill Company, 1966.

Skeoch, L.A. *Restrictive Trade Practices in Canada*. Toronto: McClelland & Stewart, 1966.

Statistics Canada. *Industrial Organizatin and Concentration in the Manufacturing, Mining and Logging Industries*. Ottawa: Information Canada, Cat. No. 31-402, December 1975.

Stewart, Walter. *Hard to Swallow*. Toronto: MacMillan of Canada, 1974.

U.S. Federal Trade Commission. *Report on Rates of Return in Selected Industries, 1961-1970*. Washington, D.C.: U.S. Government Printing Office, 1972.

U.S. Federal Trade Commission. *The Structure of Food Manufacturing*. Technical

Study No. 8, National Commission on Food Marketing, Washington, D.C.: U.S. Government Printing Office, June 1966.

U.S. Senate. Subcommittee on Anti-trust and Monopoly. 88th Congress, 2nd Session. *Economic Concentration*, 1964.

Warnock, John W. "The Food Industry in Canada: Oligopoly and American Domination," *Our Generation*, XI, No. 4, Winter 1976, pp. 52-72.

Young, Bert. "Corporate Interests and the State," *Our Generation*, XX, No. 1, Spring 1974, pp. 70-83.

2. THE MEAT INDUSTRY

The largest single food industry in Canada today is the meat packing and processing industry, and it is also the third largest manufacturing industry in terms of total sales. In North America, the slaughtering and packing of meat was the earliest food processing industry to develop a national scale of operation and sales. It was also the first industry to move in the direction of monopoly and oligopoly.

In the United States, the five largest meat packers—Swift, Armour, Wilson, Cudahy and Morris—rapidly expanded in the last three decades of the nineteenth century to the point where they had nearly monopolized the meat industry from coast to coast. When these firms began to diversify into other food processing industries, as well as wholesale and retail distribution, the U.S. Federal Trade Commission intervened. The famous Packers Consent Decree of 1920 ordered the major national packers to divest themselves of all interests but meat packing, and prohibited future diversification. This order successfully prevented the early monopolization of the food industry as a whole, and in the long run opened the meat industry to greater competition.

The move toward monopolization of the meat packing industry was also repeated in Canada. In 1905 the largest American meat packer, Swift & Co., moved into Canada by purchasing the J.Y. Griffin Company. Probably fearful of the power of the largest meat packer in the world, three of the largest Canadian meat packers merged in 1927 to form the company now known as Canada Packers. The third largest packer, Burns Foods Ltd., was incorporated in 1928 as a successor to Patrick Burns and Co.

44

Industry Concentration

Because of public outcry against its monopolistic practices, the meat packing industry came under the scrutiny of the Royal Commission on Price Spreads. Their final report, issued in 1937, found that during the depression years between 1929 and 1933, Swift had made a profit in three of these years and Canada Packers had made a profit in all five. Almost all other industries in Canada lost heavily during this period.

The Commission found that between 1929 and 1933 the value of meat sales had dropped by 51%, the amount paid by the packers to farmers had dropped by 57%, but the return to the meat packer had only dropped by 25%. They concluded that the ability of the meat packers to protect their gross margin (the difference between what they paid the farmer and what they charged at the wholesale end) was due to "the monopolistic character of the structure of the industry."

The system of industry pricing was revealed in a statement to the Royal Commission by the President of Canada Packers: "The total livestock is sold for the total sum, whatever it is; from that sum is deducted the packer's expense and the packer's profit and the farmer gets the balance."

While the degree of domination of the meat packing industry by Canada Packers alone has certainly diminished over the years, the oligopoly of the few big national packers has been able generally to retain this system of obtaining the required gross margin.

The findings of subsequent government investigations have reached similar conclusions. The Royal Commission on Prices (1949) concluded that the industry could not be called "highly competitive," as the packers claimed, due to the fact that the Big Three had 65% of the cattle kill and 61% of the hog kill, giving them control over pricing to the farmer.

The Royal Commission on Price Spreads of Food Products (1959) also stressed the ability of the meat packers to maintain a gross margin that suited their needs. This market power brought them profits which were higher than industry as a whole when considered over the long run, including the fluctuations of the primary production cycles. They noted that the high profits were achieved in spite of the fact that the red meat packing industry paid the highest wages in the food industry.

This Royal Commission found that between 1949 and 1957 the meat packers had increased their gross margin from 18.1% to 23.9% of the retail price of meat. During this same period, the farm share of the retail price for beef had declined from 68% to 54%, and for pork from 66% to 60%. In the mid-1960s, the four largest Canadian meat packers had 71% of the national market, while the four largest American firms had only 39% of the U.S. market.

By 1973, when the House of Commons began their investigation into the rise in food prices at the retail level, the Meat Packers Council of Canada could boast that the share of the national market held by the four largest packers had fallen from 58% in 1965 to 51% in 1970. This degree of concentration, they noted, was much lower than that of other major Canadian industries—in particular motor vehicle manufacturing, petroleum refining and iron and steel manufacturing.

Nevertheless, in 1971 the five largest packers (see Table IIa) slaughtered 50.6% of all hogs. This degree of concentration was still about twice as high as that in the United States and gave the large packers considerable market power.

While it is sometimes argued that the market power of the large meat packers is counterbalanced by the power of the retail chains, this does not seem to be the case in Canada. A study done for the Ontario Special Committee on Farm Income concluded that "the meat packing industry as a whole is not too greatly affected by the market power of the retailers." Because of their control over prices at the other end, they were in a position simply to shift added costs back onto the producer. The study concluded that "livestock producers, as the weakest participants in the production-marketing system, tend to bear most of the consequences associated with wide swings in supplies, as well as increases in processing and retailing costs, over the years, in the form of widely varying and often unfavourable prices."

While market control by the Big Three is normally an informal process based on mutual interest, it has, on occasion, taken the form of direct collusion. In 1969 the Combines Commissioner reported that Canada Packers, Burns Foods, and Swift Canadian had pleaded guilty to charges that over a period of five years they fixed prices in their sales to the Department of Defense Production in New Brunswick. They settled without a court case.

Another example can be seen in the case of the Manitoba Wheat Pool's venture into meat packing. They purchased the Brandon Packers meat packing plant and tried to break into the prairie meat market. They soon encountered great difficulty in gaining adequate access to retail outlets, as the major packers had well-established marketing links. When they needed to buy livestock on the market to increase their slaughter capacity, the Big Three bid up the prices, putting the squeeze on them. After losing millions of dollars, they quit the business in 1969 and sold their plants to Burns Foods.

The power of Canada Packers alone in the market for livestock was demonstrated in the Report of the Restrictive Trade Practices

46

Commission (1961). In the Maritimes, when Swift Canadian undertook buying schemes to try to get a larger share of the market, Canada Packers retaliated with "predatory pricing" until Swift surrendered.

TABLE IIa

Slaughtering and Meat Processors

Company	1971 Sales	Ownership/Control
Canada Packers	$937,720,000	Canada—W.F. McLean
Burns Foods	359,300,748	Canada—R.H. Webster*
Swift Canadian	280,440,639	U.S.—Esmark, Inc.
Intercontinental Packers	95,720,000	Canada—Mendel Family/Sask. Govt.**
J.M. Schneider	84,163,000	Canada—Schneider Family
Essex Packers	33,619,730	Canada—Hamilton Group***
Legrande Meats	30,000,000	Canada—Co-op Federee de Quebec
F.G. Bradley Co.	21,000,000	Canada—Bradley Family

* In 1964 it was reported that about 40% of the shares were held by Alexander Hill of Toronto and the Imperial Trust Company of Montreal. But the *Financial Post* reports that 41%, and controlling interest, is held by Webster.

** In 1973, the NDP Government in Saskatchewan paid $10.4 million for 40% of the equity in the company. Dun and Bradstreet's study concluded that the total shareholder equity was between $4 and $5.5 million; the Saskatchewan Economic Development Corporation said total Mendel family interest was $6.3 million.

*** Essex Packers went bankrupt in 1975. It was bought in 1976 by a group of Hamilton businessmen, according to Roman Doeyshyn, one of the purchasers.

As the RTPC Report concluded, the market power of Canada Packers "inevitably results in wider processing margins than would exist in its absence." In order to control the market, the company was "depressing meat prices and forcing competitors to lose money on their livestock purchases." They were also found guilty of "deliberately bidding up the prices which competitors have been obliged to pay for livestock" in order to maintain their position as industry leader.

It should also be noted that Canada Packers has one advantage that the other major packers do not have: close links with a large retail chain. They hold about 8% of the voting stock of Dominion Stores and have traditionally had a representative on Dominion's Board of

Directors. While this has not given them control over Dominion (which is held by Argus Corporation), it has undoubtedly helped "grease the wheels." Spokesmen for both Canada Packers and Dominion Stores have denied that these links have led to any special buyer-seller relationship, and in the case of fresh meats, it is difficult to prove otherwise without examining company records.

In March 1974 I conducted a survey of the brands of processed foods carried by the four major chain stores in Saskatoon: Safeway, Loblaw, Sakatoon Consumers Co-op, and Dominion. In the area of processed meats, the Canada Packers' Maple Leaf brand was found in all the chains. This is to be expected as Canada Packers is the largest packer, has a well-established brand name, and has a very large share of the processed meat market.

What was more interesting, however, was the way the chains dealt with the York Farms division of Canada Packers. Dominion Stores alone carried York Farms canned meats and frozen meat pies. Dominion Stores alone carried the York Farms brand of jams, frozen orange juice, canned apple juice, peaches, cherries, prunes, pears and tomatoes. In some cases, like canned raspberries, strawberries, and blueberries, the York brand was the only one carried by Dominion. The other chains carried almost no York Farms brand products.

In addition, the manager of the Dominion store told me that York Farms processing plants in Ontario and British Columbia did the packing for their house (or private) brands. In Saskatoon, this included their line of frozen vegetables. It is hard to believe that this type of relationship does not carry over to the fresh meat area.

The Role of Excess Capacity

There seems to be general agreement from all sources that the meat packing industry in Canada is characterized by excess capacity; that is, there is considerable underutilization of floor space and capital investment in general. This inefficiency, combined with the packers' ability to control gross margins, keeps prices high to consumers. This is a major part of the reason why the greatly depressed farm prices of the mid-1970s were not reflected equally in lower prices at the retail level.

The extent of this industry inefficiency is hard to measure. Harold Bronson has noted that during World War II, meat packing plants in Canada normally ran two or three shifts per day; now they normally run only one shift. The "one-shift" problem has been blamed on a shortage of chilling capacity at the plants. However, this "problem" could be easily overcome—if it were necessary to increase profits.

The study done for the Special Committee on Farm Income in Ontario noted that when Canada Packers faced a nation-wide strike in 1966, the rest of the industry easily took up that company's share of the market with only an average of 5% overtime. This would indicate a minimum of 30% excess capacity at that time, Canada Packers' share of the market. The study concluded that this was still "an underestimate since considerably more livestock could have been handled by taking on second shifts and adding to overtime."

Raymond C. Nicholson of the Department of Agricultural Economics at the University of Saskatchewan attempted to assess the extent of this overcapacity in the industry in 1965. He did so by using as a standard the demonstrated capacity of the plants in existence, rather than their physical capacity. He took the peak periods of output-per-plant and used them as a possible standard of full capacity. For the period 1956-1960, he concluded that the excess capacity for cattle was 56% and for hogs 127%. But even this could be a gross understatement, for the peak periods of production were probably well below actual plant potential.

The Food Prices Review Board conducted a survey in August 1975, through a questionnaire submitted to the meat packers. Since the packers replied that many of the plants were "basically designed for single shift operations," this was the standard used by the Board. Thus, they conclude, the "normal" capacity of the report is "understated in aggregate." For the period between January 1974 and June 1975, the average rate of utilization for cattle slaughter was 62.5% and for hogs 59%. On a regional basis, the excess of capacity was found to be much more pronounced, with only Ontario at "reasonable levels of capacity utilization being achieved."

Nevertheless, the packers continue to build more slaughtering and processing plants. Professor Nicholson offers the following explanation:

> The meat packing industry has traditionally provided capacity in excess of current requirements. This is fairly typical of this type of industry which is dominated by a few large firms that attempt to retain a certain share of the market and for which entry is comparatively easy. It is expected that the industry will continue to build in excess of requirements and consequently there will be little need to promote the construction of new plants if capacity is the only factor.

Product Differentiation and Ease of Entry

The meat packing industry in Canada has the basic characteristics typical of an oligopolistic industry. The major packers display a high degree of forbearance towards one another. They respect each other's share of the market. They avoid active competition with each other. In their bidding at the stockyards, they display a common desire to keep prices to producers at a low level. The absence of any real competition at the wholesale level permits all the major firms to keep their required gross margins.

Yet in both the United States and Canada there has been a decline in the share of the national market held by the top four and eight firms. This is in direct contrast to all the other food processing industries, where increasing national concentration is the norm. Why is this the case?

First, it should be noted that national concentration figures can be grossly misleading. This is a major point made by the Director of Investigation and Research, Combines Investigation Act in the 1971 Report on Concentration in the Manufacturing Industries of Canada. Regional concentration is much higher and in most cases a more accurate measurement as it reflects a real market. A study done in 1973 for the Economics Research Service of the U.S. Department of Agriculture revealed that while the four largest meat packing firms in the U.S. had only about 23% of the national market, they accounted for 65% or more of the market in most states.

This came to public attention during the 1974 conflict between the national packers and their trade union, the Canadian Food and Allied Workers (which, in spite of its name, is an American union). Instead of settling negotiations, Canada Packers, Swift Canadian, and Burns Foods locked out their workers in Alberta alone. This was to accomplish several ends: they would save money by not paying wages, they could unload the surplus meat that was piling up in storage, they would cut down their storage costs, and they would create a backload of livestock on the farms which would depress farm prices.

But they did not lock out their workers in Eastern Canada. In the West, the Big Three had 60% of the market; but in Ontario, only 40%. They were afraid that the smaller packers would step up their production by adding second shifts, fill the market held by the Big Three, and perhaps hold onto some of it after the lockout. Probably because most of the small packing plants are non-union, the CFAWU refused to call a national strike, and let the Alberta workers bear the full brunt of the lock-out. As far as the public can judge, the six-week lockout by the Big Three was a success.

There are two main reasons why there has been an increase in the number of smaller firms coming into the meat processing industry. There are, of course, the high gross margins maintained by the major packers. These create an artificially high price umbrella under which smaller local fresh meat packers can operate—if they can get a share of the local market. This has happened, particularly around the high population centres in Eastern Canada.

The most important factor, however, is the lack of product differentiation in fresh meats. It has not proven possible to create a brand identification for fresh meats, probably because of the lack of quality control of the product. Therefore, little can be gained from the type of massive advertising which is associated with the highly concentrated processed food industries. The consumer has been unable to determine if one brand of beef is better than another.

John M. Blair, in his study of economic concentration in the United States, found that while the share of the fresh meat market held by the national packers had declined, the opposite was true of the processed meat market, where brand identification and advertising were the norm. In Canada, the five largest packers have a preponderant share of the processed meat market, probably about 90%, although no official figures are available.

Nevertheless, while the number of firms and plants in the meat packing industry has been on the increase, the share of the market held by the large firms with the large plants has not really declined very much. R. A. Patterson notes that "the percentage of large establishments [shipments of $1,000,000 and over] and their share of shipments remained relatively constant between 1961 and 1966. In fact, these large plants held 95% of the market over this period."

In the United States, the nine national packers have been shifting their emphasis to processed meats, where profits are higher. This is another factor which has permitted the development of strong, middle-sized regional packers, who have cut into the national packers share of the total U.S. meat market.

There are two main reasons why the meat packing industry in Canada has remained largely Canadian owned and controlled. First, the industry was highly monopolized at an early date and was highly profitable to the owners. A takeover would have involved a large outlay of capital, and the Canadian owners were reluctant to surrender such a highly profitable business.

Secondly, there is the lack of product differentiation. The advantages held by the large U.S. food corporations stems from marketing, and particularly advertising. There is no overflow advertising from the United States that has created a ready market for U.S. meats. This is probably the main reason that the meat industry has not followed the

51

sell-out pattern of other food industries in the late 1950s and 1960s.

Industry Profits

During the early part of this century, when Canada Packers held almost a monopoly position in the industry, profits were much higher than they were to become. But profits have been unusually high even in the period after World War II. The Royal Commission on Prices reported that Canada Packers profit in 1948 represented a 23.4% return on net worth. The Restrictive Trade Practices Commission found that between 1935 and 1958, Canada Packers' net income averaged a 11.3% return on total assets; this was almost twice as high as the return on assets for the four largest American firms: Swift, Armour, Wilson and Cudahy. A study by the Ontario Government, released in April 1974, concluded that between 1967 and 1972 Canada Packers, Burns Foods, and J.M. Schneider averaged an increase in profit of 15.6% per year, which made meat packing the "biggest profit makers in the food industry."

Nevertheless, the spokesmen for the companies have claimed that their returns are poor relative to other manufacturing industries. This position is supported by R. A. Patterston in his survey of the food industry for the Federal Task Force on Agriculture.

If returns are low, the obvious solution would be to increase company efficiency by eliminating unnecessary excess capacity. However, the Big Three evidently are wary of such a solution; excess capacity has served as an important tool for the oligopoly, helping to maintain a high share of the national market.

As Harold Bronson has pointed out, the profitability of a firm cannot be measured solely by the annual return on the investor's equity, the approach taken by Patterson and the Food Prices Review Board. An investor also takes into consideration the increased value of the stock that is bought. This is normally a reflection of increased company assets.

Bronson uses Canada Packers as an example. If one invested $100.00 in that company in 1956, by 1965 (10 years later) the stock would have brought a dividend return of $45.10, or a return of only 4.51% on investment. That is the low rate of return often cited by the defenders of the corporations. But what was the value of the stock? By 1965 the $100.00 was worth $232.40; this returned the investor another $22.24 per year.

Over the same period, a $100.00 investment in Burns Foods would have brought $35.00 in dividends plus another $16.71 per year in annual growth in the value of the stock. J.M. Schneider only "went public" in 1969, and so comparable figures are not available for that firm. However, this meat packer, which specializes in processed meats (with product differentiation and brand advertising), would have had an even higher rate of return. Patterson notes that between 1962 and 1968 the industry rate of return was about 1% on the sales dollar, yet J.M. Schneider averaged between 1.75% and 2.29% over that period.

It is now generally recognized that meat production in Canada, on the primary level, goes through periodic cycles due to "free market" forces. Prices to producers peaked in the fall of 1973 when cattlemen were receiving over $.50 per lb. for steers. Then beef prices at the farm gate fell dramatically, by about 32%. They did not reach the 1973 level again until the late spring of 1978.

During this very tough period for beef producers, the large meat packers insisted that they were being squeezed just as hard. But was this really the case?

Between 1974 and 1977, Canada Packers' sales rose from $1,497 million to $1,700 million. They showed a profit every year. Their own reported return of stockholders' equity varied from a low of 16.2% in 1975 to a high of 21.5% in 1976.

Over the same period of time, Burns Foods reported that their sales increased from $567 million to $876 million. They returned a profit every year. Their net income increased over this period by an average of 17.5% per year.

The two largest packers insisted that profits were low in the meat packing area, but were relatively good in their other food areas. Schneider's is a far less diversified company, so its results could be considered more indicative of the state of the major packers. Between 1973 and 1977 the average return of after-tax profit on shareholders equity was 12.82%. This was an average increase of 1.2% over the return from the previous five years.

Finally, there is another factor which must be taken into account when assessing the performance of the industry. As Joe S. Bain argues in his classic study, *Industrial Organization*, in a capitalist society the rate of return is also related to the risk factor. Where the risk of investing is low, then the return to the investor also should be lower. That is the theory.

Clearly, the degree of risk in investing in the Canadian meat packing industry is low compared to manufacturing as a whole. Bronson concludes that "it appears that Canadian meat packing has been able to maintain an average rate of profit substantially higher than the standard set forth for workable competition, and higher than the rate prevailing in American meat packing."

Growth and Diversification

The 1960s and 1970s have witnessed the growth of the conglomerate food firm, and the meat packing industry has not been out of step with this development. In this country, Canada Packers was one of the first companies to recognize the value of diversification into other areas of production. In addition to meat packing they have been active in the following areas: fertilizers, leather tanneries, creameries, feeds and feed supplements, feed mills, edible oil processing, fruit and vegetable producing and canning, wholesale grocery distribution, poultry plants, hatcheries, soap plants, jute bag plants, and feather processing.

Swift Canadian Co. (its U.S. parent is now called Esmark, Inc.) has also diversified into dairy and poultry plants, feed mills, hatcheries, grocery sales, and other non-food areas like fertilizer, chemicals and agricultural pesticides. The U.S. parent is diversified into leather tanning, adhesives, motor oil refining, nitrogen production, petroleum exploration and development, insurance, and financial services.

Burns Foods, like Canada Packers, diversified its operations at a relatively early date through the acquisition of Palm Dairies and Scott National Co., a fruit and vegetable wholesaler. In 1973 Burns bought a controlling interest in Western Canadian Seed Processors (renamed Canbra Foods Ltd.), a manufacturer of edible oils, which in turn controlled Stafford Foods, a manufacturer of grocery products. In the fall of 1976, they acquired Food Services Ltd., which vertically integrated them into the restaurant and food catering business.

With the drastic decline in returns to farmers for livestock, plus the relatively high return on grain, Western Canadian production of hogs declined significantly in the mid-1970s. Burns responded by shutting down their slaughtering operations in Moose Jaw and Prince Albert. At the same time, they announced a $10 million expansion at their Kit-Wat plant in Ontario. In 1976 Burns concluded a long term contract with a hog slaughtering plant in Montana, taking almost the entire output from this American plant for sales in Canada.

J.M. Schneider has continued to specialize in the processed meat market, where it has been very successful. In the early 1970s, it purchased a cheese manufacturing plant at St. Isidore, Ontario, but this was their only venture outside the meat and poultry industry. Their plant acquisitions in 1973-1976 were all to expand their processed meat market. Intercontinental Packers, based in Saskatoon, has remained in the fresh and processed meat field, and is growing more slowly than the other major meat packers.

54

Decline of Canadian Production

Per capita consumption of pork has not risen in Canada since the end of World War II. And while Canada was at one time a major exporter of pork, it is now a net importer.

Within the industry, there has been a rather significant shift in hog production and processing from Western Canada to Ontario and Quebec over the past few years. In British Columbia, Intercontinental Packers shut down their hog slaughtering operation; only 10% of the B.C. market is supplied from within the province.

In 1977, three plants in B.C., Alberta, and Saskatchewan were processing 92% of all hogs slaughtered in those provinces. Whereas Alberta used to be a major exporter of hogs, by 1977 one-third of all pork sold in the B.C. and Alberta market was provided by U.S. packers.

In 1971, there were 4.7 million hogs slaughtered in the four Western provinces; by 1976, this had dropped to only 2.7 million. In 1961 there were 41,000 farms in Alberta producing hogs; by 1977 this had fallen to 8,000.

The cost to the West has been dear. There are farm sale losses, but in addition, there is the shift in value added to production through slaughtering to the East. In 1977, Saskatchewan's value added in meat processing was only 9.7% of farm sales; in Ontario it was 28%, and in Quebec 46%.

Western hog producers are angry because their counterparts in the two central provinces regularly obtain between five and ten cents a pound more for their product. At the same time, Ontario consumers can buy pork at lower prices than are available in Western Canada.

The other major development in the meat industry is the trend towards greater importation. Canada at the present time is a net importer of beef and veal, mutton and lamb, and pork. There is considerable concern here because meat is one food product that Canada can produce on a relatively competitive basis.

Table IIb provides some interesting data on trade in beef exports and imports. In 1973 beef imports into Canada were only about 45 million lb. This rose to 145 million lb. in 1977; of this total, 24 million lb. came from the United States, 59 million lb. from Australia, and 60 million lb. from New Zealand. In that year Canada exported 75 million lb. to the United States.

In 1976, Canada supplied 5% of total U.S. imports of pork, but took 46% of U.S. pork exports. In 1977, Canada was a net importer of almost 40 million lb. of pork, all from the United States.

It was this situation that provoked the formation of the Canadian Agricultural Movement and their boycott in the spring of 1978. In spite of pressures by many farm organizations, in April, 1978 Jack Horner, Minister of Industry and Commerce, announced that there would be no new controls on beef and veal imports.

TABLE IIb

Imports and Exports of Beef, 1975

	Exports		Imports
Country	Metric Tons ('000)	Country	Metric Tons ('000)
Australia	517.3	United States	557.3
New Zealand	332.0	Italy	320.5
France	291.6	West Germany	197.1
Ireland	270.4	United Kingdon	196.4
West Germany	137.8	France	159.6
The Netherlands	137.3	CANADA	58.3
Denmark	128.5	The Netherlands	44.9
The Argentine	93.2	Japan	44.9
Uruguay	78.7	Greece	37.4
Yugoslavia	36.7	Belgium-Luxembourg	29.2
South Africa	30.0	Spain	26.8
United States	20.9	Portugal	23.7
CANADA	11.5	Sweden	13.1
Brazil	5.3	Israel	12.0

SOURCE: United National Food and Agriculture Organization, "Monthly Bulletin of Agricultural Economics and Statistics," September, 1976.

POULTRY PROCESSING

While the poultry industry in Canada is a separate industry at the level of the producer, the processing industry is highly integrated on a horizontal and vertical basis with other major food processing concerns.

There are three different groups of food industries involved in the poultry processing business: (1) the major meat packers, including Canada Packers, Swift Canadian, J. M. Schneider and Burns Foods; (2) the large grain and flour companies, including Maple Leaf Mills,

56

Ogilvie Flour Mills, Quaker Oats, Ralston Purina and Federal Grain; and (3) the farmer-owned co-operatives.

In the past few years there has been a growing centralization of processing of broilers and turkeys. Ogilvie sold their Cham Foods Division in Winnipeg to Ready Foods of Toronto, a subsidiary of Green Giant of Canada. Quaker Oats sold their feed and poultry division to Maple Leaf Mills, which is controlled by the Norris Grain Company in the United States. In 1975 Federal Industries sold their Panco Poultry processing plant in British Columbia to the B.C Government; it was the largest packing plant in the province. And in 1976, Ralston Purina sold Checkerboard Farms to Swift Canadian.

In the mid-1960s it was estimated that farmer-owned co-operative poultry processing plants had about 25% of the Canadian market. Usually these operations are linked with other farmer co-ops, particularly creameries, and it is difficult for an outsider to obtain accurate sales figures. The largest poultry processors are United Co-operatives of Ontario (UCO) and Co-operative Federee de Quebec. These two co-operatives are large agribusiness operations, heavily involved in the farm supply industry.

Other firms are involved in the further processing of poultry, particularly turkeys. Frozen turkeys are a major food item and are distributed nationally by the large meat packers. The so-called "self-basting" turkey is a highly advertised food item and costs more than the local brands. The turkey industry is highly oligopolized with only a few major firms dominating the market.

In this field, Swift and Co. set the pace with the introduction of the "deep basted Butterball" frozen turkey. Armour brought suit against Swift for false advertising, arguing (correctly) that there was no butter in the turkey, only coconut and soybean oil.

In Canada, Swift Canadian markets the "Butterball," but no picture of butter appears on the wrapper, and the label states that only "vegetable oil" is used. Canada Packers, through its Maple Leaf brand division, is marketing the "Miracle Baste" frozen turkey. In the advertising war that has been going on for several years, Swift obviously has benefited from the overflow television and magazine advertising from the United States. Canada Packers, which has been operating under license from Armour for this product, does not benefit from overflow advertising; Armour uses a different brand name in the United States.

The Campbell Soup Co.'s Canadian subsidiary buys the preponderant share of the fowl disposed of by Canadian egg farmers. Fowl, and other poultry products, are canned and processed at their plant at Listowel, Ontario. Producers have been bitter over the near monopoly power of the Campbell Soup plant in Ontario. For example, in 1967 when there was an excess of fowl in Canada, Campbell Soups imported 1.2 million live fowl, almost all from Michigan. Michigan egg producers were dumping their fowl almost at the trucking price.

Other canned chicken is produced by Puritan, a subsidiary of Unilever, the British controlled conglomerate, and Green Giant of Canada, Ltd. The frozen "TV Dinner" market in Canada is almost completely dominated by two firms: Stouffers, owned by International Multifoods (Robin Hood), and Swanson, owned by Campbell Soup. Frozen chicken pies are mainly manufactured by Canada Packers York Farms Division and Morrison-Lamothes Foods, a smaller Canadian firm. In recent years they have experienced stiff competition from imports by Banquet Foods Corp. of St. Louis, a division of RCA. These, and other smaller firms, supply the house brands which appear in the local chain supermarkets.

Vertical Integration

The other major characteristic of the poultry industry in Canada is the degree of vertical integration. First, there are the chicken and turkey breeding firms. In Canada there is only one large chicken breeder and one large turkey breeder. Shaver Poultry Breeding Farms Ltd. of Cambridge, Ontario is the only operation of its kind in Canada. Twenty years ago there were almost 400 breeders in Canada. In 1965, Cargill Corporation bought two-thirds ownership of the lone Canadian chicken breeder. The Nicholas Company, based in Western Canada, is the only company handling turkeys.

These breeders in turn are linked, through contracts, with the hatcheries. At all levels of the poultry industry, the real market is regional. The hatchery industry is very highly concentrated and often is integrated into the poultry processing firms through mutual contracts with primary producers.

The main integration takes place between the farmer-producers and the processors. In general this integration takes two forms. First, there is the system of "owner integration," where the processing firm directly owns the farm and the poultry flock. Several firms in this category include Maple Leaf Mills, Canada Packers, Robin Hood, Swift Canadian, and Green Giant. In British Columbia, Ernie's Fine Foods operates the B.C. franchise for Kentucky Fried Chicken, which is owned by General Foods, one of the biggest American food conglomerates. General Foods also owns the White Spot restaurants in B.C. and three chicken farms in the Fraser Valley which supply about 12,000 chickens per week, about one-half of the firm's needs.

58

In a sense, the co-operatives could also be called "owner-integrated," as the poultry producers own the processing plants. While the social relationship is different, farmers insist that the style of operation is identical to that of the private firms.

However, the corporations have generally been getting out of the business of direct ownership of farms and flocks in Canada. In 1959 there was considerable "over-production" of poultry, and the very low prices brought heavy losses to the processors. This was one reason for getting out. The other is that direct farm ownership requires the outlay of capital for the farm and the payment of wages to the farmer and other farm employees. These are unnecessary expenses.

The preferred alternative is "contract-integration." By 1961, about 88% of the poultry produced in Ontario was covered by this form of vertical integration. The farmer must obtain the capital for the farm, and if he receives any return which could be called a compensation for his labour it must come from any profit he might make. This would be very rare in the case of poultry production.

Normally, a farmer's contract with the processor is on a 1-3 year basis. It rarely is long term. A floor price is established for the poultry provided by the farmer, with incentives for certain types of production. In return, the farmer normally pays extra for the feed (over the market price) and a cent or two more for chicks; both of these inputs are provided by the integrating firm.

During the "chicken-and-egg war" in 1971, smaller poultry producers tried to save themselves from bankruptcy by the creation of additional marketing boards with the power to set quotas for production. This caused considerable conflict between smaller farmers and the few very large producers who did not want marketing boards. It also caused conflicts between provinces, as each group of poultry producers tried to use their governments to protect their "home market" while expanding into other provinces to get rid of the increasing production. But the marketing boards have not protected the producer against the increase of farm input costs.

In 1976, when the National Farm Products Marketing Council held hearings on the possibility of establishing a national poultry marketing board, strong opposition came from the Consumers Association of Canada and the representatives of Kentucky Fried Chicken Ltd. This American firm operates almost 600 franchised fast food outlets in Canada, and in 1976 bought about 30% of all the chickens sold in Canada. Few farmers believe that the National Chicken Marketing Plan will reverse the trend towards larger and larger producers and fewer and fewer farmers.

Concentration Levels

Fresh poultry is one of the food products for which there is really no national market. This is due to the high degree of perishability of the product and the large distances involved in moving the product from one regional market to another. Thus, Table IIc, which shows regional concentration of processing firms in 1963, gives a far more accurate picture of the oligopolistic nature of the industry than mere national figures. As can be seen, only in Ontario is there anything approaching a competitive market. In other markets, there is a very high degree of concentration.

TABLE IIc

Concentration in the Poultry Processing Industry in Canada, 1963

Share of the Market Held by the Top	4 Firms	8 Firms
British Columbia	86.6	92.7
Prairies	59.2	83.9
Ontario	30.7	55.4
Quebec	42.3	68.9
Maritimes	90.4	99.1
Canada	20.8	33.1

SOURCE: J.T. Hill, "Structure and Concentration in the Canadian Poultry Meat Industry," *Canadian Farm Economics*, I, No. 2. June 1966, Table 6.

In 1963, about 35% of all the poultry processing plants were located in Ontario; these plants processed about 41% of all the poultry in Canada.The Ontario Special Committee on Farm Income reported that in 1962, about 85% of the broiler processing facilities in Ontario were owned by the feed manufacturing firms. In 1974 it was reported that the Tend-R-Fresh poultry plant of UCO at Petersberg, and the Canada Packers' plant at Walkerton, processed about 35% of the province's turkeys and 30% of the broiler chickens.

Because of the fact that the poultry processing industry exists as a branch operation of the larger agribusiness corporations (including the co-ops), it is very difficult to measure the profitability of the industry. In the United States, the National Commission on Food Marketing reported that between 1948 and 1964 chicken processors averaged between 4% and 14% return on net worth after taxes; turkey processors between 9% and 26%; and egg handling, distributing and processing, about 20%. Their analysis of the ten leading firms in each area in 1964 found the following average return on net worth after taxes: turkey processors, 13.3%; chicken processors, 6.2%; and egg handling and processing, 18%.

In Canada there are no figures available on profits in the industry. Industry spokesmen insist that poultry processing in itself is not very profitable, and that the profits came from selling the feed to the farmers. Plants are regularly being shut down. But in the early 1970s, considerable new capital was being invested in Quebec in the processing industry, indicating that it can't be that unprofitable.

When the wages in the industry are taken into consideration, it is hard to believe that the corporations are not making a profit. In 1966, the average hourly wage in the industry was $1.43. This compared to $2.47 in the red meat packing industry, which historically has been the only food processing industry with wages that are higher than the average for all manufacturing. The Canadian Food and Allied Workers Union traditionally bargains on a national level for its red meat employees, which are 80% male. In contrast, the same union negotiates with the same meat packers on a regional basis for the "white meat" industry, where 50% of the employees are women.

On the other hand, the poultry industry handles a very perishable product. Ewell P. Roy found that poultry prices were often low in the United States, compared to other foods, where the chain stores were most concentrated. In this market situation, the bargaining power of the chains allowed them to "set the tone of the market."

In Canada, The Royal Commission on Price Spreads in Food Products (1959) concluded that agricultural products which were not sold under brand names by the established corporations were most often subject to advertised loss leaders by the retail chains. The poultry processors, because of the very perishable nature of their product, were in a very weak bargaining position whenever there were supplies above normal. This produced lower returns to poultry processors and the primary producers.

The Importation of Chicken from the United States

In recent years there has been a significant increase in the amount of chicken imported into Canada from the United States. Between 1970 and 1973, the amount imported was less than 10 million lb. per year. In 1974 this rose to 12 million lb., in 1975 to 20 million lb., and then to 55 million lb. in 1976. In this last year imports were the equivalent of 12% of total Canadian production. With poultry producers in a tight cost-price squeeze, and with provincial marketing boards concerned about "over-production" by their licensed producers, the question of U.S. imports became a matter of national concern.

While producers and their farm organisations were pushing for controls on imports, the Consumers Association of Canada and the retail chains were advocating the right to unlimited imports.

In British Columbia, Super-Valu, the local retail chain owned by Weston interests, imported 60,000 lbs. of chicken from the United States. The B.C. Broiler Marketing Board seized some of the imported birds and declared that importers must have a permit from them before importing chickens.

In a court case supported by the B.C. branch of the Consumers Association of Canada, Super-Valu challenged the legal authority of a provincial marketing board to restrict imports. They won their case in the B.C. Supreme Court in 1977.

The threat of cheap U.S. imports to the Canadian industry, plus the inter-provincial conflicts, led to the establishment of the National Chicken Marketing Plan. However, the new Board will not have the ability to eliminate imports. U.S. pressure led to a compromise whereby the new Canadian agency will continue to allow imports at "an historical level." In practice, this was established at an average of imports over the previous three years.

Why are U.S. Prices Lower?

The Consumers Association of Canada has denounced poultry marketing boards and has demanded imports of cheap poultry from the United States. Others have taken a similar position. Why are U.S. costs lower?

First, as is the case for nearly all foods, costs of production are higher in Canada because of the climate. In this industry, where feed is the largest single cost, this is a significant factor. But U.S. poultry is also cheap because it is one of the most exploitative industries in the United States.

In 1959, about 60% of all broilers produced in the U.S. were produced by independent farmers; by 1970, 98% were produced by growers under integrated contracts with the processors. In 1950, broilers on the average cost the U.S. consumer 60 cents a pound; by 1970, this had fallen to 42 cents.

During the period since World War II there has been a tremendous concentration of poultry processing in the United States. Between 1947 and 1958, there were 233 company takeovers; 98 were by the four largest corporate integrators, Central Soya, Cotton Producers,

Pillsbury, and Ralston Purina.

This concentration and vertical integration has resulted in a tremendous squeeze on individual poultry producers. In 1966, the U.S. National Commission on Food Marketing reported that labour returns for growers varied from a high of $.91 an hour in Maine, to $.77 in Delmarva (Delaware, Maryland and Virginia), down to $.24 in Georgia. The U.S. Department of Agriculture reported that in 1969-1970 the grower received between 1.5 and 2 cents a pound for broilers. A study for 1970 done by the USDA found that in Northern Alabama, growers averaged $.36 per hour for their labour. They lived on depreciation, went further into debt, and finally went bankrupt.

The feed companies are the major integrators. They make their money on selling the farmer the feed. Through tricky incentives, they encourage overcapacity at the farm level, not caring that the "burn out" takes a heavy toll on poultry producers.

There are few Canadians who wish to work for the equivalent wages earned by their counterparts in the southern United States. Few poultry growers wish to operate at a loss. But there are also other reasons why U.S. costs are lower than those in Canada. Canadian governments have established much higher sanitary and environmental standards than are found in the American south.

The Corporate Ideal

The large poultry farm of today is the epitome of factory farming. No longer do we see flocks of birds in the field. They are all jammed together in cages. They are mechanically fed specially prepared feed, normally including arsenic to promote growth, and antibiotics to protect against disease. Leukosis, a cancer in chickens, is the most serious problem facing the industry. It is widely recognized that Leukosis is caused by stress from crowding chickens in small areas.

Aside from stress, chickens often suffer from rickets and deformed bones, as feed is often deliberately low in calcium and vitamin D in order to promote small bones in the finished product. In modern poultry farming, there is only artificial lighting. There are no windows. (Chickens will rush to the light of a window, and cannibalism is heightened.) The industry feels that because customers want a yellow tint to their chickens, the birds will be fed artificial colouring.

Is this really the product that Canadian consumers crave? Do we really want to live and work in a society controlled by a small handful of large multinational corporations?

SOURCES

Blair, John M. *Economic Concentration*. N.Y.: Harcourt, Brace, Jovanovich, Inc., 1972.

Bronson, Harold E. *Canadian Meat Packing and Farmer Organization*. Saskatoon: University of Saskatchewan. Brief prepared for the Saskatchewan Wheat Pool, October 1967.

Canada. 27th Parliament. First Session. Proceedings of the Special Joint Committee of the Senate and House of Commons on Consumer Credit (Prices). Nos. 15, 16 and 20; November 7, 8 and 22, 1966.

Canadian Agriculture in the Seventies. Report of the Federal Task Force on Agriculture, December 1969. Ottawa: The Queen's Printer; 1969.

Engleman, Gerald, and Arnold Aspelin. *National Oligopoly and Local Oligopoly in the Meat Packing Industry*. Economic Research Service, U.S. Department of Agriculture, 1973.

Food from Farmer to Consumer. Report of the National Commission on Food Marketing. Washington, D.C.: U.S. Government Printing Office, June 1966.

Hill, J.T. "Structure and Concentration in the Canadian Poultry Meat Industry," *Canadian Farm Economics,* I, No. 2, June 1966, pp. 5-13.

Hill, J.T. "Vertical Integration and the Poultry Meat Industry," *Canadian Farm Economics*, I, No. 3, August 1966, pp. 8-13.

MacPherson, Myra. "Chicken Big," *The Washington Post, Potomac Magazine*. May 11, 1975, pp. 15-16, *et seq.*

Meat Packers Council of Canada. *Meat: Canada's Largest Food Industry*. 1973-4 edition.

Mitchell, Don. *The Politics of Food*. Toronto: James Lorimer & Co., 1975.

Morris, J.L., and D.C. Iler. *Processing Capacity in Canadian Meat Packing Plants*. Ottawa: Food Prices Review Board, August 1975.

Ontario Special Committee on Farm Income. Research Report No. 11, "Marketing of Beef and Pork in Ontario," 1969.

Ontario Special Committee on Farm Income. Research Report No. 12. "Marketing Poultry and Eggs in Ontario," 1969.

Patterson, R.A. *A Survey of Selected Segments of Canadian Agribusiness*. A Study for the Federal Task Force on Agriculture. Unpublished, September 1969.

Reiger, George. "It Takes a Tough Man to Fowl a Tender Creek," *Audubon*, LXXIX, No. 6, November 1977, pp. 142-145.

Report of the Royal Commission on Price Spreads. Ottawa: The King's Printer, 1937.

Report of the Royal Commission on Prices. Ottawa: The King's Printer, 1949.

Report of the Royal Commission on Price Spreads of Food Products. Ottawa: The Queen's Printer, September 1959.

Restrictive Trade Practices Commission. *Report Concerning the Meat Packing Industry and the Acquisition of Wilsil Ltd. and Calgary Packers by Canada Packers Ltd.* Ottawa, 1961, RTPC No. 16.

Reynolds, Neil. "Food Unfit for a Swine," *Harrowsmith*, I, No. 6, March/April, 1977, pp 18-27, *et seq.*

Robbins, William. *The American Food Scandal*. N.Y.: William Morrow & Co., 1974.

Roy, Ewell P. *Contract Farming, U.S.A.* Danville, Ill.: Interstate Printers & Publishers, Inc., 1963.

U.S. National Commission on Food Marketing. *Poultry and Egg Industries*. Technical Study No. 2. Washington, D.C.: U.S. Government Printing Office, June 1966.

Wellford, Harrison. *Sowing the Wind*. N.Y.: Bantam Books, 1972.

Williams, Willard F. "The Meat Industry," in John R. Moore and Richard G. Walsh, eds., *Market Structure of the Agriculture Industries.*Ames, Iowa: The Iowa State University Press, 1966.

3. THE CEREAL INDUSTRIES

Throughout Canada's history, the grain industry has been central to the development and expansion of the economy. In the food industry, it has traditionally been more important than the meat industry. With the opening of the West to settlement, there was a mercantile boom in exports of grains to Europe. But there was also an industrial development in Canada linked to the expanding wheat economy.

In 1878 the railroad from St. Paul, Minnesota to Winnipeg was completed. Soon after, A.W. Ogilvie & Co. began selling wheat to Minnesota for milling, and in 1881 opened the first flour mill in the West, in Winnipeg. Nevertheless, most of the flour mills were built in Ontario and Montreal.

In the 1880s the grain trade in the West was dominated by the CPR, which controlled the country elevators and the major elevator at Fort William. Ogilvie and the CPR were closely linked through the Montreal Anglo-Saxon business establishment, including the Bank of Montreal and the Sun Life Assurance Co.

The complete control of the grain shipping industry in the West, and the Winnipeg Grain Exchange, was broken in 1906 when the first of the farmers' co-operatives, the Grain Growers' Grain Co., was admitted to the exchange. The co-operative elevator companies grew quickly and soon dominated this area of the cereal business.

By 1971, the four farmer-owned co-operatives had about 58% of all the grain elevators on the prairies. When the Saskatchewan Wheat Pool bought the grain handling facilities of Federal Grain, this gave the co-ops about 85% of the prairie elevators. By 1976, the elevators were divided as such:

Saskatchewan Wheat Pool   1,317

Alberta Wheat Pool	789
United Grain Growers	701
Pioneer Grain	443
Manitoba Pool Elevators	284
Cargill Grain	253
N.M. Paterson & Sons	89
Parrish & Heimbecker	65

In 1974, Cargill Inc. bought National Agri-Services from Peavy of Minneapolis. On the prairies, the American company had fewer elevators than Pioneer Grain, owned by the Richardson family. Yet, the sale created a growing concern among the prairie grain farmers.

Cargill Inc. is the largest grain trader in the world, with annual sales in the mid-1970s of over $10 billion. Along with Continental Grain Company, a New York-based firm owned by the Fribourg family, Cargill handles over 50% of the world's grain trade. There are three other companies in the trading business: Cook Industries, based in Memphis; Bunge Corporations, owned by Bunge & Born, now located in Brazil; and Louis Dreyfus Corporation, based in France and owned by the famous Dreyfus family.

While these companies are largely playing a merchant's role, they are major speculators in the grain commodity futures markets. In 1971, Cargill rigged the wheat market in Chicago, artificially raising prices. In 1973, Cargill helped precipitate the soybean embargo in the U.S. by cancelling 40% of its futures contracts, creating panic buying in the industry. According to Joel Solkoff, this drove up prices and brought a fortune in profits for the traders. The farmers got relatively low prices, and the public paid in higher food prices.

But the power of these companies, and their influence in high government circles, was most clearly revealed in the infamous Soviet grain deal of 1972. The five giant firms had inside knowledge of Soviet grain shortages and of the Soviets' intention to buy heavily in the U.S. market. They obtained this information from U.S. Department of Agriculture officials. No one else knew of this until the corporations had made the deals with the Soviet buyers.

U.S. farmers contracted their grain from $1.25 a bushel; when the deal was made public, grain prices skyrocketed, and the profits all went to the middlemen, mainly Continental Grain and Cargill. Furthermore, the grain companies received $300 million in export subsidies from the U.S. government.

The U.S. Senate Subcommittee on Investigations reported that Cargill sold wheat to a wholly-owned subsidiary in Latin America in order to collect the forty-seven cents a bushel subsidy; this company in turn sold it to another subsidiary in Europe, which made the final sale.

66

The whole affair was simply a paper transfer, as the grain never left the ship bound for the buyer.

Thanks to the Wheat Board, Canadian farmers are protected from this sort of manipulation and exploitation. But the corporations are pushing to cut back the powers of the Wheat Board and to bring in a "free market" in wheat sales, and they have found supporters in the federal government, particularly Otto Lang.

For these reasons, Canadian farmers fear the impact of Cargill and its friend, Continental, on the Canadian system of marketing grains. No sooner had they bought out National Grain than they announced that they were going to build large inland terminals on the prairies, bypassing the traditional system of local country elevators and local rail transportation. They were also going to build "high through-put" elevators, which would serve larger areas. Farmers not only fear the destruction of their elevator investment, they fear that this centralization will further destroy the remaining rural communities.

By 1976, Cargill had built two inland terminals. Through a large advertising campaign, they attacked the central marketing system of the Canadian Wheat Board, urged farmers to build their own inland terminals, and pushed farmers to contract sales to local markets outside the Wheat Board.

A group of farmers around Weyburn, Saskatchewan swallowed the line, many feeling that the Wheat Pools had become too large, overly bureaucratized, and inefficient. They raised the capital and built their own terminal, seeking to be "independent." When it was opened in 1976, they announced that they had hired a manager from Cargill and that they had contracted with Cargill to ship all their grain!

On top of this, the Trudeau Government, under pressure from Otto Lang, began to lease federal grain elevators on the prairies to Continental Grain. There is a genuine fear among farmers that they will not be able to confront the economic and financial power of the huge American grain companies and their friends.

Worldwide sales for Cargill in 1976 were around $11 billion, and they reported a profit of $179 million. Their earnings were more than two and a half times the total earnings of all the Canadian co-operative elevator operations. We can also understand some of the concern of the prairie farmers when we remember that total sales by the Canadian Wheat Board in 1976 were around $3 billion.

In January 1977, Cargill issued its first annual report on operations in Canada since the acquisition of National Grain. On an investment of $50 million, it reported sales of $574 million and a net income of $8.9 million, a return on equity of 18%. That is not a bad start.

Many prairie farmers find themselves in a difficult position at this time. On the one hand they fear that the invasion of Cargill and

Continental will cause further attacks on the Canadian Wheat Board, posing a major threat to the pool elevators, in which they have a large financial investment. At the same time, they are not very happy with the performance of their own elevator companies.

In practice, the pool elevators are not very different from the private firms in the field. All the elevator companies work together in a united front, as the grain handling employees know only too well. When it comes to raising fees for handling, storing, drying, or cleaning grain at the country elevator level, all the elevator companies take the same position.

In May 1978 the Alberta Pool decided to push ahead with the building of a second grain elevator for Prince Rupert, B.C. Under their proposal this would be accomplished by a consortium of the elevator companies, including Pioneer Grain, Parrish & Heimbecker, and Cargill Grain.

While everyone agrees that the grain elevator system of grading is far superior to the old days of "free enterprise," there are still occasional problems. In April 1978, four companies in Manitoba were charged under the Canada Grains Act for accepting high-quality red spring wheat as utility grain. The four charged were Manitoba Pool Elevators, United Grain Growers, N.M. Paterson and Sons, and Pioneer Grain. The two co-ops pleaded guilty and were fined.

While the farmer-owned co-operatives dominate (for the time being) the grain handling trade in Canada, they have not significantly diversified into other areas of the grain industry, though they are significantly involved in the feed industry. But only the Saskatchewan Wheat Pool has constructed a flour mill, and that was in 1949. In the area of processing grain into food, they have felt that they could not compete with the huge conglomerate agribusiness firms, both Canadian and American.

THE FLOUR INDUSTRY

The flour industry was a natural by-product of the wheat economy; it soon became a major food and export industry. By 1890, there was such excess capacity in mills in Ontario that they were only operating two months out of the year. Ogilvie led an unsuccessful move by the four largest millers to establish a combine.

At an early period the American firms began to move into Canada. In 1910 Minnesota Mills, now known as Robin Hood, began to construct and buy flour mills in Western Canada. In 1906 the Quaker

Oats Company bought an established flour mill in Peterborough, and in 1912 it bought its first mill in Western Canada, at Saskatoon.

Despite discrimination against flour exports, and preference given to the export of grain, the flour industry grew and prospered down through World War II. From this time on, the industry has been in decline. In the years between 1945 and 1950, total flour production averaged 47 million hundredweight (cwt) per year; 55% of this production was exported. By 1968-1969, annual production was down to 37.6 million cwt, and only 28.5% of this was being exported.

While domestic consumption of flour rose over this period, the per-capita consumption of flour has been steadily declining. The other negative factor has been the loss of export markets. After World War II the European countries raised their tariffs against flour imports and encouraged the development of local mills. The Common Market (now including Great Britain) has also cut into Canada's exports. In addition, the Common Market and the United States have various schemes for subsidizing their export of flour.

The other major factor in industry decline has been the building of flour mills in the underdeveloped countries by the large multinational food companies. For example, since World War II Quaker Oats has built flour mills in Argentina, Colombia, Brazil, Venezuela and Mexico. Labour is cheap, and return on equity has been about 20%, much higher than could be obtained in North America. By 1965, the sales of Quaker Oats' twenty-two overseas plants were over $100 million, and represented around 25% of total sales. At the same time, Quaker Oats has shut down its flour mills in Moose Jaw and Saskatoon, and has concentrated its operations at its Peterborough plant.

Maple Leaf Mills is the largest flour miller in Canada, and one of the largest agri-business corporations. It was re-organized as Maple Leaf Mills Ltd. in April 1961, as an amalgamation of the original company plus Purity Flour Ltd. and Toronto Elevators Ltd. Its takeover by American interests has been relatively recent. In 1977 Norin Corp. of Miami, Florida (formerly Norris Grain Co. of Chicago) offered $18 a share to buy the 17% of the outstanding stock that they did not own.

Maple Leaf Mills has been slow to follow the American agribusiness trend towards overseas expansion. In the early 1970s MLM signed an agreement to manage and operate a flour mill owned by the government at Port-au-Prince, Haiti. In 1972 they built a flour mill in Trinidad, jointly owned with the local government, and in 1976 they signed an agreement to build a plant at Bridgetown, Barbados, 40% of which will be owned by MLM and 60% by the government. They also agreed to build a mill at Kingstown, St. Vincent, 40% owned by

MLM and the remaining 60% by local interests and the government of St. Vincent. In 1977 the corporation announced that it was negotiating with the governments of Barbados and Haiti to establish livestock and poultry feed plants, and was studying the possibility of entering the grain handling industry in Brazil.

In recent years, the industry has relied more and more on shipments under the overseas aid and relief programmes of the federal government. However, this government support has been insufficient to maintain a growing industry. In 1971, 54% of Canada's flour sales were to the USSR, for export to Cuba. This caused problems for some mills in Canada, as the U.S. Trading with the Enemy Act prohibits branch plants of American corporations to sell to countries on the "unapproved list." Quaker Oats, Robin Hood, and Pillsbury Canada were cut out of this export market. However, there were enough Canadian-owned firms around to supply the needed commodity.

Today, the U.S. government permits its corporations to trade with Cuba. But they must still obtain prior approval from the U.S. government. In the fall of 1976, Cargill made a major deal to sell corn to Cuba, and in 1977 Maple Leaf Mills announced that sales to the USSR represented 21% of their total production.

Economic Concentration

Between 1934 and 1971, the number of flour mills in Canada declined from 435 to fifty-one. Concentration of sales and power in the hands of a few large conglomerate food firms has been increasing at a rapid pace.

In 1948 the Combines Division of the Justice Department completed their investigation into the flour milling industry in Canada. They found that, at least since 1936, members of the Canadian National Millers Association had regularly conspired to make agreements to control and fix common prices for the sale of flour, rolled oats, millfeeds, and course grains. The prominent firms in this effort are the same ones which dominate the industry today: Maple Leaf Mills, Ogilvie, Robin Hood, and Quaker Oats.

When, contrary to law, the Mackenzie King Government refused to publish the report the Combines Commissioner resigned in protest. Public pressure led to the delayed publication of the Report, but the Liberal Government, loyal to big business and foreign interests, refused to take any action.

The degree of concentration in the industry today is very pronounced. Using Joe S. Bain's classification, it is a "very highly concentrated oligopoly." In the late 1960s, Maple Leaf Mills, Ogilvie,

70

and Robin Hood had around two-thirds of the flour milling capacity and about 80% of total sales. Quaker Oats, once a dominant firm, had been reduced to only 2% of the domestic flour market.

In recent years, the major flour mill operators have been concentrating their efforts in more specialized areas, reflecting some sort of agreement between themselves. This type of an arrangement, even though informal, is common where tight oligopolies exist.

First, Quaker Oats sold off its poultry and feed division to Maple Leaf Mills. It decided to concentrate on breakfast cereal and pet food manufacturing. Ogilvie sold its poultry division to Green Giant and has decided to specialize in flour, feed, and the grocery products. Robin Hood Multifoods has remained in the flour industry, where it has kept its 50% share of the market in Western Canada. However, with flour sales down, the Minnesota firm has expanded rapidly into frozen foods, grocery products, and specialty meats, while keeping its feed, hatchery, and poultry operations.

Maple Leaf Mills is clearly the dominant firm in the cereals industry. When it bought Quaker Oats' agricultural division, it became the industry leader in poultry and feeds in central Canada. As well, it is the largest flour miller. In 1976, it expanded its share of the Western Canadian market by purchasing the Calgary flour mill and bakery mix division of Pillsbury Canada Ltd. It is only marginally active in the grocery products industry, except for oil seed crushing and margarine. Ralston Purina has concentrated in the feed and poultry area.

The other major change in the industry is the shift in flour production to the East, following closure of flour mills in Western Canada. In 1950, only 48% of milling capacity was in the East; this had risen to 69% by 1975.

This was a major subject treated by the Royal Commission on Grain Handling and Transportation, headed by Emmett Hall. A staff study by T.G. Johnson concluded that part of the reason for the shift was the myriad of government subsidies and Wheat Board payments and charges which discriminate against Western millers. This was estimated to represent an additional cost of forty cents per hundredweight. Being close to the wheat did not give Western millers any advantage.

THE FEED INDUSTRY

The feed industry has shown a remarkable growth in Canada since the end of World War II, matching the growing Canadian consumption of red meats and poultry. Between 1961 and 1971, industry sales increased from $291 million to $631 million.

At the same time, the number of plants in the feed industry declined, and the major corporate enterprises expanded their domination of the industry. R.A. Patterson reports that in 1966 independent operators of feed mills held only 7.3% of total industry sales. In all regions of Canada farmer-owned co-operatives have been in the feed business for a long time. In 1966, they had 22% of the plants and 23% of the market. Patterson notes, however, that the co-ops were only maintaining their share of the market; the large corporations, with the advantages of vertical integration, were steadily expanding their share of the feed industry.

Concentration and Regional Markets

The feed industry is one of the agribusiness industries in which there is no national market, in spite of some degree of product differentiation by the major firms. The product is bulky and heavy and shipping costs are very high. Entry into the field by new local firms is relatively easy.

In his study of the feed industry in the United States, Daniel Padberg notes that "the unit of effective competition between manufacturers in the sales of their output can be restricted to a rather small geographic space . . ." The "relevant market" in most cases is smaller than the size of the state. Transportation costs are the key.

The regional nature of the industry is reflected in statistics on the share of the national market held by the major feed firms. In the United States in the 1930s, the four largest firms had 25% of total shipments; by 1964, this had dropped to 17%. Of the twenty largest firms in the industry in the U.S. in 1964, only five or six could have been described as national firms, marketing feeds across the country. The top twenty firms had only 31% of the national market.

In Canada in 1965, the top four firms had 28% of the national market, and the top twenty firms had 51%. This higher rate of concentration is usually attributed to the smaller size of the Canadian market. In Western Canada, National Grain (now owned by Cargill) has been the industry leader. The co-operatives have a fairly large share on the prairies. Buckerfields (owned by the Richardson family) is the dominant firm in British Columbia.

In spite of the fact that cattle and hogs are a major farm product on the prairies, the feed industry is concentrated in Ontario and Quebec due to the large poultry operations, dairy farms, and increasing hog production. In 1966, Ontario and Quebec accounted for 75% of the feed industry shipments.

In Eastern Canada, the dominant firms are Maple Leaf Mills and Ralston Purina. The latter is the largest feed company in the United States. Canada Packers was one of the earliest firms in the feed business in Canada and still ranks as the third largest firm in central Canada and as the dominant firm in the Atlantic provinces. In Ontario, United Co-operatives of Ontario is also a major feed producer, with regional feed mills, 120 local mixing mills, and 140 local retail outlets in 1968.

In November 1974, a spokesman for the Newfoundland Egg Marketing Board complained that the four feed companies in that province had "stopped offering competitive prices." He asked the House of Commons Special Committee on Egg Marketing to request the Combines Division to make an investigation. For eighteen months, none of the four companies (Fortress Feeds, Canada Packers, Hillcrest Feeds, and Maritime Co-operative Services) had offered competitive prices.

Therefore, in spite of national figures that show low levels of concentration, the real market has a much higher degree of concentration. The few large firms which dominate local markets also engage in some degree of product differentiation. Padberg reports that in twenty-four of the thirty-three American states for which data is available, the four largest companies have 50% or more of the business. He found that "the major brand companies probably have significantly more than half of the business in most localities. The small companies provide the competitive fringe." The real market is "composed of a few very large firms engaged in nonprice competition and containing many small firms which are motivated toward price competition."

The Advantages of Integration

In this era of corporate-style farming, in animal and poultry production, there has been a change in the style of operation of the feed industry. Feed was originally provided as a by-product of the grain milling process: the screenings, bran, shorts, and middlings were sold to farmers.

The other main source of feed was the by-product of meat packing—the inedible parts were sold as high-protein feed supplements. Canada Packers was the early company in this field, but only Swift Canadian sold concentrates in all regions of Canada. By 1958, according to the Restrictive Trade Practices Commission,

Canada Packers' feed supplements represented about 38% of all the feed supplements provided in Canada.

At first Canada Packers provided only feed concentrates, which were sold to small manufacturers of complete feeds. In the late 1930s they moved into the field of chopping mills, which mixed concentrates with grain brought in by the farmer. From there it was only natural to move into the field of owning and operating feed mills as well as undertaking licensing arrangements with franchised local mills. With this integration came the extension of credit. By 1958, Canada Packers had arrangements with 661 feed mills across Canada for the production of their advertised product, Shur-Gain feeds.

Similar arrangements are available from the other major feed manufacturers who also market advertised brands. Maple Leaf Mills and Ralston Purina have their own feed mills, but sell their feed supplements and brand products through franchised dealers. These integrators have non-price competitive advantages: advertised feed products of supposed high quality, services provided by a large organization, and credit. In addition, they have market power arising from their vertical integration into the hatchery and poultry processing industry. A few large co-ops, like UCO and Co-operative Federee de Quebec, are trying to maintain a similar system which will allow them to compete with the large corporate firms.

The Ontario Committee on Farm Income found that the large corporations "have substantial advantages over independent operators in the purchasing of ingredients." The integrators have the advantages of access to feed to meet growing demand, a more captive outlet, less competition, lower selling prices, more efficient scheduling of operations, and lower inventory costs. The large feed companies buy most of their antibiotics, vitamins and other feed supplements from the large European pharmaceutical companies. Their volume purchases provide economies of scale, if not quality.

In both the United States and Canada, the industry suffers from excess capacity. Padberg cites a study of the grain handling industry of the North Central United States. In 1954, it was judged to have 52% excess capacity; by 1960, excess capacity was set at 53%. Integration, he concludes, was inspired by the problem of excess capacity, as manufacturers sought outlets for their differentiated products.

A study by the Economic Research Division of the U.S. Department of Agriculture in 1965 concluded that "data obtained in this survey and previous ones clearly indicate that many feed mills should be removed to provide for more efficient operations."

The Ontario Farm Income Committee found a similar situation in that province. The number of local feed mills was "excessive." The move towards more centralized bulk operations was expected to result in a removal of many of the local mills—and in a higher degree of concentration by the large corporations.

The situation had not changed by 1978. Nicholas Florakas, Chairman of the Board of the Canadian Feed Industry Association, reported in Saskatoon in January that the feed processing industry was only operating at about 50% efficiency. He argued that this was mainly due to the 50% reduction in pork production in Western Canada, overproduction of feeds by the dairy farmers in Quebec and Ontario, and the reduced demand for poultry in Eastern Canadian markets.

THE BAKING INDUSTRY

The bakery industry has undergone significant changes in the last twenty years, mainly reflecting the shift to large shopping centres serviced by the large retail food chains. The delivery of door-to-door bakery goods has all but disappeared in Canada; only in Quebec does it still have some life. The small retail bakery, owned by the independent operator, is also rapidly disappearing. Those who have managed to survive are now identified as local "specialty shops." whose baked goods offer a quality and variety which is generally not available at the major chain stores.

The largest segment of the industry consists of the wholesale bakeries. These large bakeries distribute their baked goods through the chains and the small independent stores. According to the Bakery Council of Canada, between 1952 and 1967 they increased their share of the market from 52% to 69%.

The other new development in the industry has been the rise of bakeries owned by the retail food stores. Several of the big chains operate large, centralized bakeries. This is true of Steinberg's and Loblaw. All the other chains operate in-store bakeries. With the growth of these two segments of the industry, by the late 1960s the share of the market held by the family-run business, which operates on a local or regional level, dropped to about 20%.

The industry as a whole is concerned because per capita consumption of baked goods is declining. Between 1976 and 1977 bread volume dropped by 7%. All of the large bakeries are complaining that they are having a hard time continuing business, let alone expanding or upgrading manufacturing facilities. There are several reasons advanced to explain this situation.

All of the large chain stores have their own bakeries and continue to sell bread as a loss leader. The decline in consumption is blamed on rising personal incomes and the rapid proliferation of fast food outlets. Fewer people seem to be packing lunches to take to work. The large bakeries complain of rising labour costs (as do all companies); but they have been very hard hit by rising fuel costs, particularly in the West and the Maritimes, where delivery trucks have to travel long distances.

In contrast, the specialty bakers are doing well. For example, Rudolph's Specialty Bakeries Ltd. of Toronto has annual sales of $7.5 million, and services 1,500 outlets with a fleet of refrigerated vehicles. Over the past five years, sales volume has risen by 120%. The owner, Rudolph Paech, argues that the real reason for their success is that "our products taste so good." There still is a small market of people who want their food to have some taste.

Vertical Integration

The major characteristic of the bakery industry today is the degree of vertical integration. First, there is the integration of the flour companies. Over the years Maple Leaf Mills has protected its share of the market by integrating forward into the baking business. Today they are dominant owners of several of the largest chains of bakeries in Canada, including Corporate Foods, Canada Bread, Eastern Bakeries, Hillcrest Farms, and Gainsborough Kitchens. They are also co-owners, with their "competitor," Ogilvie Flour Mills, of McGavin Toastmaster, a chain of bakeries with a retail delivery system that is the largest in the four Western Provinces.

The other form of integration has been at the retail level. George Weston (which has its own flour mills) has a captive market for bread and biscuits through their large chain of retail stores as well as their system of wholesale distribution to independents. Dominion Stores is the dominant shareholder in General Bakeries, a large baking chain which controls Inter-City Baking Co., Consolidated Bakers, Wonder Bakeries, Walker Bakeries, O'Mally's and Marra's Bread. In 1978 General Bakeries bought the bread division of Christie Brown. Steinberg's has its own baking companies to serve its stores. In fact, according to the bakery Council of Canada, between 1965 and 1975 Steinberg's was the only company to build a new large bakery in Canada. The other major chain stores—Safeway and A & P—have either developed in-store bakeries or have contracted with bakers for private brand baked goods. Canada Safeway has a couple of bakeries run by its subsidiary, Empress Foods.

Degree of Concentration

The bakery industry is one of the food industries for which there is no national market. The product is so perishable that it would be impossible for a company to try to establish large centralized plants. The president of Morrison-Lamothe Bakeries of Ottawa argues that large bakeries are actually at a disadvantage as they must incur substantial transportation costs. Moving bakery products more than 100 miles is considered too costly.

The other reason for the failure to create a national market is the difficulty in establishing brand name products. There is very little difference in the commercial bakery product between firms; only the types of bread differ. Therefore, advertising is a low factor in this industry.

The degree to which the industry is characterized by a local market is reflected in the fact that the distribution of bakeries across Canada closely mirrors the distribution of the population. This is not the case for more highly manufactured food products.

Nevertheless, there is a definite trend towards centralization in the ownership of the bakery industry. This is accomplished through national firms which own and operate a chain of bakeries and a wholesale distribution system. In the United States, the National Commission on Food Marketing (1966) reported that the top two bakers, Continental Baking Co. and American Bakeries Co., sold 14% of all commercial bread. The eight largest baking companies controlled 40% of all commercial bread. Most of these companies are expanding outside the bakery industry. Continental, the largest bakery, was purchased by International Telephone and Telegraph. The other large bakeries are active in the biscuit industry and are expanding into the frozen goods and snack food area. General Host Corporation believes that the only future for the bakers is to expand into convenience and snack foods.

In 1963, the U.S. Federal Trade Commission did a survey of bakery concentration in seventeen American cities. They found that the four largest bakeries averaged 63% of the local market. Thus, the true market reflected a much higher degree of concentration than the national market.

The largest baker is Continental. It has attempted to establish brand identification through a massive advertising campaign for Wonder Bread and Hostess cakes. In the mid-1970s, ITT was spending 5 million dollars a year on national television advertising alone. As a result, Wonder Bread held 12% of the national bread market. In 1971, five independent bakers in California filed an antitrust suit against Continental; the result so far has been a temporary court injunction prohibiting ITT from acquiring any additional bakeries.

The baking industry in Canada is more concentrated than in the United States. The Royal Commission on Price Spreads of Food Products (1959) noted that in 1948 the five largest firms had 33% of the national market, and by 1956 the six largest had 37%. The Combines Commission Report found that in 1965 the top four firms had 32% of the market and the top eight firms had 44%. Today, the wholesale industry is heavily dominated by Weston, Maple Leaf Mills, and General Bakeries. McGavin Toastmaster is the dominant firm in Western Canada.

Quebec has traditionally been the market which supported many local, independent bakeries. But even here, the growth of large firms through merger is the trend. In 1969, only 33.5% of bakery sales were by firms owned by French Canadian businessmen. The dominant firms were Nabisco, Weston, Grissol Foods, General Bakeries, and the bakeries of Maple Leaf Mills. In 1976 two of the largest bakeries merged, Robin-Le Pain Moderne and Durivage. Combined sales were expected to be around $25 million, making this the largest bakery group in Quebec, and giving them about 35% of the Montreal market.

As the Bakery Council of Canada has noted, there has been a steady fall in per-capita consumption of bread, although it still remains as a basic food for lower income groups. For the larger bakeries, white bread remains the staple item, accounting for about 90% of bread production. The other 10% covers the various non-white bread products. In Western Canada, there is a strong shift in consumption patterns to whole wheat bread; in 1977, white bread held only 54% of this market, with whole wheat bread taking 23.5%. The industry claims that the shorter runs of non-white bread is a major factor in its higher prices. A study of the baking industry in Ontario in 1967 by the Federal Department of Industry found that bread accounted for 56% of the value of shipments in the industry, and "sweet goods" accounted for another 25%.

There has been a rapid increase in the sale of frozen bakery products in Canada in recent years, particularly in the "sweet goods" area. The market for fresh baked "sweet goods" has been declining about 10% per year. Other food firms are active in this area, as product differentiation and transportation of the product is more feasible.

Today's supermarket includes Pepperidge Farm Frozen baked goods (owned by Campbell Soups), frozen "sweet goods" produced by Kitchens of Sara Lee (Canada) Ltd., McCain's frozen pies and desserts, Kellogg's frozen waffles, and Quaker Oats' frozen waffles and french toast. Morrison-Lamothe bakery is moving into the frozen baked goods area, and Maple Leaf Mills has kept its place in this market through their Gainsborough Kitchens division. Morton brand frozen pies and cakes are manufactured by ITT.

The Bakery Council of Canada insists that profits in the bakery industry are quite low. For example, in 1976 General Bakeries reported they had a return of only 1.1% on sales and 6.7% on capital investment.

In 1973, the Liberal Government in Quebec introduced legislation designed to combat loss leader selling by the large food chains. The Quebec Professional Bakers Association and the Montreal Bakers Association supported the legislation, noting that predatory pricing by the chains was driving down the price of bread and forcing the closure of small bakeries.

Another problem, mentioned in the federal study of the Ontario industry, is the presence of excess capacity. The excess capacity at the wholesale level, plus the inability to create a differentiated product, has led to significant price competition in these markets. Normally, this is reflected in low returns on capital investment.

Nevertheless, R.A. Patterson concludes that "the industry is profitable and . . . can make a greater return on equity than most segments of the food industry." This conclusion is supported by figures from the Canadian Imperial Bank of Commerce showing a return on net worth in the period 1961 and 1964 ranging between 7.1% and 11.4%. But this may be changing. Without a doubt, the small bakeries, with the exception of the specialty bread bakeries, are rapidly going out of business. The large conglomerate firms are the ones increasing their share of the market.

THE BISCUIT INDUSTRY

The biscuit industry has traditionally been distinguished from the bakery industry according to the extent of perishability of the product. Statistics Canada limits their classification of "biscuit manufacturers" to those firms primarily engaged in the manufacturing of biscuits, crackers, pretzels and similar "dry" products.

The much longer shelf life for biscuits has enabled the firms in the field to distribute on a much wider scale, establish national markets for some products, and engage in a significant degree of product differentiation through volume advertising. Thus, in contrast to the baking industry, the biscuit industry in Canada is one of the most highly concentrated, with oligopolistic results.

High Concentration Oligopoly

According to an industry spokesman quoted by R.A. Patterson, George Weston Ltd. and Christie Brown and Company account for 40% of the national market. The next three firms, Dare Foods, David et Frere, and Peak Frean account for another 35% of industry sales.

In fact, the industry may be more highly concentrated than this suggests. The Report of the Combines Commissioner (1971) found that the top four firms in 1965 accounted for 67% of industry sales, and the top eight firms, for 84% of the market.

The industry is also highly concentrated in the United States. The U.S. National Commission on Food Marketing reported that in 1964 the top four companies accounted for 61.8% of national sales. The top three firms in the 1960s were the same as in the 1930s: Nabisco, Sunshine Biscuits, and United Biscuits.

The leading firm in Canada is George Weston Ltd. Most Canadians are aware of the phenomenal growth of this giant corporation, which began as a baking and biscuit manufacturing concern. It is today the largest food conglomerate in Canada and one of the largest in the world. In the 1970s, the Weston Empire consisted of about 188 companies, owned as subsidiaries; the route to corporate power for the Weston family has been through the takeover of other firms.

Between 1900 and 1948, J.C. Weldon reports that George Weston Ltd. took over fifty-five companies in the vegetable foods area. (The other major companies in the merger field were Canadian Canners, with fifty-three; Maple Leaf Mills, forty-eight; and Canadian Breweries, twenty-two.) While the other three major Canadian conglomerates were in turn taken over by foreign corporations, George Weston Ltd. remains controlled by the Weston family.

Furthermore, the Weston takeovers were not only small concerns. Wallace Clement notes that six of the corporations taken over were already dominant firms in their field. In the biscuit industry, there was not only George Weston Biscuits but also Interbake Foods, McCormick's, Paulin Chambers, Marven's, and Kambley Canada, all of which were major biscuit manufacturers before absorption.

In 1972, Weston Foods Ltd. changed its names to Interbake Foods Ltd., to improve marketing in the biscuit and confectionery area. A company marketing study found that Canadians viewed Weston as a foreign-owned company because Garfield Weston lived permanently in England. In contrast, the public believed Nabisco to be a Canadian company, because its Shredded Wheat package had always featured a picture of Niagara Falls. In 1970, Weston biscuit and confectionery subsidiaries had sales of $104.5 million.

The other major firm in the biscuit field is Christie Brown. In 1927

National Biscuit Co., the largest biscuit manufacturer in the United States, came to Canada in the classic manner by purchasing Telfer Biscuit Co. In 1928 they bought Christie Brown & Co., one of the largest and best known Canadian food corporations. Nabisco wisely chose to maintain the established Canadian brand name. In 1929 they consolidated their position in this industry by purchasing the Shredded Wheat company factories in both Canada and the United States. Today, Nabisco's Christie Brown subsidiary runs a close second to Weston in the biscuit field.

The third largest biscuit company by sales in Canada is Associated Biscuits of Canada, a British firm, which markets Peak Frean and David Biscuits. Dare Foods, a private Canadian company, is considered to run fourth, slightly ahead of United Biscuits (Canada) Ltd., another British firm. Grissol Foods, a subsidiary of IMASCO, is already established in the field and is expanding through the takeover of other smaller biscuit and confectionery firms, mainly in Quebec.

A number of other smaller Canadian firms have been able to keep a foot in the biscuit market by concentrating on the manufacturing of more specialized products (those not carried by the large manufacturers, and which are portrayed as having a special quality) or by gaining a share of a smaller regional market.

The success of the biscuit manufacturers is clearly aided by the fact that the chain stores have not entered the manufacturing field, as they have in baked goods. For the most part they have not even tried to establish private brands. Therefore, the national manufacturers have a virtual free run at the supermarket shelf space. R.A. Patterson quotes an industry spokesman who estimates that twenty accounts handle about 80% of Canada's total sales.

George Weston has an obvious advantage, and the products of its companies clearly have priority shelf space in the Weston supermarkets. Weston wholesalers also distribute Weston biscuits to the smaller independent stores.

As a general company policy, Canada Safeway carries almost no Weston biscuits in their stores. Instead, they grant more shelf space to U.S. brands with smaller lines—items which are often not found in the other supermarkets.

For example, in my survey of Saskatoon supermarkets in the spring of 1974, I found Safeway carried a full line of products by David & Frere Ltd.; none of the other three chains carried any products by this company. David & Frere was owned by Hershey Foods. Other biscuit goods carried by Canada Safeway, and generally not available in the other chains, included products by General Host, General Mills, Kellogg's, Quaker Oats, Cadbury, Schweppes & Powell, as well as single products manufactured in Europe.

81

The biscuit industry is therefore characterized by a high degree of product differentiation and a very high degree of corporate concentration. They do not even have competition from supermarket private brands. Under such circumstances, profits should be high. Unfortunately, there are no Canadian studies in this area. However, the study by the National Commission on Food Marketing (1966) found that the four largest biscuit manufacturers in the United States averaged a profit rate of 10.1% on sales and 13.3% on shareholder equity. For the food industry, this is quite high.

BREAKFAST CEREALS

The breakfast cereal industry is one of the most interesting food industries. It is the epitome of the economic model which holds that high advertising, high market concentration, high product differentiation, and high profits go hand-in-hand. For Canada, it is also an industry which is almost 100% foreign-owned.

In the era of "convenience foods," the ready-to-eat or dry cereals provide about 80% of industry sales. In Canada, Kellogg's is the leading firm, with about 50% of the total market. If you check the local supermarket, you will find that Kellogg's regularly has around 50% of the shelf space. The other two leading manufacturers in Canada are Nabisco and Quaker Oats. These three together reportedly have 90% of the Canadian market.

There are a few other firms in the dry cereal market as well. General Foods (Post's Cereals) is the next largest, followed by General Mills and Weetabix, a British firm.

When people used to cook porridge, Quaker Oats was the clear industry leader. They are still the leader in this area, but its importance is declining. Other firms in the cooked cereal field include Ogilvie, Robin Hood, and Nabisco. The baby cereal market is shared by two American firms, Bristol Myers (Pablum) and Heinz.

The industry is concentrated in other countries as well. In Great Britain, the Monopolies Commission reported that in 1971 Kellogg had 55% of the market, Weetabix 22%, Nabisco 12% and Quaker Oats 4.5%. The remainder of the market was provided by a manufacturer of house-brand cornflakes, a market phenomenon that is absent in Canada and the United States. Kellogg's Corn Flakes alone accounted for 33% of industry sales.

In the United States in 1971, Kellogg's had 45% of the market, General Mills 21%, General Foods 16%, Quaker Oats 9%, Nabisco

82

5% and Ralston Purina 3%. Kellogg's Corn Flakes was still the market leader, with 9.2% of all sales. Thus, the top four firms had 91% of the market, which would make the industry a "very highly concentrated oligopoly" according to Joe S. Bain's classification.

The Role of Advertising

Advertising has always been a most important part of the breakfast cereal industry. Arthur F. Marquette's official history of the Quaker Oats company notes the pride it has in having pioneered in many of the advertising techniques now accepted as normal in the American food industry: scientific endorsements, customer testimonials, cash-prize contests, sampling, market testing, giveaways and boxtop premiums.

Quaker developed the special package, easily identifiable, which shrunk to maintain its 10 cents-a-box tradition. In more recent times it was quick to sponsor radio shows for children, including Sergeant Preston of the Yukon, Roy Rogers, and Rin Tin Tin. It introduced selling gimmicks in the supermarkets (six for ninety-nine cents rather than the individual price of fifteen cents). It learned which areas of the stores were best for displays, and then gave kick-backs for the best locations.

A proxy battle took place within the Quaker Oats company, with Ferdinand Schumacher, one of the original owners, arguing that low prices sold breakfast cereal. Henry Parsons Crowell, another early owner, argued that advertising was the most important factor in selling. You don't have to read the book to know who won.

In 1970, in the United States, the breakfast cereal manufacturers spent 13% of total sales on advertising, by far the highest of any food industry. The Food Prices Review Board, in their non-scientific survey of a few food firms, concluded that breakfast cereal manufacturers in Canada spent only 3.8% of sales on advertising in 1971. However, Kellogg Canada reported that in 1970 they spent "about $4 million" on advertising, which was about 10% of sales. It should also be recalled that American food firms, and in particular breakfast cereal manufacturers, benefit from overflow advertising through cable TV and magazines from the United States.

Why spend so much on advertising? The industry approach is summarized by C.W. Post, the founder of the company now known as General Foods: "You can't just manufacture cereal. You've got to get it halfway down the customer's throat through advertising. Then they've got to swallow it."

A number of critics have concentrated on the fact that breakfast

83

cereal advertising is aimed at youth, and therefore is a form of brainwashing the innocent. The cereal industry has broken down its market as follows: the under thirteen age group, 38%; fourteen to forty-four age group, 31%; and the over forty-five age group 31%. One industry source says that 70% of the dry cereal product is consumed by the under twenty age group.

The advertising dollar goes much farther when it is aimed at the children's market. Saturday morning television advertising time is much cheaper than prime time; so is the after-school time. Prime time in the United States, according to the U.S. Federal Trade Commission, costs about seven times more than Saturday morning. Thus, the introduction of a new brand of sugar-coated munchies requires a much smaller outlay in marketing than for other new food products.

In 1970 the dry cereals came under strong attack for their lack of food value. In the good old days, when everyone ate Quaker's rolled oats, breakfast was a very nutritious meal. But the ready-to-eat cereal is something else. Dr. Robert B. Choate, a nutritionist, popularized the facts in testimony before a U.S. Congressional Committee. The dry cereal, he found, was almost devoid of vitamins, minerals and high quality protein, which were largely destroyed in the heating process of manufacturing.

For a short time, the manufacturers feared a consumer reaction. They came out with "fortified" brands with some vitamins added. But the consumer reaction was short-lived. By 1972 the cereals that were ranked very low in nutrition (Kellogg's Corn Flakes, Rice Krispies and Sugar Frosted Flakes; General Mills' Cheerios) were again the most popular brands. In spite of the attack on adding sugar, sales of the cereals with sugar coating were on the rise. This example reveals the power of advertising and the almost complete lack of nutritional education in North America.

In Canada, the federal government announced in January 1978 that they were going to make cereal manufacturers list the percentage of sugar in the product on the label. Needless to say, this was vigorously opposed by the cereal manufacturers and the Grocery Products Manufacturers Council. They argued that it wasn't fair to single out their industry when sugar was a major ingredient in most processed foods. Arnold Langbo, president of Kellogg Salada Canada, pointed out that children obtain a much greater amount of sugar in soft drinks, and there was no requirement that sugar content be listed on the container.

TABLE IIIa

Major Cereals Companies

Company	Ownership/Control	1971 Sales
Maple Leaf Mills	U.S.—Norris Grain	$202,154,000
Ogilvie Flour Mills	Canada—Brascan	140,680,000
Weston Companies	Canada—George Weston	106,767,000
Robin Hood Multifoods	U.S.—Int. Multifoods	104,881,000
Ralston Purina (Canada)	U.S.—Ralston Purina	82,896,000
Nabisco-Christie Brown	U.S.—Nabisco	74,023,000
Quaker Oats of Canada	U.S.—Quaker Oats	45,680,000
General Mills Canada	U.S.—General Mills	44,000,000
General Bakeries	Canada—Argus/Dominion	36,225,000
Vachon Inc.	Canada—Vachon Family	35,000,000
McGavin Toastmaster	Canada/U.S.—Ogilvie/MLM	35,000,000
National Agri-Services	U.S.—Cargill	32,623,000
Kellogg Co. (Canada) Ltd.	U.S.—Kellogg	30,000,000
Canadian Food Products	Canada—Aneas Investments	19,370,000
Dover Industries	Canada—M.M. Campbell	17,793,000
Associated Biscuits of Canada	U.K.—Associated Biscuits	13,137,000

Monopoly and Profits

On January 22, 1972, the U.S. Federal Trade Commission (FTC) issued a complaint contending that the Big Four in dry cereals had "illegally monopolized the market for breakfast cereals." They were charged with "unfair methods of competition and unfair and deceptive trade practices." The two smaller firms, Nabisco and Ralston Purina, were not specifically charged but were named as "co-conspirators."

The main charge was that between 1950 and 1970 the four introduced a profusion of about 150 brands of cereals. Through advertising directed primarily against children, they "artificially differentiated" and exaggerated "trivial variations such as colour and shape." The trademarks were used "to conceal basic product similarities." Furthermore, they were charged with making claims for their products (i.e., diet control, physical strength) which could not be supported in fact.

The companies were also charged with manipulating shelf space allocation in supermarkets, a practice aimed at eliminating small and regional manufacturers. Their numerous company acquisitions over the years were alleged to have "enhanced the shared monopoly structure of the industry." Kellogg's was the recognized price leader.

The result of these monopoly practices was "artificially inflated cereal prices, excessive profits, limitations on product innovation, and, in general, a lessening of competition." The case finally went to trial on April 28, 1976.

In Canada, there is a higher degree of economic concentration than in the United States. But no federal government action of any kind has ever been taken against these large foreign corporations.

Kellogg's is the clear leader in the ready-to-eat breakfast cereal industry. But it is primarily a breakfast cereal company and thus has limited sales and assets. Even if it wanted to, it could not win a price war with industry giants like General Foods and General Mills. As the FTC points out, because of this it was very important for the corporations to agree not to package private brands for the supermarkets.

What are the profits in the breakfast cereal industry? In Canada, this is very hard to determine. The conglomerate firms do not provide their own stockholders (let alone outsiders) with a breakdown of profits between divisions within the companies. There are no government studies. The foreign-owned corporations in the food industry are normally 100% owned by their parents, and it is difficult even to get sales figures from them.

But there is no reason to believe that industry profits here are very different from those in the United States and Great Britain, which have similar markets with the same firms. In the United States, the National Commission on Food Marketing reported that the Big Four had the following percentage return on net worth (investment) in 1968: Kellogg's, 24.3%; General Foods, 20.2%; General Mills, 16.8%; and Quaker Oats, 12.4%. The industry as a whole averaged a return on net worth of 19.4%.

The Monopolies Commission in Great Britain reported even higher profits in that country. On the other hand, it found that the breakfast cereal industry was making very efficient use of its capital investment, normally running three shifts on a five or six day week. For Kellogg, net profit as *a percentage of sales* ranged from 23.8% in 1967 to 13.4% in 1971, a phenomenal rate of profit. In 1971, this was translated into a 31.7% return on net worth.

The other companies (Weetabix, Quaker Oats, and Nabisco) reported that their average rate of profit on net sales was only slightly below that of Kellogg. Quaker Oats, as in the United States, reported a lower return. Nevertheless, the economic performance of the breakfast cereal companies is indeed incredible; it is a profit situation that can only occur through monopoly control.

Taken as a whole, from grain handling through processing, the cereals industry is the most important food industry in Canada. It is an industry which is characterized by a high degree of concentration of economic power in the hands of a few corporations and is integrated on a horizontal and vertical basis. Only in the baking industry is there a fairly competitive situation, and even here concentraton on the local level is high. As with other food industries, when the basic food is processed, it increases in price. The more highly processed products are more widely advertised, and return a much higher rate of profit to the food corporations.

SOURCES

Canada. Department of Industry. Food Products Branch. *A Survey of the Bakery Industry*. November, 1967.

Cohn, William. *Out of the Cracker Barrel: The Nabisco Story, from Animal Crackers to Zugus*. N.Y.: Simon & Schuster, 1969.

Cook, G.R. "Feed Manufacturing Industry in Canada," *Agricultural Institute Review*, March-April 1964.

CUSO Manitoba. *The Sun Never Sets on Cargill*. Winnipeg: CUSO Manitoba, 1978.

Director of Investigation and Research. Combines Investigation Act. *Concentration in the Manufacturing Industries of Canada*. Ottawa: Department of Consumer and Corporate Affairs, 1971.

Dougherty, Phillip H. "Battle of the Breakfast Table," *The New York Times*, October 22, 1972, pp. 1, 15.

Fowke, Vernon C. *The National Policy and the Wheat Economy*. Toronto: University of Toronto Press, 1957.

Gray, James. *Business Without Boundaries: the Story of General Mills*. Minneapolis: University of Minnesota Press, 1954.

Hamilton, Martha. *The Great American Grain Robbery*. Washington, D.C.: Agribusiness Accountability Project, 1973.

Hightower, Jim. *Eat Your Heart Out*. N.Y.: Crown Publishers, 1975.

Luttrell, Bill. *Have You Got $10,000 to Burn? The Commodity Future Link in the International Food Chain*. Toronto: GATT:fly. February 1977.

Marquette, Arthur F. *Brands, Trademarks and Good Will: The Story of the Quaker Oats Company*. N.Y: McGraw-Hill, 1967.

Mitchell, Don. *The Politics of Food*. Toronto: James Lorimer & Co., 1975.

National Commission on Food Marketing. *Food From Farmer to Consumer*. Washington, D.C.: U.S. Government Printing Office, June 1966.

Marshall, Herbert, Frank Southard Jr., and Kenneth W. Taylor. *Canadian-American Industry*. Toronto: McClelland and Stewart Ltd., 1976 edition.

National Commission on Food Marketing. *Grocery Manufacturing*. Technical Study No. 6, Washington, D.C.: U.S. Government Printing Office, June 1966.

National Commission on Food Marketing. *Milling and Baking Industries*. Technical Study No. 5. Washington, D.C.: U.S. Government Printing Office, June 1966.

Naylor, Tom. *The History of Canadian Business, 1867-1914*. 2 Volumes. Toronto: James Lorimer & Co., 1975.

North American Congress on Latin America. "U.S. Grain Arsenal," *NACLA Report,* IX, No. 7, October 1975.

Ontario Special Committee on Farm Income. *Farm Supply.* Research Report No. 1, 1969.

Padberg, Daniel I. "The Mixed Feed Industry," in John R. Moore and Richard G. Walsh, eds., *Market Structure of the Agricultural Industries.* Ames, Iowa: Iowa State University Press, 1956.

Patterson, R.A. *A Survey of Selected Segments of Canadian Agribusiness.* Ottawa: Study for the Federal Task Force on Agriculture, September 1969.

Restrictive Trade Practices Commission. *Flour Milling Industry.* Report No. 32. December 29, 1948.

Robbins, William. *The American Food Scandal.* N.Y.: William Morrow & Co., 1974.

Royal Commission on Grain Handling and Transportation. *Final Report.* 2 Volumes. Ottawa: The Queen's Printer, 1977.

Royal Commission on Prices. *Final Report.* III. Ottawa: The King's Printer, 1949.

Royal Commission on Price Spreads. *Report.* Ottawa: The King's Printer, 1937.

Royal Commission on Price Spread of Food Products. *Report.* Volume II. Ottawa: The Queen's Printer, 1959-1960.

Solkoff, Joel. "The Grain Drain: Cargill's Private Empire," *The Western Producer,* April 14, 1977, p. 7.

United Kingdom. Monopolies Commission. *Breakfast Cereals.* London: Her Majesty's Stationery Office, November 1972.

Warnock, John W. "Honesty is our Policy: The Quaker Oats Shutdown," *Next Year Country,* I, No. 1, October 1972, pp. 20-23.

Weldon, J.C. "Consolidations in Canadian History, 1900-1948," in L.A. Skeoch, ed., *Restrictive Trade Practices in Canada.* Toronto: McClelland & Stewart, 1966.

4. THE DAIRY INDUSTRY

Without a doubt, the dairy industry is the most complicated food industry in Canada and the most difficult for the average person to understand. Of all the food areas, it has the highest degree of government intervention, including import controls, general subsidies and marketing boards. It has the highest degree of farmer participation in the processing end, through the growth of producer-owned co-operatives.

Yet, in spite of all this, everyone seems greatly dissatisfied with the industry as it now stands. Consumers feel that prices are too high. The industry is characterized by a growing centralization. The bankruptcy rate of milk processors is perhaps the highest of any industry in Canada, and large multinational food corporations are increasing their control of manufactured milk products. Industry spokesmen complain of low returns on investment.

While dairy farmers are more protected than any of their Canadian brothers, they are leaving the farm in droves—faster than any other class of farmers. They complain that the price they receive is far below what is necessary to carry on a viable operation. In 1976 there were large protest demonstrations in Ottawa by dairy farmers from Ontario and Quebec—the only group of farmers to stage such protests in the mid-1970s. Why is there such dissatisfaction?

Decline of Consumption

Much of the crisis in the industry can be traced to the decline in the consumption of dairy products in Canada. Between 1961 and 1971, the per capita consumption of milk products dropped from 453.4 lbs.

to 365.5 lbs., a decline of 21.4%. There was a drop in consumption of fluid milk, cream, butter, evaporated milk and skim milk powder. There was a slight increase in the amount of cottage cheese and ice cream consumed and a significant increase in cheddar and specialty cheeses. Unfortunately for Canadian farmers, much of the increase in cheese consumption has been in imported specialty cheese. These have shown the most dramatic increase in per capita consumption.

For many reasons, this is a distressing trend. First, milk is the most complete food; it contains all the essential amino acids, balanced in a ratio ideal for human consumption. It is rich in minerals, especially calcium. North Americans generally have no difficulty digesting milk sugars, although this is sometimes difficult for older people who lack the enzyme lactase. But almost everyone is able to consume cultured products like buttermilk and yogurt. Furthermore, whereas milk products are a very good nutritional food, their substitutes (particularly soft drinks, coffee, tea and alcoholic beverages) are positively harmful to the human body.

Why, then, has there been such a drop in consumption of milk? First, it is claimed that the high price of milk at the retail level drives away customers. But the price of substitutes has risen as fast as milk prices, so this cannot be the entire reason. Consumers with families are aware of the amount spent on dairy products, as it easily shows up in the household budget. In addition, consumer groups and government officials have concentrated public attention on the rise of the price of milk while generally ignoring the rise in the price of substitute beverages, particularly soft drinks.

A second reason could be the fear of cholesterol. Many doctors and fad diet advocates have urged people not to eat eggs or milk products. Many people have stopped consuming milk products, believing that this will cut down cholesterol levels.

Finally, there is the fact that the dairy industry spends almost nothing on advertising, whereas the other beverage industries spend massive amounts. The gross margins in the fluid milk area are so low that equivalent advertising could not be carried out without a substantial increase in the cost of milk. On the other hand, cheese is a highly differentiated product. Its marketing is controlled by large conglomerate food corporations which are among the highest advertisers. This is the only segment of the dairy industry that has shown any increase in sales. It is not just a coincidence.

Nevertheless, the dairy industry is still the second most important food manufacturing industry in Canada. Industry sales in 1971 were $1,509 million, and it employed 29,855 people, second in both cases only to the meat industry.

The Industry at the Producer Level

The most notable fact about the production of milk in Canada is the dramatic drop in farmers producing milk in Canada. In 1961 the census reported there were 309,000 farms with milk cows; this had dropped to 222,000 by 1966, and to 145,000 by 1971. Over the ten year period 146,000 farmers quit the business, representing a 53% decline. This trend is definitely continuing. For example, in 1972 it is reported that 7,356 Quebec dairy farmers alone left the business.

With this there has been a shift to larger farms with larger herds. Between 1966 and 1971 the number of farms with fewer than eight cows dropped by 31%; those with between eight and thirty-two cows dropped by 11%; farms with more than thirty-three cows more than doubled. During the same time, farmer efficiency has shown a remarkable growth. Between 1960 and 1971 the output-per-cow rose by around 33% to 8,000 lbs. of milk per year. However, a problem here is the wide variation between provinces in output-per-cow. In 1972, a cow in Ontario produced around 8,700 lbs. of milk, while one in B.C. produced 12,000 lbs. Clearly, weather variations make a national programme more difficult; they also go far to explain why the cost of milk products is higher in Canada than in the United States.

At the farm level, there is a major breakdown between types of producers: in 1971, about 16% of farms were producing fluid milk for direct consumption, and the other 84% were producing industrial milk for the processing industry. There are substantial differences in costs between fluid and industrial milk producers. Studies done in 1971 showed that on the average the capital investment for fluid milk production in Ontario was 50% higher than for industrial milk production; a study in the same year for Quebec found average capital investment to be 14% higher.

The two studies also reveal that basic capital costs (real estate, machinery and equipment, and livestock) are more than 100% higher in Ontario than in Quebec for fluid milk producers, and more than 60% higher in Ontario for industrial milk producers. There is no doubt that the wide variations in farm production costs between provinces makes any national policy more difficult, particularly when it is based on an income stabilization policy. When subsidies (in lieu of import controls) paid to farmers for the same product differ between provinces, farmers question them. But when they are the same, regardless of region and cost differences, then inequities obviously develop.

91

The other major characteristic of the industry is the concentration of farmers and processors in the two central provinces. In 1974, Ontario and Quebec had 62% of the processing establishments, about 60% of all milk producers, and their processing plants accounted for 73% of total national sales. In 1972, Quebec accounted for 45% of the Canadian total of industrial milk. The $300 million which went to farmers represented 40% of total farm income in Quebec, making it by far the most important farm group in the province. No other province relies on milk production to the same extent. That may be one reason why in 1976 about 15,000 Quebec dairy famers descended on Ottawa and in an angry, bitter mood threw milk in the face of Eugene Whelan, the Minister of Agriculture.

There are reasons for this centralization in Ontario and Quebec. First, fluid milk is produced and distributed in a ratio very close to that of the population in general. As a perishable product, it can't be moved long distances. Secondly, the large multi-national milk processing firms have located their plants in Ontario and Quebec to be near population centres, the supply of milk, and large pools of labour.

In spite of the fact that dairy farmers have co-ops, marketing boards, and various forms of federal subsidies and import controls, the returns to dairy farmers are among the lowest in Canada. This fact was noted by the Food Prices Review Board in their quarterly report on March 22, 1974. The discovery created a contradiction for them as they had chosen to single out marketing boards with production controls as the prime culprit in rising food prices.

David MacFarlane and Lewis A. Fischer cite a 1971 study undertaken by the province of Quebec on the costs of producing fluid and industrial milk in that province. Allowing the farmer a return on his labour of $2,900 a year (which must work out to less than $1.00 an hour), they concluded that the industrial milk producer lost $2,019 per year and the fluid milk producer made $44.00 a year.

Furthermore, this study involved a sample of 483 industrial milk producers and 421 fluid milk producers, all of whom had "better than average farms." Yet even these "more efficient" producers could only produce very low returns. It is therefore not surprising to learn that the 1966 Census for dairy farmers found that 64% obtained a majority of their income from off-farm work or sources other than dairy farming.

Government Support for the Industry

The ironic aspect of this area of the food industry is that while dairy farmers have been leaving the farms in droves, while net income to dairy farmers remains very low compared to other farmers, and while the local and regional milk processing plants have been disappearing at a fantastic rate, this food industry has the longest and most complete system of government subsidy and support.

During the depression, dairy farmers pressed for protection and support. While their demand was rejected by the Mackenzie King Government, when the Tories under R.B. Bennett took office, changes were implemented. After 1930, import restrictions became a regular feature of the industry. First, this was a recognition that the cold Canadian climate created additional costs of production; Canadian dairy farmers could never compete with the dairy industry in more temperate climates. Secondly, the Bennett Government argued that this oldest of Canadian farming enterprises was worth saving, along with the related manufacturing and jobs that went with it. Self-sufficiency in this basic food area was deemed a desirable policy.

The other major programme established by the Bennett Government was direct dairy subsidies to producers and manufacturers. This was intended to keep retail prices down so that the lower income families could afford dairy products. While these subsidies were revoked by the return to office of Mackenzie King, under farmer pressure they were re-established during World War II and maintained as a permanent programme through the Agricultural Price Support Act of 1944.

Presently, price supports are maintained through the Agriculture Stabilization Act of 1958. A floor price for milk is established under this programme, 80% of the most recent ten-year average. These floor prices under the federal programme have been limited to industrial milk; price supports have been regularly extended to butter, cheddar cheese and skim milk powder.

In 1966, the Canadian Dairy Commission was created to try to bring order and change to the industry. The following year Parliament Hill was mobbed by angry dairy farmers from Ontario and Quebec demanding increased returns for their labour. The CDC was given control over imports; it was to export surpluses, even at substantial losses. The new policies were also directed towards the elimination of the smaller farmers. In 1971, the CDC introduced the Market Sharing Quota, which imposed heavy penalties on dairy farmers for producing more milk than their quota allowed.

At the same time, direct subsidies have been increasing. In 1962, manufacturers were granted a 12 cents a pound subsidy on butter. In 1973 the federal government introduced a 5 cents a pound subsidy on fluid milk. These programmes were designed to lower prices to consumers.

Fluid milk production is controlled on the provincial level through marketing boards which exist in all provinces. All of these operate on the basis of quotas allotted to producers based on "historical production." The problem here has been that farmers are very efficient, and through their efforts are regularly able to increase production from their cows. It is hard to make a farmer restrict the natural inclination to produce more. However, as per capita consumption of milk has declined, problems of "overproduction" have become normal. Some provinces have also introduced subsidies for fluid milk, trying to keep the price down to consumers.

In April 1978, the Trudeau Government modified its dairy policy. While farmers were asking for the chance to produce specialty cheese, the import quota from Europe was reduced by only 5 million pounds. Common Market tariffs have eliminated traditional Canadian exports of cheddar cheese, and Canadian farmers were asking for reciprocal treatment.

The federal dairy subsidy was to be cut substantially from $477 million in 1977 to $329 million in 1978. But the major protest came from consumer groups, as the federal government eliminated the subsidy of 34 cents a pound on skim milk powder.

In spite of all these efforts, the industry remains in serious trouble. And while dairy farmers struggle along at very minimum income levels, the Consumers Association of Canada, the Food Prices Review Board, and a number of "free enterprise" professors have concentrated their attacks and public attention on marketing boards. By doing so they have diverted attention away from the larger problems associated with the food industry in Canada.

The Growth of Industry Concentration

The milk industry in Canada has demonstrated a tremendous shift towards centralization in the period since the end of World War II. This has been the case for both fluid milk distribution and the processing of industrial milk into other end products. Furthermore, the trend continues at a rapid pace: in 1961, there were 1,710 dairy factories in Canada; by 1974, this had declined to 557.

The study for the Federal Task Force on Agriculture, released in 1971, found that around 45 fluid milk plants were disappearing per year, a drop of 5% annually; industrial milk plants were disappearing at about 25 per year, or a rate of 3%. At the same time, employment peaked in 1969 and has been declining steadily since then.

In Quebec, the centre of the dairy industry in Canada, there were 2,240 dairy factories operating in 1938; by 1951 this had fallen to 1,080; by 1965 there were 455, and by 1973 only 160. Philippe

Pariseault, General Manager of Agricole Co-operative de Granby, predicts that by 1980 there will be only 20 industrial milk plants and only 10 fluid milk pasteurizing plants left in Quebec.

However, if we are to look at industry concentration only at a national level we will get a very distorted picture. The Combines Investigation study on concentration found that in 1965 the top four firms had only 25% of the national market, the top eight 35%, and the top 20, 49%. By most standards, this would appear to be a highly competitive industry when compared to concentration levels in other industries.

But the milk industry is not a national industry because of the perishability of its product. Some of the more highly processed products (like skim milk powder) can be marketed nationally, but this is not a basic characteristic of the industry.

The real market is the local market, particularly for fluid milk and other highly perishable milk products. Transportation costs in refrigerated trucks and railroad cars also limit the extensiveness of the real market.

For example, Duncan Allan found that in Ontario in 1961 the Big Three (Silverwood's, Borden and Dominion Dairies) had 35% of the fluid milk sales, 42% of cream sales, and 42% of buttermilk sales. But they only operated in seventeen markets in Ontario, the larger ones; and here the Big Three had between 50% and 75% of total sales. In Toronto, they had "only" 60 % of the market due to the existence of four "independents." One of these has been swallowed up by Silverwood's. Furthermore, in the late 1960s and early 1970s Beatrice Foods began a major takeover programme in Ontario and emerged as one of the four major firms in the field.

The dairies that have disappeared have largely been taken over by the larger ones. Allan found that between 1945 and 1961, bankruptcies were rare. Of the 97 dairies that disappeared, 26 were bought out by the Big Three. In Quebec, most of the dairies that have disappeared were taken over by the large co-operative at Granby, or else were integrated into larger co-ops under the umbrella of Co-operative Federee de Quebec.

Similar patterns have been apparent in the United States. In 1970, the Big Four were Borden, Kraftco, Beatrice Foods and Carnation. The National Commission on Food Marketing reported that between 1922 and 1964, the eight largest firms acquired some 2,000 independent dairies, and 63% of this total was acquired by Borden and Kraftco. In the late 1960s the U.S. Federal Trade Commission ordered the four largest firms not to acquire any additional dairies for 10 years. It was because of this order that Beatrice Foods moved into Canada, buying up sixteen dairies in Ontario, to become a major force in that market, and Modern Dairies, which gave the company 60% of the Manitoba dairy market.

In the area of processed milk products, the industry is much more highly concentrated. The Royal Commission on Price Spreads (1959) found that in 1956 the four largest firms had 59% of the condensed milk market, with Carnation and Borden being the two dominant firms. In the processed cheese field in the same year the top five firms had 87% of the national market, with Kraft Foods being by far the market leader.

Today, the cheese market is totally dominated by Kraft, which reportedly has 80% of the market. The other large marketers are major food firms: Brooke Bond Foods, Ault Foods (Brascan), Burns Foods, Canada Packers, J.M. Schneider, and Nestle (Canada) Ltd. The co-operatives are generally forced to sell most of their cheese to these firms or else to the retail stores which market it under a house label.

At the local level, ice cream sales are dominated by the chain stores, most of which market house brands provided by their own or local dairies. Independent firms, including the co-ops, often have a difficult time getting shelf space for their dairy products in the chain supermarkets. Silverwood's is the only firm which tries to market ice cream on a national level.

But in direct retail sales of ice cream, the large corporations are again dominant, with many of them foreign-controlled. The national leaders are as follows: Laura Secord (Brascan), Baskin-Robbins (UK—J. Lyons), Orangeroof Canada Ltd. (US—Howard Johnson's), Bresler's 33 (US—Corn Products Inc.), Maynards (Canada) Ltd. (UK—Maynards), Good Humour (UK—Unilever), and Dickie Dee Ice Cream (Canada) Ltd. (US—Dickie Dee).

The trend in the processing field is to large firms which can produce all the various lines of dairy products and operate on a year round basis. For fluid milk pasteurizing, the longer lines and increased flow bring significant economies of scale, despite higher capital and transportation costs. Furthermore, with marketing being the key, diversification is growing. For example, Kraftco and Borden are engaged in so many other food lines that it would be misleading simply to think of them as dairy firms.

The other recent development is vertical integration. First, the chain supermarkets are acquiring their own dairies. (This is eliminating shelf space for the independents.) Even when they do not have their own dairies, they prefer to have long-term contracts with large firms, packaging products to sell under the house brand name. For example, in 1972 Silverwood's explained a decline in earnings due to the fact that the large chains in the Toronto area had shifted to Borden and

96

Dominion Dairies (Kraftco), which undercut them in contracting.

Direct retail sales have also been an outlet for the large dairies: most of this has been through the convenience "jug milk" outlets. Silverwood's is a major leader here, with the large chain of Mac's Milk and Mini-Marts, and now Bantam Stores acquired in 1976 from Royal Oak Dairies. Becker's Milk has also been successful with well over 400 outlets. In Quebec, Perrette stores have been dominant. The advantage here is the returnable 3-quart jug, which provides a saving to consumers due to lower packaging costs. All of these trends, however, have led to a higher degree of concentration of the milk market into the hands of a few large corporations.

The Role of the Co-operatives

The milk industry has the highest degree of producer-owned co-operatives. In 1973 the National Dairy Council reported that the co-operatives had 44% of the milk processing market in Canada, compared to 43% for corporations and 13% for the smaller family-owned operations. This applies to both fluid milk and industrial milk.

Co-operatives and small family-owned operations are dominant in the Atlantic provinces. The Dairy Producers Co-operative dominates in Saskatchewan. Two co-ops, Central Alberta Dairy Pool and The Northern Alberta Dairy Pool, dominate the market in Alberta. In British Columbia, the Fraser Valley Milk Producers Co-operative is the largest operation, and with Shuswap Okanagan Dairy Industries Co-op has a strong presence in the B.C. market. Silverwood's and Palm Dairies, and the dairies owned by the two major chains, Canada Safeway and Super-Valu, have a strong role nevertheless. In Manitoba, the Manitoba Dairy and Poultry Co-operative (Manco) is the only alternative to total domination by Beatrice Foods.

While the co-ops have a very small presence in Ontario, they are by far the dominant force in Quebec. In 1950 the co-ops had 40% of the industrial milk production in Quebec; this rose to 80% by 1973. They are also moving quickly into the fluid milk area, previously held by smaller family-owned firms. Many of the smaller regional co-ops are grouped together under the umbrella of the Co-operative Federee de Quebec.

Special note should be made of Co-operative Agricole de Granby, the largest dairy operation in Canada, owned by 9,200 Quebec dairy farmers. In 1973 it processed 43% of all industrial milk in Quebec through 12 plants. The Granby cheese manufacturing plant is the largest in the world; in 1976, it produced 65 million pounds. It is also moving into the fluid milk area; in the Quebec-Lait fluid milk enterprise, it operates as a partner with private business interests.

Nevertheless, it markets most of its cheese through an agreement with Kraft Foods Ltd. This is a reflection of the fact that it does not have the market power of the big corporations. It could not win an advertising war with the U.S. giant.

Furthermore, it is at the marketing level that the high profits are made, not at the manufacturing level. This is a problem that the dairy co-ops face everywhere: the squeeze from the large manufacturers on the one hand and the chain stores on the other.

But farmers will tell you many stories of the troubles they have had with their co-operatives. Producers quickly lose control over them as they grow in size. They are dominated by an independent management which often acts contrary to the interests of the farmer-owners. For example, the co-operatives in Quebec joined with the private business associations to oppose the creation of a single farmers' organization. They also opposed any form of collective bargaining rights for the new farm organization. Co-ops in the rest of Canada have taken a similar position, opposing efforts by the National Farmers Union to obtain collective bargaining rights. During the Kraft boycott, led by the National Farmers Union, the large dairy co-operatives (which were members of the National Dairy Council) often stood in the forefront of the opposition to the position taken by the NFU and its supporters.

The Role of the Ontario Milk Marketing Board

Many studies have concluded that the most successful government management of milk production and processing has been in Ontario. Here there are two institutions: the Ontario Milk Marketing Board, comprised of producers, and the Ontario Milk Commission, a government-appointed organization which has the power to overrule the OMMB. Farmers and other critics have pointed out that the two boards have operated to benefit the large multinational corporations at the expense of the farmer and the smaller regional co-operative and private firms. David Cayley, who has done extensive research into the Kraft boycott, explains how this is accomplished.

Ontario used to be a major producer of cheddar cheese, of a quality that was world renowned. In the later nineteenth century there were over 1,500 local factories producing cheddar cheese, most of which was exported. In 1973, total Canadian production was only 189 million lbs., and of this only 6 million lbs. was exported.

During this early period dairying was a major farm occupation in Ontario, and there was competition by the factories for farmers' milk.

The big change stemmed from the intrusion of the large dairy corporations, including Borden, Silverwood's and Kraft. Because they were able to produce a multiple line of dairy products, they were able to offer dairy farmers milk deliveries on a year round basis. After farmers shifted deliveries to the larger plants, they found that the price dropped, as did the test grade on their milk.

Farmers were caught in a dilemma. They wanted to keep the local plants in operation, but they wanted the steady income offered by the large plants. When there was competition for milk at peak periods, the large corporations could offer higher prices and take milk from the smaller plants. Their market power enabled them to pass off these temporary additional costs to their consumers; the small plants could not do this.

In 1967 the Ontario government established the Ontario Milk Marketing Board; two years later, the Board established a quota system for milk products. Milk was classified in seven basic categories, from fluid milk down to Class 5, which included cheddar cheese. The small plants were convinced of the equity of the programme; they were "guaranteed" 98% of their production for the year 1968. Most concluded that this was the best they could hope for, given their weak bargaining position.

However, problems soon developed. Milk prices to farmers remained low in relation to costs. With declining net income, farmers continued to leave the land, and milk production dropped. With a shortage of milk, the OMMB distributed it according to the priorities of the original classification. Thus, Class 5 milk, used for cheddar, was lowest on the priority list. The quota for this category was cut from 98% in 1969 to 56% in 1972-1973. With such a low quota, the small plants could not remain in production. They were forced to close, and their quotas were transferred to the large corporations.

In contrast, the large corporations had control over the milk they received; they were able to use their overall quota as they saw fit. Thus, they could shift milk provided under the first six categories to the production of cheddar cheese. This they did, as cheese was the only sector of the milk industry experiencing significant growth. The small plants, making only cheddar cheese, simply could not do this. They didn't have the milk.

For the cheddar cheese processing plants, the situation is getting worse every year. Production of milk is dropping in Ontario. More is now being diverted to manufacturing specialty cheeses and yogurt. In April 1978, the OMMB told the cheddar cheese plants that they would have to accept another 10% cut in their milk supply.

The plant supply quota, established according to what milk the plants utilized in 1968, had dropped to 51% in 1978. Some plants were operating at 48% of capacity. Only the large corporate establishments will be able to survive the squeeze.

The Kraft Boycott

It was the realization of how the system was working that inspired many farmers in Ontario to try to institute a system of collective bargaining. Only through collective bargaining, they concluded, could their gross margins be raised to a level high enough to earn a decent living. It was also the realization that the OMMB, whether intentional or not, was working primarily to the benefit of the large corporations. The main power in the cheese industry, of course, was Kraft Foods, the branch plant of the huge American food conglomerate.

Kraft's power was in marketing. It bought most of its cheese from other factories, both large and small. As noted before, it markets most of Granby Co-op's cheese. It also buys 75% of Ault's cheese. But many of the small cheese manufacturing plants were also delivering the bulk of their product to Kraft for marketing, and this was risky business. It is similar to the vertical contracts that growers have with processing plants: the corporation can simply terminate the contract on short notice.

David Cayley cites one example. The Tourelle cheese factory at Plantagenet, Ontario delivered the bulk of its cheese to Kraft, marketing only 10% on their own. When Kraft found it could get cheese cheaper from a source in Quebec, in 1972 it cancelled the contract, and the Tourelle plant went bankrupt.

The power of Kraft in the market can also be illustrated by a recent case from Alberta. There, the Alberta Dairymen's Association sponsored an "Eat Canadian Cheese" advertising campaign to counteract the increase in sales of European specialty cheeses. Kraft followed the dairy producers campaign with one of their own and reaped most of the benefits. Sales of Kraft cheese went up and no Kraft cheese is manufactured in Alberta.

The boycott of Kraft Foods products initiated by the National Farmers Union was supported by many trade unions and other urban organizations. It was an interesting experiment, and it succeeded in opening the eyes of many Canadians to the question of corporate power and foreign ownership. But it was doomed to failure. The large food corporations and the large co-ops rallied to the side of this huge foreign corporation. Furthermore, Kraft enjoyed the support of all the existing governments, including the provincial NDP governments.

The other major factor was the split in the farmers' organizations. The individual commodity groups (and there are seemingly hundreds of these) are gathered in loose federations, on a provincial basis. The basic philosophy of this grouping of farm organizations is that the farmer and the food processor are joined together in a co-operative manner to produce and distribute food. They deny the adversary situation, and thus they opposed the Kraft boycott.

The American system of farm organizations (which the Canadian Federation of Agriculture follows) is unique; but it places farmers in a weak position, as they are divided into endless groups, pursuing their own narrow self interest, oblivious of the similar plight of their fellow farmers.

This system stands in direct contrast to the United Kingdom and the European Common Market countries. In Britain all farmers belong to the National Farmers Union, and they have used their centralized power to more effectively defend their interests. Within the Common Market, the farm organizations were actually the first group (even before trade unions) to organize, demonstrate and push for common policies across traditional national borders. As a result of their united actions, they have obtained considerable market power, high protections, and subsidies from tariffs which provide them with a standard of living roughly equivalent to that of industrial trade unionists. Not so in Canada, as the Kraft Boycott so clearly demonstrated.

In Ontario, the provincial government gave Kraft $500,000 to help build the plant at Ingleside and another $329,000 to help build Ault's plant as well. Furthermore, it instituted "closing out" grants for the small cheese factories. Their milk quotas were then transferred to the large dairy processors, the main beneficiary being Kraft Foods. It is not just a simple matter of conspiracy, of large corporations financing Canadian political parties. It is a question of the Canadian colonial mentality, which always assumes that biggest is best, and what is American has to be best.

In April 1977, K.G. Murray, President of J.M. Schneider Ltd., warned shareholders that national marketing boards would be detrimental to consumer interests. Costs would rise to processors. But he feared that the new national commodity marketing boards would end up like the cheese industry in Ontario, where Schneider's was operating a processing plant. He noted that "the combined effect of the Ontario Milk Marketing Board and the federal dairy policy is that about 90% of all cheese produced in the province is produced by two firms." The two were, of course, Kraft and Ault's.

For the consumer? Well, there used to be a time when the cheddar cheese produced in Ontario won world competitions. Now that they have adopted J.L. Kraft's system of emulsifying cheddar into the rubber product that is bought in the stores in sandwich-sized, individually-wrapped slices, everything has changed. James S. Turner quotes one U.S. Food and Drug official who believes that "Kraft has been responsible for a major decline in the quality of cheeses made in the United States." Even the old "Cracker-Barrel" now contains artificial food colouring. That may be why there is such an increase in imported specialty cheese coming from Europe. For many cheese eaters, taste still means something, and that only results from the historic techniques and fresh milk. That era may be over for Canada.

Industry Profits

For the dairy industry as a whole, the profit level has not been out of line with the overall food and beverage industry profit picture. Between 1965 and 1970, the return on net worth for the industry as a whole ranged between 8.4% and 10.7%. This was just slightly below the average for the food manufacturing industry. But it was considerably below the return for the other beverage industries. Soft drinks averaged a return of about 13%, breweries about 15%, and distilleries a phenomenal 27%.

But as in all the food and beverage industries, overall figures can be grossly misleading. In the dairy industry, profits have varied greatly between the large firms and the small firms. While industry-wide figures are not available for Canada, a study by the U.S. Internal Revenue Service for 1965 found that the small firms actually lost money, the medium sized firms averaged a return of 4.6% on equity, while the larger firms averaged 9.1%.

In Canada, the large public corporations have had a higher rate of return than the small factories. In the 1960s, Silverwood's averaged between 10% and 12% return on net worth. Dominion Dairies, which is 84% owned by Kraft Foods, averaged a return between 11% and 16% over the same period. Kraft Foods, which is dominant in the marketing end for the more highly processed dairy foods, has done much better. They were able to realize an 18% return on net worth. In 1973 Kraft Foods was also the largest advertiser in magazines in Canada, and along with General Foods the top food company in television advertising.

The public at large has been led to believe that marketing boards operate mainly to the benefit of farmers and that they result in higher prices for consumers. In the milk industry, despite strong marketing boards and government subsidies, dairy farmers are still among the poorest farmers in Canada. While the industry is also characterized by a high degree of producer-owned co-operatives, again this does not seem to have helped the dairy farmer very much.

Only the cheese industry, controlled by Kraft Foods and a few other large conglomerate corporations, shows high industry profits. In this era, marketing is the key, as well as market control. Dairy farmers and their perishable products simply cannot compete with the other beverage industries. They are also in a weak bargaining position at the retail level due to the development of vertical integration by the large chain operations.

TABLE IVa

The Dairy Industry's Leading Firms

Company	Ownership/Control	1971 Sales
Kraft Foods Ltd.	U.S.—Kraftco	$161,442,000
Beatrice Foods (Canada) Ltd.	U.S.—Beatrice	135,000,000
Silverwood Industries Ltd.	Canada—Silverwood Family	118,043,000
Co-operative Federee de Quebec	Canada—Quebec Co-op	83,000,000
Co-operative Agricole de Granby	Canada—Quebec Co-op	82,061,000
Dominion Dairies Ltd.*	U.S.—Kraftco	77,621,000
Borden Company Ltd.	U.S.—Borden	66,903,000
Brooke Bond Foods Ltd.	U.K.—Brooke Bond Foods	59,681,000
Fraser Valley Milk Producers	Canada—B.C. Co-op	58,888,000
Becker Milk Co. Ltd.	Canada—Love Family	56,956,000
Palm Dairies	Canada—Burns Foods	45,969,000
Carnation Co.	U.S.—Carnation	40,969,000

* As Kraft Foods is a wholly-owned American subsidiary, and publishes no annual report on its Canadian operations, it is not known if the filings with the Federal Department of Consumer and Corporate Affairs include revenues from Dominion Dairies. Given the diversification of Kraft into other food areas, it is assumed that they are not.

SOURCES

Allan, Duncan. "Concentration and Competition in Ontario's Fluid Milk Industry," *Ontario Economic Review,* III, No. 7, November 1965, pp. 3-14.
Canada. Department of Industry Trade and Commerce. *The Canadian Dairy Industry.* Ottawa: Department of Industry Trade & Commerce, 1971.
Canada. Director of Investigations and Research. Combines Investigation Act. *Concentration in the Manufacturing Industries of Canada.* Ottawa: Department of Consumer and Corporate Affairs, 1971.
Canada. Statistics Canada. *Handbook of Agricultural Statistics.* Part VII. Dairy Statistics, 1920-1973. Catalogue No. 21-515.

Cayley, David. "The Battle of Plum Hollow," *This Magazine*. X. Nos. 5 & 6, Nov.-Dec. 1976, pp. 32-36.

Clark, J.H., R.G. Marshall, and Brian B. Perkins. *Canadian Dairy Policies: A Research Report to the Federal Task Force on Agriculture*. Ottawa: The Queen's Printer, 1969.

"Dairy Industry Report," *Food in Canada*. Toronto: Maclean-Hunter Publications, XXXCI, No. 3, January 1976, pp. 34-37.

McCormick, Veronica. "A Comparison of the Dairy Industry in Canada and the United States," *Canadian Farm Economics*. IX, No. 6, December 1974, pp. 1-8.

MacFarlane, David L., and Lewis A. Fischer, *Canadian Dairy Industry: Short Term Perspectives*. Ottawa: Food Prices Review Board, March 1974.

Mitchell, Don. *The Politics of Food*, Toronto: James Lorimer, 1975.

National Commission on Food Marketing. *Food From Farmer to Consumer*. Washington, D.C.: U.S. Government Printing Office, June 1966.

National Commission on Food Marketing. *Organization and Competition in the Dairy Industry*. Technical Study No. 3, Washington, D.C.: U.S. Government Printing Office, June 1966.

National Dairy Council of Canada. "Observations & Comments on Pricing Trends of Dairy Foods." Brief presented to the House of Commons Special Committee on Trends in Food Prices, March 6, 1973.

Pariseault, Philippe. "The Quebec Dairy Industry in 1981." Speech to the Ontario Dairy Council, November 21, 1973. Unpublished.

Robbins, William. *The American Food Scandal*. N.Y.: William Morrow & Co. 1974.

Royal Commission on Price Spreads of Food Products. *Final Report*. Volume II. Ottawa: The Queen's Printer, 1959.

U.S. Federal Trade Commission. *Report on Rates of Return in Selected Manufacturing Industries, 1961-1970*. Washington, D.C.: U.S. Government Printing Office, 1972.

Wong, W.Y. "Changes in the Manufacturing Milk and Cream Industry Under the Canadian Dairy Commission, 1969-1970," *Canadian Farm Economics*, V, December 1970, pp. 38-42.

5. PROCESSING FRUITS AND VEGETABLES

Processing of fruits and vegetables has historically been a very important local manufacturing activity in Canada. In contrast to the larger heavy industries, it was not centralized at an early date. The plants were located near the source of supply, and since fruits and vegetables have been grown on a commercial basis in every Canadian province with the possible exception of Newfoundland, the industry was widely decentralized.

In the early period, the proliferation of small, local canneries was assisted by the municipal bonusing system. In the late nineteenth century this practice resulted in too many plants, with a high failure rate, and a general problem of over-capacity. In 1883 the fruit and vegetable processors met in their first attempt to create a system of price fixing. This was institutionalized in 1894 with the formation of the Canadian Packers' Association, which included all but one canner. They agreed to sell only through wholesale grocers and recognized brokers; anyone who broke the combine would be subject to a cash penalty. The attempted combine failed as new plants continued to open, and there were a number of bumper crops which cut its price stabilization system. In 1905 the first steps were taken to move towards monopoly: the formation of Canadian Canneries Company, a merger of twenty-four Ontario factories.

The industry is quite different today. The number of firms in the field is steadily declining, and a handful of large corporations have a dominant position. Foreign ownership by conglomerate firms, operating on a multinational basis, is the dominant characteristic. On the other hand, the large retail chains are heavily involved in processing and selling their own private house brands. The small, Canadian-owned, local firms have seen their day. Production is heavily concentrated in Ontario. The Federal government's commitment to support "free trade" in this food area has opened up Canada to imports from around the world and has obviously been of great assistance to the large foreign-owned corporations which operate on an international basis.

Market Concentration

In both the United States and Canada, the industry has seen a relatively recent move towards market concentration and growth of conglomerate activity. In the United States, the four largest firms held about 40% of the market in the 1960s. As the product is more defined, the degree of concentration becomes much more significant.

For example, Hunt Industries is the largest packer of tomatoes in the world, and along with Heinz, dominates the market in both the United States and Canada. Three firms—Gerber, Heinz, and Beech-nut—completely control the baby food market. Five firms control the frozen vegetable market, and four firms control the canned goods market.

The U.S. National Commission on Food Marketing found that the most significant development is the conglomerate corporation. Of the thirteen largest American food firms, sales in the fruit and vegetable area accounted for only 25% of company revenues. All of them are active in a number of other food areas, as well as in non-food industries.

In Canada, the Royal Commission on Prices (1949) reported that in 1947 the seven largest fruit and vegetable packing firms accounted for over 40% of sales. The Royal Commission on Price Spreads (1959) reported that by 1956 the four largest firms had 43% of total sales. The study by the Combines Commissioner on concentration in manufacturing reported that in 1965 the four largest firms had 38% of the market and the eight largest had 52%. While concentration levels have been higher in Canada than the United States compared to other manufacturing in Canada, the level of oligopoly on the national level appears to be relatively low.

The dominant firms are largely the same as in the United States: Campbell Soups, Heinz, Del Monte (Canadian Canners), Green Giant, and Libby. The only independent, Canadian-owned firm which is in the same league with the foreign-owned giants is McCain's Foods, the family-owned enterprise based in New Brunswick. The other major Canadian packer is York Farms, a division of Canada Packers.

Product domination in Canada, as in the United States, is more highly concentrated. Heinz has a near monopoly on baby foods. Green Giant, Libby and Del Monte are the dominant firms in canned vegetables, while Libby and Del Monte control the canned fruit market. Kraft dominates the area of jams and jellies.

Canned soup, as in the United States is almost completely controlled by Campbell Soup. Actually, there is more "competition" in Canada, as Del Monte, Green Giant (Clark's Soups), and Heinz are also found in most supermarkets. As in the United States, T.J. Lipton (Unilever) has a virtual monopoly in the dry soup field. In the mid-1970s, Nestle decided to try to break into this market.

In a rather unusual development in this industry, in the fall of 1976 Heinz sued Campbell Soups in the United States for $105 million in damages for "attempting to monopolize trade in the manufacture and sale of canned soup at the retail level." This attempt was accomplished, according to Heinz, through predatory pricing practices, high advertising, and promotional discrimination with retail stores, particularly in the allocation of shelf space for display of products.

In the area of frozen products, Green Giant appears to be the most widely distributed nationally-advertised brand in Canada. In the United States, General Foods (Bird's Eye brand) is the leading firm, but it does not distribute nationally in Canada. As in the United States, Coca Cola, through its Minute Maid Division, dominates the frozen juice market. In canned juices, Libby dominates with some competition from Sun-Rype, the company owned by the Okanagan fruit growers.

Advertising and Profits

It is difficult to determine how profitable the fruit and vegetable processing industry is in Canada. All the large corporations are foreign-owned and do not reveal figures on their Canadian subsidiaries. The sole exception is Canadian Canners, 97% owned by Del Monte, but which still must publish an annual report to satisfy its few remaining Canadian stockholders. Their published returns on equity are low relative to other areas of the food industry.

There are a number of reasons for this. First, the large chains are heavily involved in selling their own house brands; as they are not advertised, they can be sold at lower prices. Furthermore, there has been stiff competition in recent years from imports from low wage countries or countries where the national government heavily subsidizes exports. The small firms are in real trouble as most of them depend on packing for the chain supermarkets.

107

The plight of the small packer is cited in R. A. Patterson's study. One industry spokesman stated that the large food chains put tremendous pressures on the small packers. "If the small processor does not come down to an extremely low price on private brand pack for a chain, it will often take the processor's own brand off the shelf and he loses both sales."

We can get some indication of profitability in the industry by looking at the situation in the United States, the home base of most of the large Canadian processors. The studies by the U.S. Federal Trade Commission and the National Commission on Food Marketing all reveal a regular pattern: the returns are much higher for the large companies, and they are the large advertisers.

The 1962 study by the FTC on the frozen foods industry found, not surprisingly, that the largest firms had the highest profits. On the average, they spent 6% of sales on advertising. The 1965 study of the canning industry by the FTC found that the twelve largest firms accounted for 81.4% of all profits, and they averaged a return of 8.8% on sales. In contrast, a survey of 343 firms with sales of under $1 million per year found that they averaged only .7% return on the sales dollar.

The small firms spend very little on advertising. The large firms, according to the U.S. National Commission on Food Marketing, spend between 3.4% and 7% of total sales on advertising. One can only conclude that advertising pays off in higher profits. Furthermore, as many spokesmen for the large firms have noted, advertising had to be increased with the rise of the supermarket house brands in order to retain a share of the shelf space. Caught in this squeeze, there is little hope for the small processor.

The Rise of Foreign Ownership

As with all the American industrial giants, the expansion of the food and beverage firms into Canada was merely a natural move to a new North American region. Most of them expanded into Canada before going overseas. The 1936 study on Canadian-American industry concluded that names such as Campbell, Heinz, Libby, etc., "are as familiar, probably, in Canada as in the United States." Yet they found that in the fruit and vegetable industry, the American branch plants had only between 10% and 15% of the market. Local Canadian businesses still were dominant.

This has changed dramatically. The Report of the Federal Task Force on Agriculture (1969) estimated that "over 70% of the pack of fruits and vegetables is processed in American-owned plants." It concluded that "the increasing domination of the industry by American companies" has created a "major public policy issue."

The Task Force study cited a few of the problems. The parents of the branch plants "appear reluctant to use in Canada the advanced machinery and technology used in its American plants." They also found that some American parents "restrict their Canadian subsidiaries in the export field, preferring to handle this business from U.S. plants." This was particularly true of multinational enterprises; Canadian subsidiaries were not allowed to export to any country where the parent had a local plant.

The American expansion and consolidation in Canada is undoubtedly due to the fact that Canada is a cultural dependency of the United States. Mass overflow advertising has given these corporations a tremendous marketing advantage over Canadian firms. But their expansion into Canada has also been aided in no small measure by their policy of takeover of existing Canadian firms. This takeover policy continues right down to the present, despite the existence of the Foreign Investment Review Act. A few examples will serve to illustrate the point.

In 1965, Green Giant bought Clark Foods Ltd., a major Canadian food processor with a well-established market in canned soups. In May 1975, Green Giant took over Readyfoods Ltd., which had established a market of fully prepared chicken, turkey and convenience food products. Readyfoods had previously acquired the Chan Foods Ltd. operation in Winnipeg from John Labatt. The Foreign Investment Review Agency said this was "in Canada's best interest."

In June 1956, Del Monte Corporation of California, the largest fruit and vegetable packing firm in the world, acquired majority control of Canadian Canners. At the time, Canadian Canners was by far the largest Canadian company in the field, with sales larger than its next two rivals combined. Since then Del Monte has added Boese Foods, Pyramid Canners, and St. Williams Preserves.

Trudeau's "nationalism" notwithstanding, the process has gone on. In March 1976, the Weston Empire announced that it was selling Nabob Foods Ltd. of Burnaby, B.C. to Jacobs AF of Zurich, Switzerland. At the time, Nabob was one of only three remaining large Canadian companies in the fruit and vegetable processing field. In July of that same year, the Foreign Investment Review Agency approved the takeover without giving reasons or making public any demands on the new owners.

The Expansion of Private Branding

One of the major developments in the field of fruit and vegetable processing has been the integration of the retailers back into the manufacturing industry and the rise of private brand labels sold by the large chains and voluntary groups. Most of the research on this development is based on the U.S. experience, but the same trends are obviously apparent in Canada.

In the area of frozen products, the expansion of private brand sales has been most pronounced. All the major chains in Canada and the United States prominently display their house brand frozen vegetables. The trend is towards increased packing in this manner. In the frozen foods area, the house brands are taking a growing share of the national market.

In canned fruits and vegetables, the national packers have a much greater share of the market. The U.S. Federal Trade Commission concludes that this is because of more emphasis on product differentiation. In the U.S. in 1963, packer's labels held 76% of the sales in canned fruits and vegetables. In both the United States and Canada, the private brand packing is largely done by smaller or medium sized regional firms—not the large packers. The U.S. Federal Trade Commission's 1965 study of the industry found that the large national packers did very little private brand packing; some did none.This finding was re-affirmed by the U.S. National Commission on Food Marketing.

Private brand sales in both countries have been concentrated in the large retail chains and in the few large voluntary chains like IGA. In 1963 in the United States, the ten largest chains purchased, on the average, one-third of all their canned products under private house brand labels. The three largest chains (A & P, Safeway, and Kroger) actually accounted for 65% of all private brand sales in 1963.

The other development has been the entrance of the large private chains into manufacturing itself. In the United States in 1963, eight of the ten largest chains also owned fruit and vegetable manufacturing operations. In Canada, the Weston Empire has always been directly involved in the manufacture of many food products. Canada Safeway (through Empress Foods), Steinberg's, and A & P have manufacturing operations in Canada. The U.S. firms can also benefit from importation of private brands from their parents.

The major result of this development has been the decline and fall of the small food manufacturing firm. As the U.S. Federal Trade Commission concluded, the large packers with the nationally advertised brands have been able to hold their own in the battle for shelf space in the supermarket. The impact of retailer integration into the food manufacturing area has been "a weakening of smaller manufacturers relative to larger ones." Certainly the same conclusion can be made for Canada.

Contracting the Growers

In the late 1960s, a considerable amount of publicity was given to a number of large conglomerate food corporations moving directly into farming. However, corporate farming in North America seems to have reached its peak, and now is actually on the downswing. This is true for several reasons.

First, when the corporations go into farming they must buy the land and finance other capital costs. They have to pay farm managers' salaries equivalent to other business enterprises. When they hire employees to do the farming, they must pay them wages; with the rise of the United Farm Workers movement in the United States, higher wages had to be paid.

Most of the corporations soon found that farming was not profitable (something farmers always knew). They have, instead, opted for contract farming. Under this alternative the farmer must supply the capital, and if prices are so low that not enough is earned to provide for wages, the farmer must take the loss. Furthermore, contract farming gives the processor the liberty of choosing to purchase his basic food items from any source, and in this period of expansion into the Third World, this is an attractive alternative. Contracts with fruit and vegetable growers are normally on a one year basis, re-negotiated each year.

This does not mean that the large corporations have completely pulled out of farming. They may decide to buy farms where the land purchased has a good chance of increasing in value (here the reason for purchase is primarily speculation). In addition, having some share of the product under direct control gives the corporation an added weight in the bargaining system.

In 1971, a U.S. Department of Agriculture survey found that only 10% of the produce used by fruit and vegetable processors was from farms under direct ownership of the corporation. About 78% of crops purchased for processing were through contracts with growers. There is a definite trend in this direction, in all areas of farming. The American Agricultural Marketing Association estimates that by 1985, 75% of all food in the United States will be under direct corporation-grower contracts.

In Canada, marketing boards have been created by growers to protect the small farmer from the powerful corporations. However,

111

unless the marketing board can control supply, and has control over imports, it has little power. In this area of production, marketing boards in Canada serve only as sales agents. We can see how this system works by looking at several different examples of contracting in Canada.

The largest potato processor in Canada is McCain's Foods, based at Florenceville, New Brunswick. They are also in the business of selling fertilizer and farm machinery; as well they have an integrated potato processing and delivery system. In normal times they buy between 60% and 75% of the New Brunswick potato crop. They also own a substantial amount of farm land (Valley Farms Ltd.) where they grow their own potatoes. The extent of their farm holdings is not precisely known, but estimates range between 8,000 and 10,000 acres. Between 1965-1969, an average of 61,000 acres were planted to potatoes in New Brunswick. As local farmers point out, McCain's direct farm holdings gives them an edge in price control.

In recent years, as McCain's Food has expanded in Canada, the United States (Maine in particular), and abroad, New Brunswick farmers have been protesting the importation of potatoes by the company, a practice which enables it to depress the prices on the local market.

But most of McCain's potatoes are raised through contracting with local farmers. Each year the contract is negotiated. It requires the farmer to deliver a certain amount of potatoes to the factory on a certain date, at a pre-determined price. If, due to crop failure, the farmer cannot fill his quota, the contract specifies that McCain's may buy the shortfall on the open market and charge the farmer the difference between the contract price and the price McCain's had to pay on the open market. It is a vicious system, one which clearly reveals the difference in power between the corporation and the individual farmer.

In recent years, vegetable production has increased in Southern Alberta. Here, the growers work through the Alberta Vegetable Marketing Board, which oversees the production of vegetables for canning and freezing plants. But it has no power to set prices. A 1973 study by the Alberta Agricultural Products Marketing Council concluded that the central problem was "the dominant role of Safeway as the largest retail chain in Alberta." It is integrated vertically into the vegetable processing industry through the Empress Foods plant at Lethbridge. Because the processing industry was "largely in the hands of one company," Alberta products were "not readily available in food stores other than Safeway." Furthermore, diversification of farm production was "not likely," because of company policy which dictated what was grown in the area. In such a situation, they found that "few producers would purposely antagonize either MacDonalds Consolidated [Safeway's wholesale distributor] or Empress Foods."

In 1976, Empress Foods contracted with most of the 133 vegetable growers in Southern Alberta. They took 27% of the corn raised for canning; most of the rest was marketed fresh in Safeway stores. Empress Foods took a majority of the pea crop (part was sold to York Farms Ltd.). They processed all the bean crop.

In British Columbia, most fruits and vegetables are marketed through producer-controlled marketing boards. While these are important sales agencies, they have no power in the marketplace. For example, in 1976 the B.C. Interior Vegetable Marketing Board "negotiated" prices with Canadian Canners. They sought 45 cents a pound for asparagus but received only 41 cents. They were paid $72.00 a ton for tomatoes, no increase over 1975. The threat by the processors to import the produce from the United States, Mexico, or Taiwan kept the price down.

In the Fraser Valley prices and quotas are "negotiated" with a number of processors by the B.C. Coast Vegetable Marketing Board. But power rests on the side of the processors. When the wholesalers and retailers imported large amounts of fresh and processed vegetables in 1975, the following year prices to farmers dropped between 3% and 11%, depending on the vegetable. Acreages were also cut in 1976 between 25% and 40%. The packers claimed that this was necessary because of inventory holdovers.

The strawberry and raspberry growers in the Fraser Valley are also under one-year contracts with local processors. In 1974, for example, the processors simply refused to negotiate contracts with many strawberry growers, most of whom had been delivering to the plants for twenty years. Instead, they imported them from Mexico. Why? A case of canned strawberries produced and canned in B.C. wholesaled at $12.00; a similar case from Mexico cost $3.00.

In 1973, raspberry growers were paid on the average 45.8 cents a pound for their fruit by the processors; in the summer of 1975, this was dropped to twenty-five cents a pound. The processors said this was necessary because of the dramatic increase in the price of sugar. But the action revealed the weakness of the growers in this contracting arrangement. That is why many farmers are so disappointed with Marketing Boards and feel that collective bargaining is the only alternative under the present economic system.

The Problem of Cheap Imports

The most serious problem presently facing the fruit and vegetable

113

processing industry in Canada is the inability to compete with cheap imports from other countries. There are no quotas imposed by the government, in contrast to the practice of most countries, including the United States. There is anti-dumping legislation, but even when a case has been proven (as with cherries imported from Washington in 1975), the federal government refuses to take action. In recent years the processors have lost export sales to Western Europe, and in particular to the United Kingdom, previously an important export market.

Canadian duties on processed fruits and vegetables were established over thirty-five years ago and were set on a poundage basis. For example, the tariff on canned peas, corn and beans is 1.5 cents per lb., and in 1976 amounted to about 60 cents per case. In contrast, the United States maintains a straight 17% *ad valorem* duty. On canned fruits, a poundage rate is maintained in Canada, which drops with inflation and increased production costs. In 1975, the Canadian tariff amounted to 7.9% on canned fruits, while the United States maintained a straight 20% *ad valorem* duty.

In the past few years, potato growers in Canada, particularly in Western Canada, have been nearly driven out of business because of cheap imports from the United States. There is a Canadian duty, amounting to 37.5 cents per hundredweight (cwt); the U.S. duty is exactly twice as high, at seventy-five cents per cwt. In 1976, excess potatoes from Washington and Oregon were dumped into B.C. at $3.50 cwt, whereas B.C. potato growers needed about $6.00 cwt to make a living. The potato processors actually wanted B.C. growers to ship the potatoes at around $3.00 cwt.

In 1974, the Tariff Board held hearings on imports of fresh and processed fruits and vegetables. They finally released their findings in 1977. For fresh produce, the most they advocated was a return to the previous 10% *ad valorem* duties on some fresh produce in season. No protection would be given apples, a commodity facing tremendous import pressure.

The report on processed fruits and vegetables was released in late 1977. It rejected a straight *ad valorem* tariff, as exists in other countries, and proposed varying duties for fifty-five processed products. On the whole, it recommended increased protection for fresh products and decreased protection for processed items. Spokesmen for the industry indicated that they did not feel the recommendations went far enough. In some areas, where reductions were proposed, the response was disbelief. In any case, the Trudeau Government will not take any action on the proposal until the end of the multilateral negotiations at the General Agreement on Tariffs and Trade (GATT) meetings in Geneva. Following that, there would be bi-lateral negotiations with the United States.

Why has no action been taken to protect this basic Canadian industry? First, the various Liberal Governments in Ottawa have been committed to the cheap food policy. They have also historically been committed to continental integration, particularly in the food area.

As well, the Trudeau Government was politically committed to a decrease in the rate of inflation, and in 1975 and 1976 the drop in food prices at the farm level was the major factor in the decline in the rate of inflation. Tariffs and quotas equivalent to Canada's major trading partners would have raised food prices.

Finally, there is the influence of the large corporations. They want an open border for obvious reasons. They have always been close to the Liberal Party, and they certainly have had more influence than farmers and small businessmen.

The effect of this has been a decline in farm production and manufacturing, and the loss of many jobs. Our declining self-sufficiency in the area of canned products can be seen from the following figures:

	1963	1974
carrots	95%	65%
mushrooms	90%	40%
tomatoes	74%	43%
apricots	48%	25%
peaches	41%	19%
pears	79%	62%

The canned peach market has been lost to imports from Australia, which is also rapidly moving into the canned pear market. The Australian government heavily subsidizes exports. The Australian situation is made more difficult by a 1965 bi-lateral agreement, whereby Canada agreed to importation of pears duty-free and peaches with only a 2% duty in return for concessions for Canadian forestry exports to Australia. The canned apricot market is being lost to South Africa, which has virtual slave labour. The strawberry market is being lost to Mexico. Mushrooms and tomatoes are pouring in from Taiwan and South Korea.

But we are also losing markets to products from the United States. For example, canned baked beans imported from the U.S. have a duty of one cent a pound, or about 6% on an *ad valorem* basis by weight. In turn, the U.S. has an 18% *ad valorem* duty, the European Economic Community a 24% *ad valorem* duty, and Japan a 20% *ad valorem* duty on this product.

115

Low wages are the reason for the tremendous increase in the importation of tomatoes. In 1972, only 300,000 lb. of tomatoes were imported; by 1975 this had risen to 23 million lb. York Farms (a division of Canada Packers) has announced that it is shifting its emphasis from canned goods to frozen products. Not only do transportation costs provide some protection, Canadian tariffs on frozen fruits and vegetables, for some odd reason, are nearly all on an *ad valorem* basis.

If Canadian farmers are expected to compete on an open basis with all other countries, then the game will be over. Canadian growers have to deal with a colder climate, the ability to produce only one crop a year, a shorter growing season, and much higher land costs. Labour costs at all levels are higher in Canada than in other producing nations. All other costs and inputs are higher in Canada. How many Canadians would be willing to work for the wages paid by the multinational companies in the Third World? How many would be willing to work for what they pay Mexican-Americans in California?

Who is doing the importing and why? All the major wholesalers, retailers, and the large processors are importing. As I know the B.C. situation best, I will give a few examples from that province.

In 1974 and thereafter, the packers in the Fraser Valley imported most of their strawberries from the U.S. and Mexico. In 1976 Empress Foods, Canada Safeway's packer, bought no fruit from B.C. Tree Fruits Ltd. In 1975, Woodwards and Super-Valu (Weston Empire) bought all private house brand peas, beans, and corn from the United States. In 1976, Woodwards announced they were buying all their house brand pears from Australia. Canada Safeway was also importing fruits and vegetables for its private brands.

Under these circumstances, the packers must do the same or else lose their markets. Royal City Foods used to operate two tomato canneries in B.C., but closed them and now imports all its canned tomatoes from California. Canadian Canners is also importing fruit and vegetables. In 1976 Snowcrest Packers (Burns Foods) bought no vegetables for freezing from B.C. growers. Why are they importing? Just to give the consumer a better price? Hardly.

The name of the game is profits, and higher profits can be made from importing food. For example, a case of canned apricots, grown and processed in B.C. in 1975, cost around $12.00 FOB the Fraser Valley. A case of equivalent apricots from South Africa could be landed in Vancouver, duty paid, for around $9.90 a case; in other Canadian markets, the same apricots sold for as low as $7.50 a case. The wholesalers and retailers can make a much higher profit on the imported apricots. And there is no way that B.C. farmers and factory workers can ever compete with slave labour.

116

Let us look at one more example: canned corn sold in British Columbia in the spring of 1976. Woodwards' private house brand corn, imported from the United States, cost twenty-seven cents a can; they charged the consumer thirty-nine cents, a markup of twelve cents, or 31%. Locally grown and processed corn cost them thirty-nine cents a can, and it was sold at Woodwards for forty-nine cents a can, a markup of ten cents or 20.5%.

Super-Valu also sold private label canned corn imported from the United States. They paid the same twenty-seven cents a can but charged the consumer forty-seven cents a can, a markup of twenty cents or 42.5%. They also sold the B.C. product, for which they were also charged thirty-nine cents a can; it retailed for fifty-two cents a can, a markup of thirteen cents a can or 25%. While the chain stores may claim they are importing to give the consumer a break, it is obvious that their only interest is in maximizing profits.

As a result of the imports, the processing industry in Canada has been dying. Between the mid-1960s and 1975, the number of plants processing tree fruits in B.C. dropped from fifteen to five, and in 1976 three of these were reported to be in serious financial trouble. The canned tomato industry, which once flourished in B.C., no longer exists; the Ontario industry is also being threatened, primarily by imports from Taiwan. B.C. has lost the processing industry for asparagus, cucumbers, carrots, is losing the strawberry processing industry, and is on the verge of losing the cole crop industry (cauliflower, brussel sprouts, and broccoli).

In Ontario, the number of peach processing plants dropped from nineteen in 1965 to only one in 1977. Of the four major fruit crops in Ontario (apples, grapes, peaches, and pears) only grapes are showing an increase in production. Local strawberries are no longer processed in Ontario, but are imported from as far away as Poland, Denmark, and Mexico. Significantly, only the grape industry is protected from cheap imports.

Canadian Canners—Del Monte

Special mention should be made of the historic role that Canadian Canners has had in this industry for many years and the significance of its takeover by Del Monte, the largest fruit and vegetable canning company in the world. As mentioned before, Canadian Canners was formed in 1903 through a merger of thirty firms in Ontario.

Until the takeover of Canadian Canners in 1956, the history of this firm was the takeover of other smaller Canadian firms; many were shut down in a "rationalization" of its operation. Some of the

117

highlights of Canadian Canners' past include: (1) the purchase of British Canadian Canners in 1915; (2) the re-organization of 1923, which included the purchase of thirty-four other firms in that year; (3) the purchase of the other B.C. plants in the early 1930s; (4) the takeover of Quebec Canners in 1932; and (5) its move into the prairies in 1952.

In 1955, Canadian Canners operated 11% of all fruit and vegetable processing plants in Canada; furthermore, it had the larger plants. In that year it had 16% of total industry sales: 41% of the canned fruit industry and 25% of the canned vegetable industry. It was much bigger than its second rival. It was a well established, profitable Canadian-owned operation.

Del Monte was, at the time, the largest U.S. packer, with sales larger than its next two competitors combined, but it was not an industry leader in Canada. In 1956, it purchased 93% of the outstanding stock in Canadian Canners. In 1955, Del Monte was one of the largest *importers* of canned fruits and vegetables into Canada. It held 21% of the canned fruit market and 6% of the canned vegetable market in Canada.

The takeover was reviewed by the Restrictive Trade Practices Commission, as it was felt it could lead to a monopolization of the industry. In June 1956 the Combines Commissioner ordered the inquiry to cease. His annual report in 1960 included some prophetic observations about the long run effects of the takeover.

First, the merger gave Del Monte advertising and distribution (including importation) advantages over other firms in the field. The Commissioner concluded that it would make new entry into the industry more difficult. But the main advantages would result from the parent-subsidiary operations over the border and abroad:

> The ability of the Canadian company to purchase now in the United States through the agency of the U.S. company means that . . . the merged companies stand outside the Canadian-U.S. border in a position to pick, for the Canadian market, either Canadian or U.S. produce, depending upon the circumstances of tariffs and tariff differentials on raw and canned produce and of supplies and prices.

Many would conclude that the takeover was not in Canada's best interest. In 1955, Canadian Canners operated forty-one plants in Canada; by 1976, this had fallen to fifteen.

Today, Del Monte is a growing world-wide octopus. Its advertisements claim that it can meet your needs "from womb to tomb." In the United States it owns fifty-five farms with 130,000

PROCESSING FRUITS AND VEGETABLES

acres, and has more than 10,000 other farmers under direct contract. And it is a tough customer for farmers. When asparagus contract growers organized in California, Oregon, and Washington, and demanded higher prices from Del Monte, the company just moved a large part of its asparagus operation to the Northwest area of Mexico. In California, when contract growers of peaches were pressed to the wall financially by a drop in prices, Del Monte, in a few instances, pulled out the small print in their contracts and foreclosed on the farms.

The firm, like all the big food corporations, is not willing to rest on its power in fruits and vegetables. It is going the conglomerate way. In 1971 a company spokesman announced that the firm will continue to shift product emphasis away from traditional staples to "higher-profit formulated or 'manufactured' products." Del Monte's pudding desserts, for example offer "above-average profit margins and little or no dependence on agricultural commodity prices."

Swan Valley Foods Ltd.

The plight of the small food processing firm can be illustrated by a look at one small enterprise, Swan Valley Foods Ltd. of Creston, B.C. This firm was established in 1971, mainly to process potatoes grown in the area. Later, a second plant was added at Richmond, B.C. to process meats.

The key to success was the development of a new form of food packaging, the "retortable" package, food in plastic pouches which are prepared by immersion in boiling water. The pouches can be stored without refrigeration. It was hoped that this relatively new innovation in packaging, plus the emphasis on pre-cooked convenience foods, would make the company a success.

The firm was heavily backed by the provincial New Democratic Government. The Minister of Agriculture, David Stupich, proclaimed that "this in not another Bricklin. We don't have Bricklin's in British Columbia." The Premier, Dave Barrett, proudly opened the Richmond plant and anticipated that Swan Valley would be a major success and would expand the province's primary agriculture.

The Provincial NDP originally invested several million dollars in the plant and guaranteed an additional $7.5 million in loans. Later it made additional loans on its own. Swan Valley also received a $165,000 federal PAIT grant and a $553,000 DREE grant.

The Creston operation was established primarily to process local potatoes. However, it was entering a market dominated by the house brands of the chain supermarkets, McCain's and Carnation. The latter had a marketing agreement with J.R. Simplot, the potato king of the United States, whose private company is reportedly ten times as large as that of McCain's.

The Richmond plant was turning out packages of ravioli in meat sauce, chicken a la king, beef stew, and meat balls—a total of seven precooked meals. Here they were competing with Campbell Soups, Green Giant, and the other American giants in the field. In April 1976, company officials announced that the outlook was bright and markets looked good. In October 1976, the new Social Credit Government in B.C. announced that the company was "insolvent," had an operation loss totalling $2.6 million, and "under normal business practices, would have gone into liquidation by now."

In April 1977 the Social Credit Government of British Columbia announced that it had "sold" the Creston portion of Swan Valley Foods to Hardee Farms International Ltd. of Toronto. Their subsidiary, Federal Diversiplex Ltd., had agreed to 65% of the equity, Canadian Venture Capital Corp. (1974) Ltd. of Toronto 10%, and the remaining 25% would be held by Creston Agro Enterprises Ltd., made up of local Creston potato farmers.

The "sale" price for the $12 million enterprise was $1.5 million. Furthermore, Hardee Farms did not have to make any payment for three years. If at that time the plant was not making money, the operation would simply revert to the province. For all its investment, the NDP Government had only acquired 40% equity interest.

At the time of the purchase, Hardee Farms International was reporting losses to its stockholders. The Creston plant was designed to process between forty and fifty million lb. of potatoes per year. Total consumption in B.C. in 1976 was estimated to be only twenty-five million lb. To break even the plant would need to supply 35% of the entire market in Western Canada. In 1978 the new management announced that it would start up in November but would only be processing between two and four million lb. Potato growers in the Creston area were shipping 50% of their crop to York Farms' processing plant at Lethbridge.

At the beginning of December 1977, the B.C. Social Credit Government announced that it had sold the Richmond plant of Swan Valley Foods to Standard Brands. The sale price was $3.2 million. Thus the loss from both plants was about $7.3 million, all of which was provided by the B.C. taxpayers.

How could this happen? The NDP Government had contracted with McDonald Research Associates of Vancouver to complete a market study. But anyone connected with the industry, or at all knowledgeable about what was happening, could have warned them. Only the large corporate giants have the resources to market new products. Not only was the frozen french fries market already saturated, but Swan Valley had to contend with established brand names, backed by heavy advertising.

As a contrast, let us take a quick look at the introduction of "Pringles" by Procter & Gamble. This is a "reconstituted potato chip," processed in such a manner that almost all food value is removed; a variety of additives are thrown in. The concoction costs 50% more than regular potato chips. But for Procter & Gamble it has worked. It enabled the firm to ship potato chips across the country, while eliminating the risk of their being broken, as they are packaged in a cardboard container. It made national marketing and advertising feasible. In contrast to regular potato chips, "Pringles" will sit on the shelf for a year. In 1973 alone, Procter & Gamble spent $4 million advertising this one product. How could Swan Valley Foods of Creston B.C., or any other small firm, ever compete with this kind of market power?

The fruit and vegetable industry used to be one of the most important local manufacturing industries in Canada. In recent years it has become highly centralized, dominated by a few very large firms, mainly American. The large retail chains have also moved strongly into this area. With an almost open border, the industry as a whole has a very bleak future. The farming sector is one of the most depressed in Canada. Many areas of Canada which used to produce fruits and vegetables now produce none. At some time in the future, when we are more dependent on high priced imports, Canadians will wonder what happened to this once strong and viable enterprise.

TABLE Va

Fruit and Vegetable Processors

Company	Ownership/Control	1971 Sales
Campbell Soup Co. Ltd.	U.S.—Campbell Soups	$70,505,000
H.J. Heinz of Canada Ltd.	U.S.—H.J. Heinz	66,205,000
McCain's Foods Ltd.	Canada—McCain Family	60,000,000
Canadian Canners Ltd.	U.S.—Del Monte	58,582,000
Nabob Foods Ltd.	Switz.—Jacobs AF	31,532,000
Green Giant of Canada Ltd.	U.S.—Green Giant	31,000,000
Libby McNeil & Libby of Canada Ltd.	Switz.—Nestle	31,000,000
Stafford Foods Ltd.	Canada—Burns Foods	9,040,000
Sun-Rype Ltd.	Canada—B.C. Growers	8,424,000
Canadian Home Products Ltd.	U.S.—American Home Products	8,110,000

SOURCES

Canadian Food Processor Association. Presentation to the House of Commons Special Committee on Trends in Food Prices, March 6, 1973.

Clement, Wallace, and Anna Janzen. "Just Peachy: The Demise of Tender Fruit Farmers," *This Magazine*, XII, No. 2, 1978, pp. 22-26.

Federal Task Force on Agriculture. *Canadian Agriculture in the Seventies*. Ottawa: The *Queen's Printer*, 1969.

Hightower, Jim. *Eat Your Heart Out: How Food Profiteers Victimize the Consumer*. N.Y.: Crown Publishers Inc., 1975.

Helmberger, Peter G., and Sidney Hoos, "The Vegetable Processing Industry," in John J. Moore and Richard G. Walsh, *Market Structure of the Agricultural Industries*. Ames, Iowa: Iowa State University Press, 1966.

McCann, Thomas. *The Tragedy of United Fruit*. Toronto: General Publishing, 1977.

Martin, Ron. "Fruit and Vegetable Report," *Food in Canada*. XXXVI, No. 1, January 1976, pp. 33-34.

National Commission on Food Marketing. *Food from Farmer to Consumer*. Washington, D.C.: U.S. Government Printing Office, June 1966.

National Commission on Food Marketing. *Organization and Competition in the Fruit and Vegetable Industry*. Technical Study No.4. Washington, D.C.: U.S. Government Printing Office, June 1966.

National Commission on Food Marketing. *The Structure of Food Manufacturing*. Technical Study No. 8. Washington, D.C.: U.S. Government Printing Office, June 1966.

National Farmers Union. "Submission to the Tariff Board on the Subject of Reference No. 152. Fresh and Processed Fruits and Vegetables." January 29, 1974.

Neil, J. "Marketing of Fresh and Processed Fruits and Vegetables in Ontario." Ontario: Special Committee on Farm Income, 1969.

Ontario Special Committee on Farm Income. *Marketing Fresh and Processed Fruits and Vegetables in Ontario*. Research Report No. 13, 1969.

Patterson, R.A. "A Survey of Selected Segments of Canadian Agribusiness." Research Project 21, Federal Task Force on Agriculture, Unpublished, 1969.

Royal Commission on Prices. *Final Report*. III: Ottawa: The King's Printer, 1949.

Royal Commission on Price Spreads of Food Products. *Final Report*. II. Ottawa: The Queens Printer, 1959.

Stewart, Walter. *Hard To Swallow*. Toronto: MacMillan of Canada, 1974.

Tariff Board. *Report on Greenhouse Vegetables*. No. 140. Ottawa: Tariff Board, 1969.

Tariff Board, *Strawberries for Processing*. No. 148. Ottawa: The Tariff Board, 1972.

U.S. Federal Trade Commission, Staff Report. Economic Inquiry into Food Marketing. Part II. *The Frozen Fruit, Juice and Vegetable Industry*. December, 1962.

U.S. Federal Trade Commission, Staff Report. Economic Inquiry into Food Marketing. Part III. *The Canned Fruit, Juice and Vegetable Industry*. June, 1965.

6. THE FOOD CONGLOMERATE

One of the central themes of this book is the rise of the large conglomerate food corporation, particularly during the 1960s and 1970s. This is a relatively new development, which resulted from the understanding that *marketing* of food products is the key to financial success. No longer is technological innovation a significant factor, as all new discoveries are quickly copied by other large firms. Furthermore, it became more and more apparent, with the rise of advertising and promotion, that the quality of the product offered the consuming public is not that important. People can be conditioned to eat anything.

Nevertheless, even before World War II there was the rise of a few conglomerate food firms which were tremendously successful. In both the United States and Canada, government statisticians have placed them in a special category: "miscellaneous food manufacturers." "Miscellaneous" in the sense that they operated in a wide number of industry areas and that many of the products they produced were not easily placed in other categories. The problem was that the standard breakdown of food products was made according to the basic food as produced on the farm level. Many of these products were far removed from the North American farm. In addition, a number of these firms specialized in manufacturing and distributing food grown in other parts of the world in the classical colonial plantation system. These firms dominate coffee, tea and cocoa sales in Canada.

In Canada, Statistics Canada defines "miscellaneous food manufacturers" as companies "primarily engaged in manufacturing baking powder, flavouring extracts and syrups, malt, milled rice, self-rising and blended flours, starch and its products, jelly powders, yeast, prepared coconut, powdered eggs, frozen eggs, 'health foods,'

peanut butter and other food specialties not elsewhere classified."
Included in this are companies engaged in "roasting coffee, blending
tea or grinding and packaging spices."

As you read through this list, it appears that the classification was
drawn up to fit three major food conglomerates: General Foods,
Standard Brands, and Unilever. Because these were the prototypes of
the modern conglomerate food corporation operating in Canada and
on an international level it is interesting to look at them as special case
studies of the modern food corporation.

GENERAL FOODS

The history of General Foods goes back to 1895 when C.W. Post
formed his cereal company at Battle Creek, Michigan. When he died
in 1914, his daughter, Marjorie Post Close, took over the company. In
1919 she divorced her first husband and married Edward F. Hutton, a
New York broker. Together with Goldman Sachs, they pulled off
what must be regarded as the most astounding corporate merger in the
history of the food industry, and perhaps in all manufacturing.

They drew up a list of twenty-five prominent food processing firms,
all of which had nationally advertised established brands. Between
1925 and 1929 they approached each of these companies proposing a
merger and consolidation of management. They were amazingly
successful, acquiring the Jello Company, Ingleheart Brothers
(Swansdown cake flour), Minute Tapioca Co., Baker's chocolates,
Franklin Baker's coconut, Cheek-Neal Co. (Maxwell House coffee),
Calumet Baking Powder, Certo Corporation, and the General Foods
Corporation (which had the patent to Clarence Birdseye's quick-
freezing process). In all, twenty firms were acquired, and in 1930 the
company changed its name to General Foods Inc.

By 1965, General Foods Inc. was the largest food corporation in the
United States with assets of $856 million. By 1974, its assets had risen
to $1,855 million, and with sales of $2,986 million it ranked 58th in
sales among U.S. corporations. As it introduces a significant number
of "new" food items every year, it is difficult to know exactly how
many food items it actually manufactures. In 1968, the U.S. Federal
Trade Commission estimated that it had 250 packaged food items in
its line, and thirty of these were well-established national brands.

124

The Move into Canada

All of the major food conglomerates moved into Canada at an early date. This normally followed their geographical expansion across the United States. For the large national firms, Canada was seen as simply an extension of the American market. In market planning, Canada was just another region. The relatively high standard of living in Canada and the similar language (Quebec being only a minor irritant) made advertising very simple. The expansion into Canada contrasted sharply with their market policy in Mexico.

In 1930, General Foods was also incorporated in Canada. Separate companies were consolidated under the corporation. They included Maxwell House Coffee, Baker's Coconut, Postum, Grapenuts, Post Toasties, Jell-o Pectin and other major brands. Factories existed at Windsor, Toronto, Cobourg, and Montreal. The corporation also owned Mitchell and McNeil Ltd., a fish and lobster packing company in Halifax. J.C. Weldon reports that between 1900-1940 General Foods acquired twelve companies in Canada.

The growth of the corporation in Canada has been dramatic. In 1960, sales were $55,576,000; by 1969 (the first year that the wholly-owned Canadian subsidiary published an annual report), they had risen to $154,854,000. By 1976, sales totalled $345 million and the Canadian president predicted that they would top $400 million in 1977.

From the beginning, the company strategy has been to expand by taking over other corporations. Their history in Canada has been no exception. Annual reports note a steady rise in capital additions, including those acquired by the purchase of other enterprises.

In recent years in Canada, General Foods has acquired (1) Hostess Food Products Ltd., which carries a full line of snack foods; (2) White Spot Restaurants in British Columbia, which also holds the franchise for a chain of Colonel Sanders Kentucky Fried Chicken outlets; (3) Grenadier Restaurants/Canterbury Foods in Ontario, which operates the 1867 Restaurants, extensive catering and concession services, and the Burger Chef chain of fast food outlets in Ontario and British Columbia; (4) Arbutus Food Equipment and Buscombe Supply Ltd., which were integrated into the corporation's institutional food service operation, and (5) the Viviane Woodward Corporation, in women's cosmetics. Like most of the large food corporations, General Foods has expanded into the profitable pet food market through the Gaines brand.

125

STANDARD BRANDS

The success of General Foods provided the inspiration for the formation of a second conglomerate food corporation, Standard Brands. The basic firm involved was Fleischmann Company, which had a near monopoly in the production and distribution of yeast in the United States and Canada. Yeast was at this time a perishable commodity, and the company had developed a system of refrigerated distribution to wholesale and retail outlets.

In 1929 the new conglomerate was formed by the addition of the Royal Baking Powder Co., Chase and Sanborn Co., Widlar Food Products and the E.W. Gillett Company Ltd. of Canada. The products of the acquired companies could easily be included in Fleischmann's delivery system. After the merger their major area of expansion was the distilling industry.

Unfortunately for Standard Brands, much of their dominant position at this time was due to technological advantages. To some extent this was undermined when General Foods developed the vacuum pack of coffee and when dry yeast was developed during World War II. Advertising, and a well-established brand name, kept them in the field; but they did not grow as fast as General Foods.

However, with the beginning of the conglomerate period of the 1950s, they expanded. In 1956 they acquired Clinton Foods, a large food processing corporation, and Dr. Ballard's pet food company. In 1960 they bought Planters Nut & Chocolate Co., the industry leader in this field. Between 1950 and 1965 their assets grew from $136 million to $311 million. Of this increase, $121 million represented assets of acquired companies. This placed Standard Brands sixth in the United States among all food firms in company acquisitions from 1950 to 1965.

Standard Brands and its original companies were in the Canadian market at a very early date. Fleischmann Company broke into the Canadian market in 1876. Chase & Sandborn coffee appeared in 1882. The E.W. Gillett Co. Ltd. began Canadian operations in the early 1890s.

In 1906, the Royal Baking Co. of the United States took over formal control of the E.W. Gillett Co. The 1929 merger also took place in Canada, and after re-organization, the company had four major divisions: the Fleischmann yeast and vinegar plant in Montreal; a malt plant at Guelph formerly owned by Canadian Diamalt; the Chase & Sandborn coffee and tea plant in Montreal; and the baking powder, dry yeast and lye plant in Toronto that formerly was owned by the Gillett Company.

Standard Brands, through the Fleischmann company, has

completely dominated the Canadian yeast market over the years. In 1958 the Restrictive Trade Practices Commission released a report on the takeover of Best Yeast Ltd. by Standard Brands. In 1954, before the acquisition, Standard Brands had 75% of the market, and there were only two "competitors." After the takeover, only Lallemand was left, with only 16% of the market. However, no action was taken, as the Commission concluded that the public interest had not been so affected as to justify dissolution.

The expansion of Standard Brands into Canada has paralleled the expansion in the United States over the past fifteen years. In 1962, they had ten manufacturing plants in Canada; by 1971 this had risen to twenty-four. Total assets in 1962 were $24.9 million; by 1971 they had risen to $117.4 million.

As in the United States, the strategy for expansion has centered on the takeover of established firms. In the confectionery industry, Standard Brands acquired the Walter M. Lowney Company and Moirs Ltd. In the pet food area they have become a major marketer through Dr. Ballard's pet foods. Following their U.S. experience, they have expanded in the liquor industry through the purchase of L.J. McGuinness & Co. and Weyburn Distilleries of Weyburn, Saskatchewan. In 1971 they bought Calona Wines and Pacific Vineyards (B.C.) from the Capozzi family, the largest wine manufacturers in British Columbia.

Despite the Foreign Investment Review Agency, the takeover process has continued. In 1974, Standard Brands acquired Beaver Specialty Ltd. of Toronto and Jean Demers in Quebec. In 1976 they bought Powell Foods (1973) Ltd., the tea subsidiary in Canada of the British firm, Cadbury, Schweppes Ltd.

The headquarters of Standard Brands in Canada is in Montreal. The company entered the political arena in May 1977 when they announced that they were moving their marketing staff to Toronto, a response to the new Quebec language act passed by the Parti Quebecois government. F. Ross Johnson, Chairman of Standard Brands Inc. of New York, announced at the time that the decision of whether or not to stay in Quebec or to relocate in Ontario was "very much under study."

In addition to its head office in Montreal, the corporation operates four plants in Quebec, employing 1,400 people. At the same time, the New York head office announced that they would be building a new corporate research centre. It was to be located in Wilton, Connecticut.

Today in Canada, Standard Brands distributes over 175 food and beverage items. At least fifteen of these are major products with well-established brand names advertised on a national basis. While they are not as big as General Foods, they have seen that the General Foods model is the ticket to financial success, and they are expanding on a regular basis.

UNILEVER

Unilever is one of the largest food corporations in the world, operating in more than fifty countries in 1975. It is one of the few companies which is truly multinational in ownership: 50% by British and 50% by Dutch capitalists. There are actually two companies, one based in each country, but with the same board of directors.

Unilever Ltd. (UK) began in 1894 as Lever Brothers; in 1930 it was bought by Margarine Union, and the name was changed to Unilever. N.V. Margarine Unie was formed in the Netherlands in 1927 by the Jurgens and Vanden Bergh families. Both operated extensively on an international basis, through plantation systems in their imperial colonies. In 1937 the two firms merged. The Equalization Agreement was signed in 1957. According to Arvind V. Phatak, this was to eliminate "competition for raw material." Both firms were operating plantations for palm oil, rubber and copra; as well, they were active in oil seeds, animal feeds, chemicals, packaging, merchandising foods, while at the same time maintaining an ocean fleet of ships.

In order to give the reader an idea of the size of this operation, the 1975 sales of Unilever Ltd. (UK) were 6,759 million sterling. In Canadian dollars, that would be well over $12 billion. Sales for Unilever N.V. (Neth.) for the same year were 21,088 million guilders, or over $9 billion in Canadian dollars.

Lever Brothers Ltd. in Canada is a wholly-owned subsidiary of Unilever Ltd. of London. In Canada, it is separate from Thomas J. Lipton Ltd., which is owned by Unilver N.V. of Rotterdam. This appears to be a strange situation, as the original agreement was that all subsidiary companies in the Commonwealth would be owned by the London branch of the company. However, there is a reason behind this.

The American branch was originally created by Thomas J. Lipton Inc., and in 1922 a subsidiary of the American branch plant was established in Canada. In 1938, both the American and Canadian operations of Lipton were taken over by Unilever N.V. and their "parent-subsidiary" relationship remained the same.

The Unilever groups recognized that Canada was more a part of the American food market than it was part of the Commonwealth.

Lipton's products, as well as those of Lever Brothers, benefited from large-scale overflow advertising from the United States. This had originally created the market for Lipton Tea in Canada. Furthermore, basic research for and development of Lipton (and for that matter Lever Brothers) are carried out in the United States. The company argues that "it does not duplicate research [in Canada] which can be done more cheaply and better elsewhere." Furthermore, in the consumer goods industries, where Lever Brothers and Thomas J. Lipton are concentrated, advertising is more important, accounting for more than 5% of company sales. In this case, both Lever Brothers and Thomas J. Lipton Ltd. benefit from advertising programmes developed in the United States.

The company (like other foreign companies operating in Canada) stresses that its managers are Canadians, drawn mainly from York University, the University of Western Ontario, and the University of Waterloo. The management is then trained for the company in courses established by the American Management Association.

In 1969 the Lever Brothers company underwent a reorganization programme, allowing each of its eleven companies decentralized management through a separate company. Part of this was a reaction to the bitter 1957 strike which hurt the highly centralized operation. Labour-management relations have improved since then, as union officials now participate in company management-training programmes. As the company notes, there are now "clearer communications" than in the past.

In December 1977 the New York stock exchange was buzzing over the announcement that Unilever had made a bid to takeover National Starch Co. In 1976, National Starch had sales of $339 million, of which $83 million was from seventeen overseas subsidiaries, including those in Canada. Unilever's offer was about $485 million, which would have made the takeover one of the largest on record.

Under the leadership of the Greenwall family, National Starch had developed a strong position in chemical starch and adhesives. However, in more recent years it had expanded into food additives, seasonings, and flavouring, while growing and selling hybrid corn seed.

Expansion in Canada

Most people identify the name Lever Brothers with the detergent and soap industry, for along with the American giant Procter & Gamble of Canada Ltd., it totally dominates the field. But Unilever in Canada has diversified into the food industry to such an extent that

The Financial Post now classifies the company as a food corporation.

Between 1964 and 1971, the sales of Lever Bros. Ltd. in Canada rose from $56.9 milion to $114.4 million, an increase of about 13% per year. Sales for Thomas J. Lipton Ltd. grew from $13.4 million in 1964 to $30.5 million in 1972, an average rate of growth of 16% per year. Very few Canadian-owned corporations can match that growth record.

As with most large conglomerate food corporations, the increase in growth in recent years has been accomplished to a large extent by the takeover of Canadian firms. As W.H. Giles concludes, "looking at the overall figures, Unilever in Canada does not appear to finance its takeovers through earnings. They are probably financed by Canadian banks using Canadian savings." No stock in either company in Canada is offered to Canadians. As the Canadian President explained to the Senate Banking and Commerce Committee, a "token sale" would "serve no useful purpose."

Lever Brothers operates through eleven companies in Canada, all of them except Lever Detergents acquired through the "merger" process. In 1968 they purchased Monarch Fine Foods Ltd. whose vegetable oil and margarine operation fit in with Unilewth's traditional international role in whale, soybean, ground nut, palm, fish and coconut oil operations. In 1976 it was announced that Lever Brothers and Maple Leaf Mills (an American-owned firm) would jointly build and operate an integrated vegetable oil crushing and processing mill in Windsor. This would be the largest in Canada.

The other main area of expansion in the food industry has been in processed meats. Two Montreal companies, Bourassa Ltee. and Hygrade Foods, were acquired. In 1971 they added Shopsy's Foods Ltd. in Toronto. This branch of the company experienced a significant drop in sales in the mid-1970s after the disclosure of the involvement of organized crime and tainted meat in the processed meat industry in Quebec.

In October 1977, Lever Brothers Ltd. bought all the shares of R.J. Lucas and Arthurs Ltd., a processed meats manufacturer, and its other unit, Vancouver Fancy Meats Co., from Kraft Inc. of the United States.

The latest major venture of Lever Brothers has been in the fast food industry. In 1972 they acquired control of A. & W. Food Services of Canada Ltd. from the American food giant, United Brands. In that year they operated 250 outlets across Canada, one-third directly owned by the company and the remainder operated as franchises in Western Canada.

The Thomas J. Lipton branch of Unilever in Canada has also grown through acquisition. While the U.S. branch has had about 50%

130

of the tea market, in Canada Lipton's share has dropped from 19% to 2% in recent years. Nevertheless, the company has a near monopoly in the dried soup market in Canada. Lipton developed the process in 1941 using monosodium glutamate and the microwave drying system. While Campbell's Soup has 50% of the total Canadian soup market, Lipton holds 20%, mainly due to the popularity of dried soup among the Quebecois. Lipton has about 50% of the Quebec soup market.

In 1962 Lipton bought J.B. Jackson Ltd., based in Simcoe, Ontario. This company specialized in ice cream, butter, milk, and frozen foods. Shortly thereafter, it acquired the American Good Humour brand in ice cream snack foods. In 1966, Puritan Canners was added, a firm which marketed canned meats and stews in Alberta and British Columbia. In 1970 Langis Foods Ltd., based in Vancouver, was added. This permitted the company to enter the lucrative institutional food market as Langis sold soups, bases, mixes, fountain syrups, drinks and other syrups in this market. More recently, Lipton hopes to expand in another area as the federal Department of Health has approved their synthetic textured vegetable proteins for use as meat substitutes.

TABLE VIa

Major Miscellaneous Food Conglomerates

Company	Ownership/Control	1971 Sales
IMASCO	U.K.—Imperial Tobacco	$569,629,000
General Foods	U.S.—General Foods	181,816,000
Standard Brands	U.S.—Standard Brands	148,541,000
Lever Bros/Lipton	U.K./Neth.—Unilever	142,217,969
Procter & Gamble Co.	U.S.—Proctor & Gamble	108,704,000
Brooke Bond Foods Ltd.	U.K.—Brooke Bond Liebig	59,680,618
Canada Starch/Best Foods	U.S.—CPC International	50,000,000

THE GROWTH OF THE NEW CONGLOMERATES

While the traditional food processing industries have generally shown a decline in number of firms and plants in the field, as well as a relative decline in employees and sales, this is not true of the miscellaneous food industries. While the number of firms has been decreasing (as the process of centralization marches on), the number of plants in the industry has actually risen. Between 1961 and 1971, sales rose from $409.7 million to $879.9 million, which was higher than the figures for the food industry as a whole. Furthermore, these figures do not reflect the complete picture. Many non-food firms have moved into the food area in the past fifteen years, primarily in the highly processed (and advertised) miscellaneous foods. However, these firms remain primarily in other industrial areas and therefore are not classified as food firms.

In the United States, the major non-food companies which have moved into the food area are the large soap and tobacco manufacturers. The American Tobacco Company has changed its name to American Brands, to reflect this change in direction. The Reynolds Tobacco Co. is now Reynolds Industries, and markets R.J.R. Foods in Canada. U.S. Tobacco has also diversified, and has bought Ste. Michelle Vintners.

Procter & Gamble Co. now controls both Duncan Hines and Crisco brands. The Warner-Lambert Pharmaceutical Co. purchased American Chicle Co., one of the two dominant firms in the chewing gum and confectionery industry. In one of the biggest takeovers, Norton-Simon acquired Hunt-Wesson Foods, which also controls Canada Dry beverages.

Nestle is Switzerland's largest corporation, and the second largest European food company behind Unilever. It began in 1866 as the Anglo-Swiss Condensed Milk Co., specializing in baby food. In 1929 and 1947 it expanded through major mergers to reach its present size. But today Nestle is hardly just a milk processing corporation, as it manufactures and sells on a worldwide basis almost the entire range of foods, including infant and diet foods, all sorts of drinks, chocolates, confectioneries, biscuits, soups, frozen and canned foods, and snack foods; as well it is involved in fish packing, owns restaurants, etc. It operates in most of these areas in Canada through its wholly-owned subsidiary, Nestle (Canada) Ltd.

There is a similar trend in Canada. Imperial Tobacco Company (now known as IMASCO) moved into the food area through the takeover of Pasquale Brothers Ltd., Grissol Foods Ltd., and three American food firms whose products were also distributed in Canada: Progresso Foods Corp., S. & W. Fine Foods and Toltee Foods.

132

In 1976, IMASCO acquired a 26% ownership of Hardee's Food Systems Inc., an American fast food restaurant chain. Later that year it became a major shareholder in Pop Shoppes International Inc., the U.S. operation of the Canadian-based soft drink company. This ownership was expanded to 50% in February 1978.

In July 1977 IMASCO sold its two American food manufacturing subsidiaries, S. & W. and Pinata Foods, both in California, to Standard Brands, for $39 million. It used the cash from this sale to purchase Koffler Stores Ltd., a Canadian firm which owned and operated Shoppers Drug Mart and Embassy Cleaners. The company announced that it wanted to concentrate its food operations in the northeastern United States and in Canada, especially in Ontario and Quebec.

For many people throughout the world, beer is considered a food, to be consumed with a meal. Therefore, it is probably not too surprising that John Labatt, the most successful of the breweries in Canada in terms of growth of sales, has moved significantly into the food area through the takeover of Ogilvie Flour Milling, Ault Foods, Cow & Gate, Laura Secord Candy Shops, plus a major move into the wine industry.

Mergers and the Rise of the New Food Conglomerates

As the U.S. Federal Trade Commission has stressed in their study of the American food industry, the period of 1950-1965 was characterized by the growth of the conglomerate food firm, mainly through the process of takeover of smaller firms. Not all of the firms absorbed in this period were small: four of these (Spencer Kellogg, Best Foods, Wesson Oil, and Clinton Foods) were in the top fifty largest food firms. Between 1950 and 1965, ten firms entered the list of the top fifty food manufacturers, and of these five companies were very active in the merger area: PepsiCo, Castle & Cooke, Campbell Taggart Associated Bakeries, Di Giorgio, and Foremost Dairies. The most active growing food corporations were Hunt Foods, Consolidated Foods, Beatrice Foods, CPC International (Corn Products) and Foremost Dairies. While they were the most active in the merger field, they were also moving into Canada as well.

PepsiCo is the second largest soft drink manufacturer in Canada. Castle & Cooke bought Dole and acquired Dole of Canada Ltd. They are mainly suppliers of tropical fruits from Third World countries, and along with Del Monte and United Brands completely control the banana industry.

Foremost Dairies operates in British Columbia in co-operation with the dairy industry, linked to the Weston chain of retail food stores. Hunt Foods bought Wesson Oil Corp. in 1960, acquired controlling interest of Canada Dry, and then was in turn taken over by Norton-Simon Inc. It has operated in Canada for a long time, and today is the largest processor of tomatoes in the world.

Consolidated Foods was the most active firm in the merger area in the United States between 1950 and 1965. It operates in Canada through Kitchens of Sara Lee (Canada) Ltd., and also has wide interests in the non-food industries.

Beatrice Foods, one of the largest American dairy industries, received an order from the U.S. Federal Trade Commission not to expand any further in the dairy industry, as it was approaching the point of monopoly power in many markets. It responded by moving into Canada after 1969, taking over many Canadian dairies, establishing itself in just five years as one of the four dominant firms in Ontario, and through the purchase of Modern Dairies became the dominant firm in Manitoba. It has also diversified widely in non-food industries.

One of the largest American food giants is CPC International, with sales in 1974 of over $2,500 million. It operates in Canada through the Canada Starch Co., Best Foods, Quebec Maple Products, and De Lair Foods; it is also active in non-food industries. In 1975 it was one of the few companies cited by the Anti-Inflation Board for having "excess profits." It caused a stir in the industry in 1976 when it launched a massive advertising campaign for Skippy Peanut Butter, trying to gain a larger share of a market heavily dominated by Kraft Foods Ltd. Skippy is the leading brand in the U.S. market.

The Nature of the Merger Movement

As numerous studies have noted, the conglomerate merger movement took off in the 1950s, and in the food industry, at least, it is still growing at a steady pace. The acquisition of existing companies has been almost the sole method by which an established firm enters the food industry. The costs of breaking into an already highly oligopolized industry are already far too high; the takeover of an established brand is a less costly and more attractive alternative. The study by the U.S. Federal Trade Commission reveals that most of the companies that were taken over during the 1950-1965 merger boom were in the area of canning, preserving and freezing, so-called snack foods and convenience foods.

Why has this merger movement occurred? Why has it taken this particular direction? The answer is simple, as noted before. The rate of profit is higher in the highly product-differentiated industries, where there is a high rate of advertising. In the United States, anti-trust legislation and activities of the U.S. Federal Trade Commission have been relatively active in the area of horizontal mergers (mergers within a single industry), but they have simply had no authority to act in the area of conglomerate mergers. There is of course also the absence of a political will to act. In Canada, there has been no *traditional* anti-combines action, let alone any action in the area of conglomerates.

TABLE VIb

U.S. Conglomerate Food Corporations

Company	Basic Food Industries, 1963	Number of Plants in U.S., 1963	1974 Fortune Ranking Sales	Assets
Borden	17	158	47	90
General Foods	16	37	58	74
Kraftco	16	204	33	84
Hunt-Wesson*	13	63	123	132
Beatrice Foods	12	114	42	105
Nabisco	11	38	106	153
Pet Milk	10	51	202	280
CPC International	9	16	71	112
Castle & Cooke	9	15	255	231
Quaker Oats	9	24	163	191
Standard Brands	8	38	120	172
Fairmont Foods	8	36	395	478
Carnation	7	58	103	169
General Mills	7	33	94	140
Stokeley-Van Camp	7	56	409	447

*1963 figures include those of Canada Dry; 1974 *Fortune* figures are for the subsequent parent firm, Norton Simon.

NOTE: The industries identified are the U.S. Standard Industrial Code, using four-digit product categories. These are a bit more specific than the Canadian Standard Industrial Code. Readers will quickly recognize that all of these corporations operate in Canada.

SOURCE: National Commission on Food Marketing. *Grocery Manufacturing*. Technical Study No. 6. U.S. Government Printing Office, June 1966, Table 1-2, pp. 6-7; *Fortune Magazine*. "The 500 Largest Industrial Companies," May 1975.

SOURCES

Giles, W.H. "Unilever in Canada," *The International Review*. I, No. 7, December 25, 1972, pp. 29-37.

Horst, Thomas. *At Home Abroad: A Study of the Domestic and Foreign Operations of the American Food-Processing Industry*. Cambridge, Mass.: Ballinger Publishing Co., 1974.

Marshall, Herbert, Frank Southard Jr., and Kenneth W. Taylor. *Canadian-American Industry*. Toronto: McClelland & Stewart, 1976 edition.

National Commission on Food Marketing. *Grocery Manufacturing*. Technical Study No. 6, Washington, D.C.: U.S. Government Printing Office, June 1966.

National Commission on Food Marketing. *The Structure of Food Manufacturing*. Technical Study No. 8. Washington, D.C.: U.S. Government Printing Office, June 1966.

Naylor, Tom. *The History of Canadian Business, 1867-1914*. Vol. II, Toronto: James Lorimer & Co., 1975.

Phatak, Arvind V. *Evolution of World Enterprises*. N.Y.: American Management Association, 1971.

Scanlon, Paul D. "FTC and Phase II: The McGovern Papers," *Antitrust Law & Economics Review*, V, No. 3, Spring 1972, pp. 33-36.

Shepherd, William G. *Market Power and Economic Welfare: An Introduction*. N.Y.: Random House, 1970.

Skeoch, L.A., Ed. *Restrictive Trade Practices in Canada*. Toronto: McClelland & Stewart, 1966.

Thorburn, Hugh G., and Gideon Rosenbluth. *Canadian Anti-Combines Administration, 1952-1960*. Toronto: University of Toronto Press, 1963.

U.S. Federal Trade Commission. *Economic Papers, 1966-1969*. Washington, D.C.: U.S. Government Printing Office, 1970.

7. THREE STYLES OF OLIGOPOLY

For the most part the food manufacturing industry in Canada is characterized by oligopoly, defined as the control of the market by a relatively small number of firms. The text book theory of competition simply does not apply; nor does the case of monopoly, control by a single firm. In advanced capitalist states, oligopoly is the norm.

However, oligopolies differ from industry to industry, even in this era of the conglomerate corporation. This chapter will take a look at three different food industries in Canada, all oligopolies, but each with different characteristics.

The sugar industry is a text book case study of a pure oligopoly. There are very few industries which are so closely controlled in all aspects by a small number of firms. The confectionery industry is different: product differentiation and control by large foreign conglomerate firms is the norm. Yet there is a very tight oligopoly, and entry by new firms is extremely difficult. Finally, there is the case of the edible oils industry. This industry could be described as a "loose oligopoly," as there are a number of firms in the primary processing level, and entry here is fairly easy (financial success is another matter). At the end product, however, the industry is controlled by the large marketing corporations.

THE SUGAR REFINERS

The sugar refining industry was one of the earliest Canadian food manufacturing industries. It was also one of the first to move in the

137

direction of oligopoly. Over the years, it has been the subject of a number of government inquiries and has even been indicted three times for monopolistic pricing. In Canada this is indeed a rare situation.

In recent years, the sugar industry in Eastern Canada has been completely dominated by three firms: Redpath Industries, Atlantic Sugar Refineries, and St. Lawrence Sugar Co. They have established one of the purest cases of oligopoly a textbook economist has ever seen.

The three manufacturers have had a tacit agreement on market shares. Redpath Industries sets the price and the others follow. There is absolutely no price competition at the retail level. In fact, they have an agreement on distribution in supermarkets: traditionally only one brand is available in any store. The industry has had no advertising expenses, for with such an arrangement, none is needed.

In Western Canada, a monopoly exists; in fact, it is a classic case. B.C. Sugar Refineries is the sole distributor of sugar in the four Western provinces. It has no competition from Eastern manufacturers or imports. During the strike against the company in 1975, the Eastern Canadian manufacturers did not move into the Western market; instead, the supermarkets brought in sugar from the United States. These imports disappeared from the stores when the strike was settled.

The Eastern Market

The largest sugar refiner in Canada is Redpath Industries. It was founded in 1854 by John Redpath of Montreal. In 1930 Redpath's company merged with the Dominion Sugar Company of Chatham, Ontario to form The Canada and Dominion Sugar Company. In 1955, controlling interest in the firm was sold to Tate & Lyle, and in 1959 this was raised to majority control (now at around 56%). Redpath operates two cane refineries, one each in Toronto and Montreal.

Tate & Lyle is the largest sugar refiner in the world. Originally formed in 1903, it resulted from the merger of two family concerns, each of which wished to cease competition. In the early period it concentrated on refining cane sugar in the United Kingdom, imported from abroad. In the 1930s it entered the plantation business, and in 1966 operated more than sixty-six companies in all corners of the world. It owns sugar plantations in Jamaica, Trinidad, Rhodesia, British Honduras, Zambia and South Africa, and maintains overseas sugar refineries in Canada, Rhodesia, Zambia and Nigeria. In 1975 its sales were 1,274 million pounds sterling, or well over $2 billion.

The second largest firm is the Atlantic Sugar Refineries Company.

138

The company, whose refinery is located in St. John, New Brunswick, was originally owned by Scottish and Nova Scotian interests. In 1970, controlling interest was purchased by the Glengair Group Ltd. A further change came about in 1973 when J. Howard Hawkes and a few associates bought most of the Gairdner family interests in Glengair. The company then merged with Atlantic Sugar Refineries to form the Jannock Corporation.

Aside from Hawkes, the other major stockholder is Max Tannembaum. In January 1975, Mohavny Ltd., controlled by George Mara, D.G. Willmot and William Hatch, acquired about 17% of the stock in Jannock. Jannock is a diversified company, but in 1976, 60% of total sales and 55% of earnings were provided from the sugar operation.

The third major Eastern Canadian refinery, St. Lawrence Sugar, operates a single refinery in Montreal. Now a part of Sucronel Ltd., it has always been a private company controlled by the McConnel family, which also owns the *Montreal Star*. It is the smallest of the four major refiners.

In the four Western provinces, B.C. Sugar Refineries has an absolute monopoly. The company was founded by B.T. Rogers in Vancouver in 1890, where it has traditionally operated a cane refinery. In 1931 it bought Canadian Sugar Factories Ltd., which operated two beet refineries in Alberta. In 1955 it acquired the Manitoba Sugar Company Ltd. after this company tried to undersell the B.C. firm in the Saskatchewan market. While the company is a public corporation with diversified stock ownership, control is still exercised through the stock holdings of the Rogers family.

There is a small government-owned sugar beet refining plant at St. Hilaire, Quebec, originally established in 1943 to provide an outlet for Quebec sugar beet growers. However, it has an agreement whereby it sells all of its production to Redpath Industries.

In 1963 a new sugar refinery was established at Montreal by Robin Austin of Barbados: Cartier Refined Sugars. After encountering marketing difficulties created by the dominant firms, it was sold to Steinberg's in 1966.

Finally, in 1974 George Weston Ltd. opened a refinery in Oshawa. Like Steinberg's, they saw their chain of retail stores as a captive market outlet for sugar products. The opening of the two new refineries has cut into the market shares of the Eastern trinity, has contributed to increased industry overcapacity, but has not led to any price competition.

Canadian Consumption of Sugar

Between 1910 and 1971 there was a 50% increase in consumption of sugar by individual Canadians. Per capita consumption in the mid-1970s was more than 100 lb. per year.

Of the total, only 40% was sugar consumed in the form of refined sugar bought at the supermarket. The bulk of sugar consumed (60%) is in the form of processed foods. In the food manufacturing industry, the following are the largest sugar purchasers: soft drink manufacturers, 25%; miscellaneous food manufacturers, 15%; fruit and vegetable processors, 14%; confectionery manufacturers, 13%; and bakeries, 11%.

Practically all processed foods that we eat contain sugar. This would include sauces, many baby foods, most fruit drinks, salad dressings, all forms of soups, frozen and canned fruits, pot pies, frozen TV dinners, and most cured meats. Heinz Tomato Ketchup is 30% sugar by weight. Coffee-Mate non-dairy Creamer is 65% sugar. General Foods' Jello-mixes are 80% sugar. A can of Libby's peach halves is 17.9% sugar, a chocolate cake by Sara Lee is a relatively modest 35.9% sugar.

About 90% of all sugar used in refining is imported. By the mid-1970s the major sources were Australia (42%), South Africa (26%) and Mauritius (16%). Imports from Cuba have dropped, and Canada has all but cut off sugar imports from the British Commonwealth countries in the Carribean area. Betwen 1966 and 1973, imports from South Africa increased from 127,000 to 278,000 metric tons. When the Union of South Africa was expelled from the Commonwealth for its apartheid policies, the Canadian Government signed a special agreement granting it Commonwealth Preferential Status, and this has been very important in the sugar area.

Sugar consumption around the world is directly related to standard of living; low-income countries (and individuals) simply cannot afford to waste scarce resources on a non-essential food item. Where feasible, most of the sugar-consuming countries are moving towards a position of self-sufficiency through the use of tariffs and subsidies to farmers. Many of the more advanced countries are self-sufficient, including the European Economic Community, Eastern Europe, and the USSR. In fact, in the late 1960s a bumper crop of sugarbeets was produced in the European Economic Community; the surplus was dumped on the world market, further depressing prices to producers in the Third World countries.

While almost all countries in the world maintain a system of national control of sugar production, distribution, and prices, Canada is a notable exception. There is a tariff to protect refiners. The Food and Drug Directorate has traditionally insisted that refined sugar sold in Canada must be 99.8% sucrose. This regulation appears to be designed to protect not our health, but the refining industry in Canada. Finally, sugar beet producers in Canada are subsidized to a certain extent.

These are the only controls in Canada. As a result, Canada is the fourth largest importer of sugar in the world behind the United States, Great Britain and Japan. When the Canadian Government signed the 1968 International Sugar Agreement, they pledged "to operate its internal policies so as not to provide incentives to production beyond a level representing 20% of domestic consumption."

Certainly, the sugar beet industry in Canada has been discouraged by both the private refiners and the government. In 1960, Canadian beet sugar provided 17.4% of the Canadian market. By 1974, this had dropped to 9.4%. Between 1962 and 1972, government support prices have varied according to international prices for cane sugar. But in spite of these supports, acreage planted to sugar beets is dropping. In 1963 producers received an average of $18.64 per ton; in 1972, they received $18.68. As usual, farmers are expected to hold the line on prices while everything else rises.

At one time there was a significant sugar beet industry in Ontario. However, in 1960 Redpath Industries shut down its beet refinery at Chatham. Instead, it opened a new cane refinery in Toronto to take advantage of the cheap overseas sources controlled by its parent, Tate & Lyle.

In 1977, when the international price for sugar dropped to seven cents a pound, B.C. Sugar Refineries announced that it was going to shut down one of its beet refineries, at Picture Butte, Alberta. Alberta sugar beet growers protested, but were in a very weak bargaining position. It was in the company's interest to shift production to the cheaper imported cane sugar, then a glut on the international market. Alberta growers feared that the closing of the plant would be the beginning of the end of their industry. They asked for a national policy guaranteeing 20% of the Canadian market for domestic sources.

The Consumers Association of Canada urged the Tariff Board not to impose any tariffs or quotas on imports, in order to keep prices to consumers as low as possible. If necessary, they preferred the system of subsidizing Canadian sugar beet growers.

Bill Luttrell of Gatt-fly, one of the knowledgeable people in Canada on the sugar industry, argues that the sugar beet industry in Canada should be maintained only if the following three conditions are met:

1. Access to Canadian markets by developing countries heavily

141

dependent upon sugar exports is not jeopardized;
2. It has not to rely upon "Third World" cheap labour in the form of Indian-Metis or Mexican migrants; and
3. These goals must be accomplished within the context of international agricultural adjustment; i.e., land used to grow badly needed crops should not be taken out of production to grow something which can be better produced elsewhere.

The 1971-1975 Price Fluctuations

All Canadians were stunned by the dramatic increase in the price of sugar beginning in 1971 and then by its rapid fall in 1975. It should also have been a lesson in the dangers of dependency on outside sources for food. All processed food prices rose during this period, as they are dependent on the use of sugar as a basic ingredient.

At the time the sugar beet industry was shut down in Ontario, and Redpath Industries opened its new cane refining plant in Toronto, the London Daily Price of sugar was around 3.5 cents a pound. It rose to 7.75 cents in 1963, but then dropped down to its low level. By 1972 it had risen to 9.5 cents. The dramatic upswing began in 1973, when it rose to 31.4 cents; it peaked at 57.27 cents in November 1974, and steadily dropped thereafter down to 8.0 cents a pound in 1976. Why was there such a great fluctuation? Who made the huge profits at this time?

Between 1960 and 1971, the London Daily Price was below the actual cost of sugar production as published by the International Sugar Organization. The sugar producing countries were experiencing severe hardships in the industry. In the period 1972-1973, this changed, with the London Daily Price being between 0.8 and 1.94 cents above production costs of raw sugar. There was a dramatic change in 1974, with the London Daily Price being more than ten cents a pound higher than the average cost of raw sugar.

The sugar refiners in Canada argued that the rise was due to bad weather, and there were shortfalls in some countries, particularly Cuba. But there is simply no way weather changes alone could have caused such a fluctuation. There were two other basic causes: commodity speculation and profiteering.

The best study on this was done by W.C. Labys for the United Nations' Conference on Trade and Development. In examining the futures market, he found that the normal hedging did not occur during this period of rapid increases in sugar contracts. Speculators did not sell when prices were rising; additional speculators were attracted, raising the prices even further. The turnover of future contracts rose spectacularly in this period when contrasted to the 1960-1971 period.

According to the criteria of commodity exchanges set by Labys, speculative trading is excessive when it exceeds 100% of the actual total of physical sugar traded. In 1973, the future contracts traded four and a half times the actual amount of sugar produced.

In 1974, Canadian consumers paid more than $500 million in excess prices for sugar than they normally would have expected to pay. All the sugar companies showed substantial increases in profits during this period.

When sugar prices fell quickly in 1975, the drop was not always passed on to the Canadian consumer. This was particularly true of the soft drink and confectionery industries. In contrast, prices went down proportionately on these products in the United States. The Toronto *Globe & Mail* noted that "the sticky issue of processed sugar prices seems to have drawn little consumer protest." Where were the consumer groups?

One thing is certain: the high prices were not the result of high wages paid to farm workers. Sugar cane workers are among the lowest paid and most exploited workers in the world. In the Philippines in 1970 field workers were paid $.50 a day; this rose to $1.00 by 1974. In South Africa, Africans were being paid $2.64 a day in 1974. In Jamaica in 1974 the sugar workers formed unions and secured collective bargaining agreements which paid them between $3.00 and $5.30 per day. Similar wages are paid in Trinidad and Guinea.

The highest wages in the world for farm workers are paid to Hawaiian workers. Through a long struggle, the International Longshoremen's and Warehousemen's Union (ILWU) managed to organize plantation workers. In 1972 they were making $30.00 a day, and by 1974, $6.20 an hour. The companies retaliated by mechanization and shifting production to the Philippines and elsewhere.

In the continental United States, farm workers in the sugar industry are among the lowest paid American workers. In 1974 they were averaging between $2.00 and $2.50 an hour. The preponderant majority of these workers are Chicanos and Blacks, following the classic colonial plantation situation of white owners and managers and exploited non-white workers.

Because of the low international prices, and the absence of any real protections, Canadian sugar beet farmers are being squeezed out. Their only possibility for survival is to cut costs the only place they can: at wage rates. Thus, the sugar beet industry in Western Canada has traditionally been worked by Indians and Metis, at very low pay. Recently, Mexicans have been imported as well. The present

143

government and industry policy threatens to create the racist situation which is present throughout the world in the sugar production industry.

TABLE VIIa

Sugar Refineries

Company	Ownership/Control	1971 Sales
Redpath Industries Ltd.	U.K.—Tate & Lyle	$86,341,214
B.C. Sugar Refineries	Canada—Rogers Family	71,408,000
Atlantic Sugar Refineries	Canada—Jannock/Glengair	45,000,000
St. Lawrence Sugar	Canada—Sucronel/McConnell Family	25,000,000
Cartier Sugar Ltd.	Canada—Steinberg Family	11,500,000
Quebec Sugar Refinery	Canada—Quebec Gov't.	8,000,000

Oligopoly—High Profits

In sugar refining, Redpath Industries is the established price leader. The other companies all admit that they follow the price leadership of this company, not necessarily because it is the biggest (it has 29.2% of industry capacity, and roughly 34% of the total market), but because it is the subsidiary of Tate & Lyle, the largest sugar corporation in the world. Each day, Redpath sets the Canadian price, which is the London Daily Price (LDP) converted to Canadian dollars at Montreal; this includes the cost of the raw sugar plus insurance and freight (CIF). No one really knows how the traders establish the LDP. In general, the result is that the Eastern Canadian price is about 33% higher than the LDP.

However, there is another base price: New York No. 11 Spot Price, which is also available daily and serves as a basis for pricing in the United States. In the 1970s, it has been almost equal to that of the LDP, some days a little higher, others a little lower. What this means is that Canadian refiners establish a price which is 33% higher than that of American refiners, and this is translated into higher prices for Canadian consumers.

Redpath Industries, for example, sells refined sugar in the U.S. market at New York prices, or about 33% less than in Canada. In September 1975 the U.S. Farmers and Manufacturers Beet Sugar Association of Michigan charged Redpath with "dumping" in the

American market, i.e., selling at prices lower than they sold the same product in the domestic market. The charge was, of course, true. In mid-September 1975, Redpath was selling sugar in Toronto to Canadians for 22.5 cents a pound; at the same time they were selling the same sugar in the United States for 19.6 cents a pound.

This is oligopoly at work. With the absence of price competition, Redpath Industries is free to adopt a pricing system which guarantees a high gross margin and a high profit. The other refiners gladly follow, and reap the same benefits.

Even though sugar prices were falling drastically, and primary producers were insisting that they were losing money, the Canadian refiners continued to make their profits. In 1977 Redpath reported sales were the highest ever, with an increase in profits of 11% over the previous year. The company's annual report admitted a 13% return on equity.

In contrast, Redpath had bought controlling interest in Refined Syrups and Sugars Inc., whose Yonkers, N.Y. refinery had a capacity equal to that of all Redpath's Canadian operations. In 1977 sales from this subsidiary were $22 million, but it had yet to show a profit in the more competitive U.S. market.

In 1971 the Tariff Board released its report on the sugar industry. It recommended that the duties on raw sugar and refined sugar, as low as they were, be lowered because of the high profits of the sugar refineries, the excessive gross margins, and the excess capacity in the industry.

In the period between 1966 and 1968, the Tariff Board reported that the sugar refiners realized a profit on sales of between 18.9% and 20.8%; their return on equity ranged from 20.3% to 26.6%. It noted that in the 1967-1969 period, the profits of Redpath Industries were three times as high as those of its parent, Tate & Lyle.

Similar conclusions were reported by George L. Beckford in his examination of plantation economies. Using company records for 1968, he found that Tate & Lyle had a turnover (sales) on refining and distribution in the United Kingdon of 127,166 thousand pounds, and a profit of 3,121 thousand pounds. That was a rate of return on sales of 2.45%. For its refining operations in Africa, the return was 6.6%. But the Canadian operations (Redpath Industries) reported a turnover of 18,672 thousand pounds, and a profit of 3,691 thousand pounds. The profit on sales in Canada, 19.76%, was by far the best of any of the company's operations.

In their study of the sugar refining industry, the Food Prices Review Board found that the industry had the highest rate of return on equity of any of the major categories of food processing in Canada. Between 1967 and 1972, their rate of return was almost twice as high as the food processing industry as a whole, and three times as high as the baking and fish packing industries. Their profit as a percentage of the sales dollar was over three times the average for the food processing industry.

Excess Capacity

With a guaranteed high gross margin established by a recognized price leader, a high degree of excess capacity often results. This is especially true of an industry where the product is undifferentiated; i.e., there can be no brand name advantages established through mass advertising.

The Tariff Board found that this was one of the major inefficiencies of the industry. An estimate of present excess capacity in cane sugar refining was made by the Food Prices Review Board in 1975.

The plant pounds per day capacity of output of refined sugar was multiplied by a 48 week year, operating five days a week, on a 24 hour shift operation. In 1973, under this formula, it estimated an excess capacity of 20%. For 1974, with the operation of Westcane, excess capacity rose to 33%. It also argued that with a little overtime, capacity could be raised even more, providing a 36% excess capacity rating for 1974. However, in their first report (issued in July 1974), it estimated the total capacity of the eight sugar cane refineries at 3,500 million lb. per year. At this rating, the excess capacity in 1974 would have been 45%.

There are problems with operating at full capacity all year round. There are winter storage problems, as the St. Lawrence Seaway is closed. Nevertheless, the high gross margin under the present pricing system more than compensates for these difficulties. That is why Cartier and Westcane have been built: in spite of industry inefficiencies, the high gross margin makes high profits normal.

The Court Cases

In 1957 the Restrictive Trade Practices Commission issued their report on the takeover of the Manitoba Sugar Company Ltd. by the B.C. Sugar Refining Company Ltd. They argued that allowing B.C. Sugar Refining to become the sole manufacturer and distributor of sugar in Western Canada would "not be in the public interest." They urged that the takeover be renounced. The federal government took the case to court, charging B.C. Sugar Refineries with "being parties to the formation or operation of a merger, trust, or monopoly contrary to sections 2 and 32 of the Combines Investigation Act." On August 8, 1960, they were acquitted in the Manitoba Court of Queen's Bench.

This was a most important case in Canadian anti-combines history. It was very clear cut as to the facts: B.C. Sugar Refineries had established a pure monopoly in Western Canada, the only Canadian market in which it sold its products. How could the court reach such a decision?

The court argued that the Crown had failed to establish that such a merger would lead to exorbitant or excessive profits or prices. The merger must be proven to be to the detriment of the general public—and this must also be "unduly."

In February 1960, the Restrictive Trade Practices Commission released its report on the sugar industry in Eastern Canada. The Commission found that the practices of the three refineries "with respect to common basic prices, equalized freight rates, common package differentials, and the use of price concessions" had limited competition to the detriment of the public. They gave examples from company records of keeping prices high to consumers even when cost-saving practices were introduced.

In April 1962, formal charges were laid in court by the Diefenbaker Government; the three companies pleaded guilty, and one year later they were each fined $25,000. Of more significance (to later events) was the fact that the court issued an Order of Prohibition stating that the company and its officials were not to conspire, combine, agree, or arrange together to (1) fix prices, (2) fix uniform package and grade price differentials, (3) fix agreed transportation charges, and (4) to arrange to share total sales proportionately. If they did so, then under Canadian law company officials would be subject to jail sentences, as in the United States.

But the companies did not change their pattern of behaviour, and pressures were applied for subsequent action. Much of the impetus came from Robin Austin, who had experienced great difficulty establishing Cartier Refined Sugars in Montreal. When the three Eastern refiners finally conceded the existence of Cartier, they each surrendered 2% of the market.

After eight years of investigation by the Restrictive Trade Practices Commission and the Combines Division, the same three companies were again brought to court. The Crown charged them with conspiring to fix prices and lessen competition from 1960 to 1973. They also charged that the companies had collaborated in trying to prevent the establishment of Cartier Refined Sugars.

In Canada, under the Combines legislation, it is not illegal to follow the price leadership of a particular company. There has to be a conspiracy or an actual agreement between companies for an illegal

147

act to have been committed. The Crown, in this case, tried to establish that the companies' unchanged share of the market, and the absence of any price competition, were, in fact, a combine agreement. The three accused companies argued that what existed was a "normal oligopolistic practice" and did not involve conspiracy. It was a simple case of price leadership.

Robin Austin, who was responsible for establishing Cartier Refined Sugars Ltd., testified at the trial that efforts to buy sugar from India and South Africa were "blocked" by Redpath Industries, St. Lawrence Sugar, SLSR Holdings, and Atlantic Sugar Refineries.

During the trial, the representatives from Atlantic Sugar Refineries, St. Lawrence Sugar, and B.C. Sugar Refineries all admitted that they followed the price leadership of Redpath Industries. On occasion, Redpath employees would even call the other "competitors" and inform them that they were changing their price. But this was not a "conspiracy."

TABLE VIIb

Capacity and Market Share of Sugar Refineries, 1974

Company	Capacity Lbs. per Day	Capacity % Total	Market Shares % Total
B.C. Sugar Refinery, Ltd.	4,400,000	29.7	20
Redpath Sugars Ltd.	4,300,000	29.2	34
Atlantic Sugar Refineries	2,400,000	16.3	22
St. Lawrence Sugar	1,900,000	12.9	16
Westcane Sugar Ltd.	900,000	6.1	3
Cartier Sugar Ltd.	500,000	3.4	5
Quebec Sugar Refinery	350,000	2.4	—

SOURCE: Food Prices Review Board, Sugar Prices II: *The Canadian Refining Industry.* August, 1975. Table 3, p. 6, for capacity figures; Bill Luttrell, *Sugar: Who Pays the Price?* Toronto: GATT-fly June 1975, p. 7, for market shares.

William Paton, then President of Atlantic Sugar Refineries, had a close relationship with Jim Crawford, then Chairman of St. Lawrence Sugar Ltd. This developed, so the Court was told, because their wives were close friends. They met often in social situations, and although they discussed the sugar business in general, they told the Court that they never discussed relations or transactions with their respective customers. No conspiracy existed.

During the trial, William Paton presented an example of how his company, Atlantic Sugar Refineries, was in competition with Redpath. Atlantic was the sole distributor in the Maritime provinces, although Redpath also distributed in Newfoundland. In order to utilize some of the excess capacity of their refinery at St. John, N.B., Atlantic began to export sugar to the United Kingdom, where it entered into competition with the market dominated by Tate & Lyle, the parent of Redpath Industries. In retaliation, Redpath entered the market in the Maritimes and began to woo some of Atlantic's major customers. Mr. Paton then stated that Atlantic concluded that the exports to Great Britain were "unprofitable" and discontinued them. According to the Food Prices Review Board, Redpath discontinued selling in the Maritime market.

On December 21, 1975, the Quebec Court of Queen's Bench issued its decision through Judge Kenneth MacKay. The Court ruled that the Crown had not proved that a conspiracy or actual agreement existed between the three companies. The government's case was "circumstantial," based largely on documents taken from the company files; it was not based on testimony from witnesses.

This was, in the Court's opinion, simply a case of price leadership. Judge MacKay noted that "the law does not prohibit a member of an industry from taking into account and following his competitors." He concluded that the maintenance of market shares was the result of a tacit agreement among the accused; the Crown had failed to prove that it was designed to unduly prevent or lessen competition. The purpose, according to Mr. MacKay, was to "avoid a price war."

Andre Ouellet, then Minister of Consumer and Corporate Affairs, described the decision as "a complete disgrace and completely unacceptable." He was immediately cited for contempt of court by Judge MacKay. The Judge described his comments as "false, abusive, intemperate and reprehensible."

The federal government appealed the decision shortly thereafter. In March 1978, the Quebec Court of Appeal reversed Judge MacKay's decision, at least in part. The sugar refiners were acquitted of the charge of price fixing. However, the three judges concluded that the refiners were guilty of "unduly restraining competition." The thirteen year agreement among them to maintain proportionate shares of the market was the key matter in the reversal.

No jail sentences were prescribed, only fines. Furthermore, the Eastern big three are now appealing the case to the Supreme Court of Canada.

THE CONFECTIONERY INDUSTRY

The confectionery industry is one of the most concentrated food industries in Canada and is almost totally dominated by branch plants of foreign corporations, many of them large conglomerates. It includes companies which manufacture candies, chocolates, cocoa products, chewing gum, salted nuts, popcorn, marshmallows and other similar products. In the mid-1970s, the per capita consumption of confectionery products was about seventeen lb. per year.

The industry has not enjoyed a rapid growth in sales in recent years. Some industry spokesmen attribute this to the change in snack food consumption patterns by youth, and in particular their shift to soft drinks and fast foods. The other major factor for the decline in the consumption of gum and chocolate bars has been consumer resistance to the rather dramatic increase in prices between 1973 and 1976.

The American Leaders

The Hershey Chocolate Co. was founded in the 1890s. It had only one major competitor in those early days, the Nestle firm from Switzerland. Thanks to a high tariff wall, Hershey Chocolate quickly came to dominate the field of chocolate bars as well as cocoa products. In 1970 its assets were $218 million, more than the total of the five next largest firms in the candy and chocolate business in the United States.

There are two interesting characteristics of the Hershey corporation. First, it has traditionally spent very little on advertising and has chosen instead to keep prices relatively low. With this practice it stands out as a prominent exception to the processed foods industry. But this may be due to the fact that it quickly came to dominate the confectionery industry to such an extent that its brand name was identified with the industry as a whole. Furthermore, its large sales staff kept its products on the shelves of stores.

The other characteristic of the company is that it has remained primarily in the field of confectionery and has resisted any merger or takeover by larger food firms. In recent years it has diversified into coffee, pasta products, frozen foods, and "TV dinners," but these remain minor aspects of the company operations. Again, this is in contrast to the other large firms in the field.

The chewing gum industry has traditionally been dominated by two large American firms, American Chicle Co. (Adams Gum) and the William Wrigley Jr. Company. The Chicle Company was formed in the United States by a merger around the turn of the century. The

150

Wrigley Company, which rose to be the biggest firm in the U.S. market, was formed around the same time. As manufacturing costs represented only around one-third of company revenues, massive amounts were spent on advertising to capture and control the market. This has been quite successful, as Wrigley has about 55% of the U.S. market and Adams Gum about 35%. The third largest is Life Savers.

Today Adams Brands is part of the huge Warner-Lambert conglomerate formed in a merger in 1955. Since then the conglomerate has acquired such major firms as the Emerson Drug Co., Adams Brands, Smith Brothers Cough Drops, American Optical Company, Texas Pharmacal Co., Schick Safety Razor Co., and Parke, Davis & Co.,

TABLE VIIc

The Confectionery Industry

Company	Ownership/Control	1971 Sales
Nestle (Canada) Ltd.	Switz.—Nestle	$48,844,000
Cadbury, Schweppes & Powell Ltd.	U.K.—Cadbury Schweppes	46,500,000
Hershey Chocolate of Canada Ltd.	U.S.—Hershey Foods	40,000,000
William Neilson Ltd.	Canada—George Weston	30,000,000
Adams Brands Ltd.	U.S.—Warner Lambert	25,000,000
Laura Secord Ltd.	Canada—Brascan	23,863,000
Rowntree MacKintosh Canada Ltd.	U.K.—Rowntree	20,376,000

Moving Into Canada

The Canadian market for chocolates is not so totally dominated by a single firm, although oligopoly is the rule. There are five companies which have a major share of the Canadian market; only one of these, William Neilson, owned by the Weston Empire, is nominally Canadian-owned. The others are Hershey Chocolate of Canada, Rowntree MacKintosh Canada Ltd. (British-owned), Cadbury, Schweppes & Powell (British-owned), and the Walter M. Lowney Co. (now owned by Standard Brands, an American conglomerate).

A smaller share of the market is held by Ganong Brothers (a family-owned firm in New Brunswick), Laura Secord (owned by Brascan/Labatt), Dare Foods (a Canadian-owned firm), Mars Canada Ltd. (U.S.-owned), and Trebor Canada Ltd. (British-owned).

151

The Kraft Foods Corp. has the largest share of the caramel market and totally dominates the marshmallow industry in Canada.

The roasted and salted nut field is heavily dominated by Planters, now owned by Standard Brands. Its major competition comes from National Nut & Confection Co. (Poppycock), Johnson's Nuts and Bunny Nuts, all owned by Ovaltine, an American firm with a major plant at Peterborough, Ontario. As strange as it may seem, the corn-for-popping industry in Canada appears to be dominated by two American firms based in Iowa, plus Canadian Home Products, an American branch plant.

As in the United States, the chewing gum industry is dominated by the two American firms, William Wrigley and Adams Gums. Their positions in the industry are reversed in Canada, with Adams having about 50% of the Canadian market. This is attributed to sales in Quebec, where the Quebecois prefer the sugar-coated Chiclet gum to the stick gum, which is manufactured by Wrigley. The third largest gum corporation in Canada is Life Savers Ltd., a subsidiary of Dobbs Life Savers Inc. of the United States.

Product Differentiation and Market Concentration

The confectionery industry is characterized by the complete absence of price competition plus a high degree of advertising and promotion. The figures on industry concentration in Canada do not reveal the extent to which the industry (and in particular the individual products within it) are controlled by a few large firms.

In the chewing gum industry, there are very few new products being introduced; changes are mainly in flavour. Adams introduced "Trident" sugarless gum in 1970. It was the first product innovation since the introduction of "Dentyne" in the 1920s. "Chiclets" were introduced in 1919.

William Wrigley brought in "Freedent" gum, designed not to stick to dentures, in the mid-1970s, its first "new" gum since World War II. In 1976, it followed Adams by bringing out a sugarless gum, "Blammo," through its subsidiary, Amurol Products Co.

The chocolate bar industry is quite different. According to the Confectionery Association of Canada, there are about eight new candy bars introduced every year (but only one in twenty become established in the market). This practice requires a high degree of advertising. A successful candy bar in the Canadian market will sell between fifty to seventy million units a year, bringing in substantial returns.

There are no figures on the amount of company spending on

advertising and promotion in Canada. Part of the reason for this is that the dominant firms are all conglomerates. But they are also primarily branch plants of foreign corporations, which rarely reveal anything about their activities. The Food Prices Review Board's brief look at advertising did not cover the confectionery industry.

However, we do know that confectionery products are widely advertised in the media. Furthermore, we have figures provided by the U.S. Treasury Department for the National Commission on Food Marketing. There is no reason to believe that the same firms have substantially different marketing strategies in Canada.

The amount spent on advertising is definitely increasing. For the industry as a whole, this rose from 2.6% of sales in 1947 to 4.2% of sales in 1961. For the large firms (with assets over $50 million) the percentage rose from 2.8% to 9.8%.

A 1963 survey done for the U.S. Senate Subcommittee on Antitrust and Monopoly found that the four largest chewing gum manufacturers accounted for 100% of all magazine and television advertising in that field. For all other confectionery products, the four largest firms accounted for 82.8% of all magazine advertising, 46.8% of all network TV advertising, and 65% of all spot TV advertising.

The gross margins of the confectionery manufacturers have been among the highest of all the food industries. For the large firms in the U.S., they rose from 32.5% of sales in 1947 to 42.8% in 1961. Profits as a percent of net worth after taxes for the large firms in 1961 were 17.2%. This was the highest of any food group covered in the survey published by the National Commission on Food Marketing.

Recent Industry Problems

For both chewing gum and candies, sugar is the major ingredient. When the price of sugar rose significantly in 1974, the price of candy bars was raised to 15 cents and then to 20 cents. There was significant sales resistance, with a drop in unit sales of about 25%. The companies shrunk the size of bars, and this was also resisted by consumers.

In 1975, there was a sharp drop in the price of sugar, but the price of candy bars did not go down. Despite lower sales, gross margins were maintained at a higher rate, providing regular profits. Industry spokesmen claimed other costs, particularly labour, had offset the drop in sugar prices.

In the fall of 1976, chocolate bar sales were still below the 1973 level. When the price of cocoa was increased, another rise to 25 cents was announced in December 1976. Industry spokesmen announced that they might opt for artificial chocolate, widely used in the United States.

With the rising cost of cocoa, the U.S. candy bar manufacturers are moving to synthetic substitutes. Standard Brands has been using a substitute manufactured from cotton to coat its "Baby Ruth" and "Butterfinger" candy bars. Peter Paul has also been using a synthetic substitute on "Mounds" and "Almond Joys". It is described as "an undisclosed brown substance."

The chemical giant, Monsanto Corporation, is marketing "counterfeit chocolate" as a "total candy system," to replace not only the chocolate coating but the filling as well. The company says that "it's a most lasting coating," with a "nice gloss, nice shine, nice snap to the product." In 1974 it was advertising that the chocolate substitute would save the candy manufacturers between 17% and 20% over the natural product.

There was a similar development in the chewing gum industry. In 1973, the price of a package of gum was raised from 10 cents to 15 cents. Sales dropped by 24%. In 1975, Statistics Canada reported that chewing gum sales were down by another 20% from 1974.

The Trudeau Government has aided the corporations by changing the classification of candy bars from confectionery to food. For fifty-seven years, candy was considered a luxury item, not essential to human growth and development. When the status was changed, the industry was relieved of the federal excise tax of 12%. The large, foreign-owned corporations have had considerable influence with the federal Liberal Governments in Canada.

The other main concern of the industry is the rising interest in nutritional content in foods. There has been growing publicity given to the relationship between good diets and good health, and lower medical and hospital expenditures. In a number of European countries, the system first adopted by Norway is gaining increased support. Norway places a tax on foods (like sugar-based products) which are injurious to your health and uses the tax to subsidize nutritious foods. This liberal attempt to modify eating practices is brought about by government concern over mounting health costs.

It is widely recognized that sugar, the basic ingredient of confectionery products, is the single most harmful food regularly consumed by humans. It not only causes most dental problems (as we always knew) but is the major cause of coronary diseases, diabetes, and other major ailments. The confectionery industry claims that candy bars are a "nutritious" food item when "eaten in moderation." They are a "good food" for many people with "an overall, balanced diet." They have tried to head off any campaign by nutritionists in Canada through widespread advertising and promotion campaigns.

For example, kids in minor hockey are told that candy bars offer "instant energy." Walter M. Lowney and William Wrigley Jr. have allotted considerable promotional expenses in the area of minor hockey. But as long as the Consumers Association of Canada and other spokesmen for consumers interests continue to concentrate their attack on the price of food at the farm gate and against marketing boards, the corporations have a clear field.

In 1977 the decline of the value of the Canadian dollar hit the industry hard, as the major ingredients, sugar and cocoa beans, are imported. Confectionery manufacturers were also greatly worried that the Trudeau Government would lower duties on imports during the upcoming negotiations on the General Agreement on Tariffs and Trade. They pointed out that with 85% of the industry controlled by Canadian manufacturers who are wholly-owned subsidiaries of U.S. and British corporations, any reduction in protection would bring a flood of imports of the identical products from the metropolitan centres.

THE VEGETABLE OIL INDUSTRY

Over the period from 1961-1971 the consumption of edible oils by Canadians doubled, making this one of the growing food industries in Canada. In 1973 vegetable oils held 85% of the market, animal oils 11%, and marine oils 4%. Less than one-half of Canadian production is bought by consumers in retail outlets; these products include margarine, cooking oils, shortenings, "creamers," etc. Of these, margarine is the most important, accounting for 43% of retail edible oil sales in 1974.

Over one-half of edible oil production is taken by food processors. The major users are the snack food and bakery industries. In addition, restaurants and industrial and institutional caterers are also major users. The meal by-product of oilseed crushing is a major feed supplement in animal and poultry feeds.

At the primary level, the industry faces competition from the animal fats industry, and in particular butter. In processing, lard and other animal fats can often be used as a substitute for vegetable shortenings. Marine oils are also used in food processing.

Imports also have an important impact on the structure of the domestic market. There is no duty on imports of raw materials, so when primary commodity prices rise, they face competition from external sources. For example, about one-half of all soybeans crushed in central Canada's mills are imported from the United States; the other one-half are grown in Ontario. The vegetable oil refiners, however, are protected by a 10% duty on crude vegetable oils and a 17% duty on refined oils. The manufacturers (as one would expect) enjoy the most protection. The federal government bans the importation of margarine.

Imports of oils are also important in the manufacturing industry in Canada. The Canadian farmer and oilseed crushers and refiners must also compete with imports of coconut oil, palm oil, corn oil, peanut oil, and cottonseed oil. In the 1970s, the imports of vegetable oils have accounted for about 17% of the Canadian market.

In the 1960s and 1970s there has been a rapid expansion of the rapeseed industry in Western Canada, both at the level of farm production and in seed crushing and refining. In 1973, rapeseed oil accounted for about 34% of the total edible oils used in the Canadian market, exceeding soybean oil. The primary production of soybeans and rapeseed depends to a large extent on market prices, not only for the oil seeds, but also for the substitute crops available to farmers. When wheat prices are low, rapeseed production increases; when cereal grain prices in general go up, rapeseed production drops off.

The Manufacturing Industry

The manufacturing industry is characterized by only a few firms in the field, a total of only nineteen in 1974. Of these, there are seven companies which completely dominate the industry, both in selling advertised brands at the retail level and providing edible oils for industrial processors. Kraft Foods completely dominates the salad dressing field, and is a major marketer of margarines. Standard Brands, through the "Blue Bonnet" and "Fleischmann's" brands, is a major marketer of margarines and salad oils. Both of these companies stress manufacturing and retailing and do not operate crushing or refining operations. Best Foods, a subsidiary of the U.S. giant, CPC International, through the "Mazola" brand, completely dominates the corn oil market.

Procter & Gamble, through the "Crisco" brand, is a strong force in the salad oil and cooking oil markets. It also markets other retail products, and is a major oilseed crusher and refiner. The "Monarch" brand is also well established at the retail level by Lever Brothers: the company maintains an oil refinery but it is not in the crushing end of the operation. Canada Packers has traditionally been a force in the oil seed market in crushing, refining, and manufacturing; however, it does not have the brand identification at the retail level that is enjoyed

156

by the four major retail firms, all of which are foreign-owned.

There are three other major manufacturers and retailers: Burns Foods, Swift Canadian, and Agra Industries. They are vertically integrated operations. Burns and Agra lack the market power of mass advertising, and like Canada Packers, suffer from a lack of overflow advertising from the United States. Swift Canadian has long been involved in refining and manufacturing but has concentrated on industrial sales. The remaining firms are minor factors in the manufacturing industry.

This does not mean that the nationally advertised brands completely dominate the industry. According to L.R. Rigaux, they have only 40% of the national margarine market. This is partly due to the fact that there are small firms in the field. But the main reason is the availability of private store brands at the retail level, particularly in margarine. The local brands, which are not advertised, usually sell at a lower price. For the consumer, there is not that much difference between brands of margarines or vegetable oils, and therefore price considerations may be significant. Furthermore, the chain stores often use the non-advertised brands as loss leaders.

Nevertheless, the retailers cannot afford not to carry the major nationally advertised brands. Furthermore, retailers know that brand identification is very important at the retail level, and the failure to carry popular brands may result in lost sales.

The manufacturers of these products must be aware of price differences at the retail level. Edible oil products are perishable, and no manufacturer can allow inventory to build up too high. The large manufacturers all engage in traditional marketing practices, offering discounts for large orders and promotional allowances.

Crushing and Refining

The crushing and refining of oil seed in Canada has traditionally been concentrated in central Canada. In 1963, the Tariff Board reported that three crushing mills in Ontario (Maple Leaf Mills, Procter & Gamble, and Canada Packers) had 80% of the crushing capacity in Canada. The refineries operated at that time in Ontario and Quebec by Canada Packers, Colgate, Unilever, Procter & Gamble and Swift Canadian accounted for 80% of the refining capacity in Canada.

Most of the large manufacturers of edible oil products also have refineries located near their manufacturing plants. The exceptions are Kraft Foods and Standard Brands, who buy refined oil from other industry sources. In Western Canada, Canbra Foods Ltd. crushes and

TABLE VIId

Major Edible Oil Manufacturers

Company	Ownership/Control	Crushing Plant	Refinery	Margarine	Shortening	Salad Oil
Monarch Fine Foods Ltd.	U.K.—Unilever		x	x	x	x
Proctor & Gamble Co. of Canada Ltd.	U.S.—Proctor & Gamble Inc.	x	x	x	x	x
Kraft Foods Ltd.	U.S.—Kraftco Inc.			x	x	x
Standard Brands Ltd.	U.S.—Standard Brands			x	x	x
Canada Packers Ltd.	Canada—W.F. McLean	x	x	x	x	x
Canbra Foods/Burns Foods Ltd.	Canada—R.H. Webster	x	x	x	x	x
Agra Industries Ltd.	Canada—B.B. Torchinsky	x*	x	x	x	x
CSP Foods Ltd.	Canada—Wheat Pools	x	x	x		
Swift Canadian Ltd.	U.S.—Esmark		x		x	

* Sold to CSP foods

158

refines rapeseed at Lethbridge. Its oil products are manufactured into various products at Burns Foods' operation at Calgary.

In the early 1970s there were only seven oil seed crushing plants in Canada. The three plants in Ontario were still dominating the industry. The industry in central Canada primarily crushed soybeans, but, with the expansion of the rapeseed industry in Western Canada, has engaged in rapeseed crushing as well.

Maple Leaf Mills has been active only in the crushing business, selling its crude oil to Monarch Fine Foods, which is the largest refiner of edible oils in Canada. In January 1976, Maple Leaf Mills and Lever Bros. Ltd. announced that they would be jointly building "the largest integrated vegetable oil plant of its kind in Canada," to begin operations in 1978. Maple Leaf Mills will use the mill for its large feed division. Lever Bros. is a major manufacturer in Canada, and its parent, Unilever, is a major world power in the field of oil extraction.

In this case the federal government provided the United Co-operatives of Ontario a grant of $9 million to help construct a grain storage terminal to serve the new Windsor plant. As there was already significant overcapacity in the industry at the time, the announcement came under heavy attack from Western Canadian farmers and industry leaders.

In Western Canada, the dominant firm traditionally was Western Canada Seed Processors, at Lethbridge, Alberta. Now known as Canbra Foods Ltd., it has come under the control of Burns Foods. The other major crushers were the Saskatchewan Wheat Pool, with a plant at Saskatoon; Co-op Vegetable Oils, at Altona, Manitoba; and Agra Industries, at Nipawin, Saskatchewan.

In October 1974, Agra Industries sold its rapeseed crushing plant at Nipawin to the Saskatchewan Wheat Pool. The Pool was to lease the edible oil refinery and packaging plant, which was to be jointly operated with Agra. This was a wise move on the part of Agra Industries, for the industry in Western Canada was beset by overcapacity at the crushing level and was suffering from federal discrimination in freight rates. Agra decided to concentrate on crushing at its Montreal plant. In 1977 Agra sold the rest of their Western Canadian vegetable oil interest to CSP Foods.

In March 1975 CSP Foods Ltd. was formed, an amalgamation of the crushing and refining operation of the Saskatchewan Wheat Pool and the Altona plant, which at the time was owned by Manitoba Pool Elevators. This gave the co-ops three of the four crushing plants in Western Canada and a capacity of 11.4 million bushels. The Canbra operation at Lethbridge had a capacity of 12 million bushels.

The Western Canadian co-operatives obviously got carried away with the rapeseed boom following the record harvest of 95 million bushels in 1971. This was an unusual situation, brought about by large seedings due to the low price of wheat. When grain prices rose, rapeseed production dropped to 52 million bushels in 1974. In spite of these fluctuations the co-ops went ahead and built new rapeseed crushing plants.

Alberta Food Products at Fort Saskatchewan was a joint venture between the Alberta Wheat Pool (60% equity) and a consortium of three major Japanese oil, feed and distribution companies (40%). It was assumed that this plant would mainly serve the Japanese market. It has a capacity of 7.2 million bushels.

Another plant has been located at Sexsmith, Alberta, in the Peace River area. It is 60% owned by the Northern Alberta Rapeseed Producers Co-operative and 40% by a West German group, Euro-Cana Trade Ltd. The plant's capacity of 9.5 million bushels can almost completely handle the 10.3 million bushels of rapeseed grown in 1974 in the entire Peace River area. This plant expected to market 80% of its feed meal in Canada, but to export 70% of the edible oil.

In 1975 CSP Foods Ltd. announced that it would be building an additional crushing plant at Canora, Saskatchewan with an 8 million bushel capacity. United Grain Growers also established a plant in 1976 in partnership with British Columbia Packers (33%), Mitsubishi Corporation (23%), and Nisshin Oil Mills Ltd. (10%). It suffered "severe financial losses" in its first year of operation at Lloydminster.

In all, the capacity of the Western Canadian plants, including the Canora plant, was rated at 48.1 million bushels. To fully utilize this capacity, it would be necessary to crush almost all rapeseed in Western Canada. This would require a substantial change in the oilseed industry, for in 1973, with a crop of about 54 million bushels of rapeseed, the four Western Canadian crushers had only 25% of the market. Why was this?

Corporate-Government Power

In 1973 the four Western oilseed crushers petitioned the federal government asking for equal freight rates between rapeseed oil, meal, and raw seed moving to Eastern and offshore markets. They admitted at that time that the four plants could double their annual output. Since 1969 the crushers have been pleading for the change. Raw rapeseed and meal are shipped to Eastern Canada at the same rate as other seeds in standard boxcars. If rapeseed meal is shipped in covered hopper cars, an additional 15 cents per hundredweight was added. Rapeseed oil, which moves in large tank cars, was charged an additional $1.10 per hundredweight, considerably higher than seed rates.

At a hearing before the Canadian Transport Commission held in Saskatoon in 1972, the governments of Ontario and Quebec, and the oilseed crushers from central Canada, strongly opposed any lowering of the freight rates on rapeseed products manufactured in Western Canada. It was a case of the co-operatives and Western farmers in political conflict with the large corporations (mainly foreign-owned) and their supporters in the Quebec Liberal and Ontario Conservative Governments.

The final blow came in May 1976. The Trudeau Government issued an Order in Council requiring the Canadian Transport Commission to establish a "minimum compensatory rate" for moving processed rapeseed to Eastern Canada. This means a rate above the railway's variable costs, those that are attributed to a particular traffic; and this rate goes up as the variable costs go up.

The president of CSP Foods Ltd., R.W. Siemens, denounced the move and said it was a blow to Western Canada and the rapeseed industry there. He predicted that it would require his firm to shut down one or two of its crushing operations. They had already postponed building the Canora plant in 1976. CPS Foods was already losing its markets for crushed and refined oil in Eastern Canada and was now going to have to operate at about 40%-50% capacity.

For political reasons, the Trudeau Government then announced an additional programme to ensure that the gap between the Crow rates and the new compensatory rates would not get worse. In February 1978, even with a $2.5 million subsidy, Western crushers said the rate differential was costing them $7 million a year. In April, Jack Horner announced the federal government would raise the rail subsidy to $3 million if each of the three prairie provinces would kick in $1 million. At this point, the issue turned into another typical federal-provincial squabble.

For the co-ops, the railroad rate controversy has been a bitter lesson in private enterprise marketing; it revealed once again, the power that the large manufacturing concerns have in Canada. In the oilseed industry, vertical integration through manufacturing has proven to be a necessity for profitable operation.

Gross Margins and Profits

It is impossible to present any strictly empirical evidence on the rate of profit in the edible oil industry. All of these industries are integrated to some degree, and they are all part of conglomerate operations where costs and returns are hidden in consolidated figures. The only study to date which tries to make any assessment here is the

161

background study done for the Food Prices Review Board by L.R. Rigaux. Table VIIe presents his calculations for the value added in the process of manufacturing and retailing margarine. The other method of analysis he uses is to look at the gross margins of each sector in the chain of production and distribution. Both assume the use of soybean oil.

TABLE VIIe

Percent Value Added by Sector Towards Retail Margarine
April-June 1975

Soybeans	15%
Crushing	15%
Refining	10%
Manufacturing	42%
Retailing	15%

SOURCE: L.R. Rigaux, Table XI, p. 67

The period covered in Rigaux's analysis was a volatile one, from December 1972 to April 1975. Soybeans experienced a tremendous price increase in mid-1973. The industry tried to protect itself from wide fluctuations in commodity prices through forward purchasing and term contracts on sales. During this period, the price of margarine at the retail level rose from thirty-one cents a lb. in January 1973 to peak at sixty-eight cents a lb. in February 1975, and then dropped to fifty-nine cents a lb. by August 1975.

Between January 1973 and the end of June 1975, the price of a bushel of soybeans on the Commodity Exchanges ranged from a low of $4.28 in January 1973 to a high of $10.96 in June 1973. Over the thirty month period, the average price was $6.44 per bushel. During the period, the gross margin per bushel obtained by the crushers ranged from $.88 in March 1973 to a high of $3.63 in July 1973. The average over the period was a gross markup of the equivalent of $1.66 per bushel, or 25.7%. This markup was clearly enough to yield a substantial profit. In May 1976, R.W. Siemens, President of CSP Foods Ltd., complained that his crushing operations were operated at only about 50% capacity, and that the industry in Western Canada was "facing 30 cents per bushel gross margin conditions, which does little more than cover direct costs." At the same time, soybeans were selling for about $5.25 a bushel on the international markets.

162

Estimates of gross margins at the refining level are more difficult due to hedging and the difficulty of obtaining data from industry sources. Nevertheless, Rigaux makes estimates based on data from soybeans obtained from a few industry sources. Margins during this volatile period of the market ranged from zero in the January-March quarter of 1974 to a high of 29% in the quarter of April-June 1975. In mid-1973, refining margins were almost zero; this was the period of "record crushing margins." But in early 1975, when crude vegetable oil prices dropped, the refiners recouped their losses.

Over the thirty month period, the gross margin between the price of a pound of crude vegetable oil and the refined product, blended margarine oil, ranged from a loss in early 1974 to a high of 8.2 cents per pound in the April-June quarter of 1975. Over the entire period, the markup averaged 3.3 cents per pound, or 10.7% over the crude oil price. Relative to the other sectors of the manufacturing process, gross markups appear to be low at the refining level.

The highests margins are at the manufacturing level, as one would expect, for this is the area of oligopoly and market control through product differentiation. The cents-per-pound markup between the cost of refined oil and the wholesale price of margarine to retailers varied from a low of 15.5 cents in the quarter of July-September 1973 to a high of 32.7 cents in the first quarter of 1975. The average gross margin during this period was 20.7 cents, or 72.7%.

Retail margins are more difficult to estimate because of the regional differences in markets. For example, price competition at the retail level is generally believed to be much greater in the metro Toronto area than in Western Canada, where Canada Safeway is the recognized price leader and where profits at the retail level are higher. Furthermore, retailers often use margarine as a loss leader. Manufacturers' discounts are often an important factor. Rigaux found cases where the reported wholesale price of the nationally advertised brands was higher than the actual retail price of non-advertised brands in the metro Toronto market. Discounts and allowances by the manufacturers range up to 20%. If the average discount is 10%, then to gain an accurate picture it would be necessary to reduce the manufacturers high gross margins by this amount and add it to the margin of the retailers.

At the retail level, margins were lower in the first three quarters, falling to around 8%, when oil seed prices were high. The cost of the basic product was carried through the manufacturing chain. When international commodity prices fell in the first half of 1975, retail margins increased up to 18%. This may be a close approximation of average retail markup.

Unfortunately, figures were not available to compare the gross margins with the actual costs of production at each level of the chain, from farmer to retailer. But it is clear that the "marketing" costs make up by far the largest share in the spread from the cost of soybeans at the farm gate to the price the consumer must pay for margarine.

The relative strengths of the sectors of the industry can be seen in the markups between January 1973 and June 1975. Over that period, the international commodity price of a bushel of soybeans increased 26.8%; the price of crude vegetable oil increased 167.6%; the price of refined oil increased 123.4%; the price of manufactured margarine increased by 92.9%; and the retail price of nationally advertised brands in the Toronto area increased by 80.6%.

At the crushing level, there is no problem with entry of new firms; this also seems to be the case at the refining level. The obvious problem is having a market for the product. And it is here that the integrated firms have a definite advantage. Financial success also appears to be greatest at the manufacturing level, where advertising and product differentiation have produced an oligopolistic market. In this respect, the edible oil industry follows the general pattern of food manufacturing in North America.

Commodity Speculation

There is one other factor which has been mentioned in both the sugar and soybean industries: international commodity speculation. Originally, merchants, manufacturers and producers bought and sold commodity futures contracts as a hedge on their operations, to make sure that they had an adequate supply when needed and that they would not be wiped out by wide fluctuations in international market prices. In a private enterprise situation, it offered a possibility for a degree of stabilization, and this was the original objective.

However, the commodity futures market has been turned into a circus for speculators and a game for the idle rich. Furthermore, despite what some promoters claim, it is not a "zero-sum game"; there are not equal winners and losers. In the food area, prices are driven up by mass speculation; there are those who profit and those who lose. But in all cases, a large amount of the cost of this form of trading in food is paid by the consumers through higher prices in food. It is a rare case when it is the farmer who benefits.

For example, when the international price of soybeans rose from $3.50 a bushel in July 1972 to an incredible $12.90 in July 1973, it was not the farmers who benefited, but the speculators. After the Russians bought large amounts of grain in the U.S. in 1972 at $1.80 a bushel, speculators drove the price up to $5.50 a bushel. A subsequent investigation by a U.S. Senate Committee headed by Senator Henry M. Jackson estimated that the rise in cereal grains and soybeans cost the average American consumer an addition 15% for food.

The same thing occurred during the speculation on sugar; the consumer paid for much of this through higher food prices. Shortage of supply was obviously a factor; but profiteering by commodity speculators unnecessarily increased the cost to consumers.

In contrast to the stock exchanges, the commodity exchanges are very poorly governed and have weak regulations. It is possible for a group of wealthy people to manipulate the international price of a commodity for personal gain. For example, Nelson Bunker Hunt, of the famous multi-millionaire oil family of Texas, drove up the price of silver in 1973 from $2.80 an ounce to $6.00 and reaped a reported $300 million in windfall profits.

In the spring of 1977, the U.S. Commodities Futures Trading Commission indicted the Hunt family for conspiring to rig the international soybean market. They had acquired futures contracts for 22.1 million bushels of the 1976 soybeans crop; the total remaining was only sixty-five million bushels. They were then planning to sit back and wait until prices rose, as other speculators and legitimate manufacturers would be forced to buy at higher prices in a short market to meet real commitments.

U.S. regulations prohibit any individual or group from purchasing more than three million bushels of soybeans. But as the *Financial Times* pointed out, the loopholes in the regulations allow one speculator or a group to buy additional 1976 futures by selling yet unproduced 1977 soybean futures. Four speculators, under the system, can buy twenty-seven million bushels. The entire Hunt family was apparently involved in the soybean case, with the CFTC charging that they were acting as a group.

The absurdity of this system was dramatized in May 1976. Jack R. Simplot, the largest potato grower and manufacturer in the world, had been speculating in the potato commodity market along with a few others. They didn't like the price they were going to have to pay to meet their futures contracts, so they just defaulted. They refused to come through on 1,000 contracts, the equivalent of fifty million pounds of potatoes. Although they were fined by the U.S. Commodities Futures Trading Commission, the total fines appeared to be less than the profit earned by the defaulters.

In January 1977 there was another example of rigging of the commodity market by the very same participants who had defaulted on the potato contracts in May 1976. Simtag Farms spread rumours that they had sold 150,000 tons of potatoes to Europe. Prices rose on the exchanges as a result of the announcement. Then Simplot and Peter J. Taggares announced that in fact the original figure was wrong, and that they had only sold 15,000 tons. Prices fell and many people lost. It is doubtful that Simplot lost.

Cases such as these reveal the exploitative nature of the international commodity exchange system. In many cases the high prices were in no way a reflection of the real supply and demand of the commodity. Furthermore, for the people of Canada, and the Third World, food is too important an item to be treated in such a manner. Its prices should never be dictated by a few wealthy people playing a game, trying to make a fast buck.

SOURCES

Al-Zand, Osama A. "Canada's Oilseed Sector: An Overview of Marketing and Trade," *Canadian Farm Economics,* IX, No. 2, April 1974, pp. 9-16.

Batler, Emanuel. "Commodity Trading: The Incredible International Guessing Game," *Saturday Night,* XC, No. 2, June 1974, pp. 36-41.

Beckford, Georg L. *Persistent Poverty: Underdevelopment in Plantation Economies of the Third World.* Toronto: Oxford University Press, 1972.

Canadian Agriculture in the Seventies. Report of the Federal Task Force on Agriculture. Ottawa: The Queen's Printer, 1970.

Confectionery Associaton of Canada. *Confectionery News.* Various issues provided by the association.

Duncker, J.W. "The Increase of Palm Oil in World Markets," *Canadian Farm Economics,* XI, No. 2, April 1976, pp. 10-19.

Eaton, E.S. "Sugar," *Canadian Farm Economics,* III, No. 6, February 1969, pp. 4-6.

Eaton, E.S. "Sugar and Sugar Beet Production in Canada," *Canadian Farm Economics,* II, No. 1, April 1967, pp. 31-36.

Eichner, Alfred S. *The Emergence of Oligopoly: Sugar Refining as a Case Study.* Baltimore: Johns Hopkins University Press, 1969.

Fletcher, Lehman B., and Donald D. Kramer. "The Soybean Processing Industry," in John R. Moore and Richard G. Walsh, eds., *Market Structure of the Agricultural Industries.* Ames, Iowa: The Iowa State University Press, 1966.

Food Prices Review Board. *Sugar Prices and Policies.* Ottawa: Food Prices Review Board, July 1974.

Food Prices Review Board. *Sugar Prices II: The Canadian Refining Industry.* Ottawa: Food Prices Review Board, August 1975.

Gott, Philip Porter. *All About Candy and Chocolate.* Chicago: National Confectioners' Association of the United States, 1958.

Hightower, Jim. *Eat Your Heart Out: How Food Profiteers Victimize the Consumer.* N.Y.: Crown Publishers Inc., 1975.

Horst, Thomas. *At Homes Abroad: A Study of the Domestic and Foreign Operations of the American Food-Processing Industry.* Cambridge, Mass.: Ballinger Publishing Co., 1974.

Institute of Edible Oil Foods. Various briefs presented to the author.

Luttrell, William L. *Have You Got $10,000 to Burn? The Commodity Futures Link in the International Food Chain.* Toronto: GATT-Fly, February 1977.

Luttrell, William L. *Sugar: Who Pays the Price?* Toronto: GATT-Fly, June 1975.

Mitchell, Don. *The Politics of Food*. Toronto: James Lorimer & Co., 1975.

National Commission on Food Marketing. *The Structure of Food Manufacturing*. Technical Study No. 8. Washington, D.C.: U.S. Government Printing Office, June 1966.

Restrictive Trade Practices Commission. *Report Concerning the Meat Packing Industry and the Acquisition of Wilsil Ltd. and Calgary Packers Ltd. by Canada Packers Ltd.* Report No. 16, August 3, 1961.

Restrictive Trade Practices Commission. *Report Concerning the Sugar Industry in Eastern Canada*. Report No. 69, February 3, 1960.

Restrictive Trade Practices Commission. *Report Concerning the Sugar Industry in Western Canada and a Proposed Merger of Sugar Companies*. Report No. 59, January 7, 1957.

Rigaux, L.R. *A Preliminary Paper on the Canadian Edible Oils Industry*. Ottawa: Food Prices Review Board, February 1976.

Tariff Board. *Oil Seeds, Vegetable Oils and Related Products*. Report No. 131. Ottawa: The Tariff Board, 1963.

Tariff Board. *Sugar in Canada*. Report No. 146. Ottawa: The Tariff Board, 1971.

U.S. Federal Trade Commission. *Report of the Federal Trade Commission on Rates of Return in Selected Manufacturing Industries, 1961-1970*. Washington, D.C.: U.S. Government Printing Office, 1972.

8. THE BEVERAGE INDUSTRY

Some might question whether the beverage industry should be included in a study of the food industry in Canada. Consider first alcoholic beverages. In Europe, the drinking of beer and wine with the meal is normal. But in North America, this practice is much more limited. Alcoholic beverages are more likely to be consumed at social events. Nevertheless, the European tradition is growing in both Canada and the United States.

But what about distilled spirits? Only in the Northern European countries are distilled spirits consumed in large amounts and in a regular manner with the consumption of food. Nevertheless, the worldwide consumption of spirits is increasing steadily.

It also must be remembered that the ingredients for all alcoholic beverages are produced on the farm; the beverage industry is an important outlet for sales of these farm products, and the manufacturers are becoming more integrated into the conglomerate food corporations.

In fact, one would be on firmer ground questioning the traditional classification of soft drinks as food. Aside from the sugar which is the basis of the syrup, the only other ingredients in soft drinks are water and a variety of chemicals produced in the laboratory. Farmers (and some nutritionists) are quite concerned over the tremendous increase in the consumption of soft drinks in Canada, because such drinks are replacing the consumption of milk.

All four of the beverage industries are characterized by a high degree of concentration and product differentiation. The distillery industry offers an interesting study of the rise of two major Canadian-owned corporations. The beer industry shows how governments can support the development of monopoly power. The wine industry in Canada is a case study of the collapse of the family-owned firm. And finally, the soft drink industry offers a clear illustration of how the franchise system has perpetuated monopoly control and foreign domination of a highly decentralized food industry in Canada.

THE DISTILLING INDUSTRY

The distilling industry in Canada is really a late arrival on the manufacturing scene. It did not really get off the ground until the U.S. government established prohibition during the First World War and continued it until repeal in 1933. During this period the two major Canadian distillers, Distiller's Corporation (now known as Seagrams) and Hiram Walker, rapidly grew due to the bootleg trade over the border into the United States. When prohibition was lifted in 1933, they were both quick to move into the U.S. market with fully-aged whiskey, manufactured in Canada; at the same time, they established large distilleries in the U.S. This lead on the American distillers permitted both of these firms to establish a brand identity for high quality Canadian-blended rye whiskey and to gain a substantial share of the lucrative U.S. market in spirits. Today, for both companies, the preponderant majority of sales are in the United States.

In both Canada and the United States, whiskey is the preferred spirit drink. However, in the 1960s and 1970s there has been some shift in Canadian consumer preference; whiskey consumption has dropped, while consumption of rum, vodka, and gin has increased substantially. With the rise of personal disposable income, Canadian consumption of wine, brandies, and liqueurs has increased.

Similar consumption trends have been noted in the U.S. market. Yet whiskey remains the American favourite. In 1971 the consumption breakdown was as follows: 62% were varieties of American whiskeys, 22% was imported Scotch whiskey, and 16% was imported Canadian whiskey.

In 1977, whiskies held 56.5% of all liquor sales in the United States. The leader was still American whiskies with 30% of total sales, with Canadian whiskey at 13.4% and Scotch whiskey at 13.1%. Vodka sales had risen to 16.8%.

Of the total of Canadian whiskey sold in the U.S. market, the two large Canadian firms have traditionally had about 65% of the market. However, in recent years the major U.S. distillers (National Distillers & Chemical Corp., Brown-Forman Distillers, and Schenley's

Industries) have established or acquired distilling plants in Canada in order to export brands of "Canadian" whiskey to the U.S.

For the distilling industry in Canada, the export market is the key. In 1971 about 70% of all whiskey manufactured in Canada was exported. In that year total exports for the spirits industry were around $195 million, while imports totalled only around $40 million.

While consumers feel that they are paying heavily for the privilege of consuming alcoholic beverages, few really realize the extent of which government taxes cut into their dollar. In 1971, the distillers received only about 20% of the price of a bottle of distilled spirits. For example, for a 25 oz. bottle of "Seagrams V.O."or Hiram Walker's "Canadian Club," retailing in 1971 for around $6.50 per bottle, the distillers received $1.25. Another $.10 went for freight. The federal sales tax amounted to $.34 and the federal Excise Tax was $1.55. At the provincial level, the sales tax averaged $.31, and the provincial markup for sales and profit averaged $2.95.

TABLE VIIIa

Canadian Distillers

Company	Ownership/Control	1971 Sales
Seagrams Ltd.	Canada—Bronfman Family	$687,000,000
Hiram Walker Ltd.	Canada—H.C. Hatch	345,000,000
Distillers Co. (Canada) Ltd.	U.K.—Distillers Co. Ltd.	40,400,000
Alberta Distillers Ltd.	U.S.—National Distillers	18,600,000
Canadian Schenley Ltd.	U.S.—DWS Corporation	20,000,000
Gilbey Canada Ltd.	U.K.—International Distillers	17,900,000
Melchers Distillers Ltd.	Canada—Marchand/Desruisseaux*	9,300,000
Bacardi & Co. Ltd.	Bermuda—Bacardi Family	3,200,000
Potter Distillers Ltd.	Canada—H.J.C. Terry	1,100,000
L.J. McGuinness & Co. Ltd.	U.S.—Standard Brands	1,000,000
Canadian Mist Distillers Ltd.	U.S.—Brown Forman Distillers	1,000,000

NOTE: It is not certain whether these figures are gross sales, including federal excise tax or net sales, excluding them. Seagrams and Hiram Walker are net sales. The foreign firms do not issue annual reports, and the figures are Dun & Bradstreet (Canada) Ltd. estimates.

* In December 1977 Melchers was bought by a consortium consisting of John De Kuyper & Son (Canada) Ltd., Meagher's Distillery Ltd., American Distilling Co., Corby Distilleries Ltd., and Calvert of Canada Ltd.

Because of high government taxes, the wholesale price of distilled spirits has been kept low by the manufacturers in an attempt to retain their share of alcoholic beverage sales. Between 1961 and 1971, the retail price of spirits at the wholesale level rose only 10%, or 1% per year. As a result, distillers have increased productivity by larger scale operations, closing down small distilleries, and replacing labour with capital. Employment in the industry has declined over the ten-year period. Because of the squeeze, stock prices have also been falling.

At the same time, the squeeze has been particularly hard on the small distillers. They have less efficient operations and cannot compete with the extensive advertising of the major firms. For example, in the early 1970s Melcher's Distilleries Ltd. of Montreal, a company controlled by the Marchand family and Senator Paul Desruisseaux, lost money for three consecutive years. In 1975, its main distillery at Bertierville, Quebec was operating at only 22% capacity. In January 1977 they tried to sell their subsidiary, Manitoba Distillery Ltd., to a group of Winnipeg businessmen, but the deal fell through. This plant had been closed since 1973. In March 1977 they were forced to declare bankruptcy. In December 1978, Melcher's was bought by a consortium of five companies, dominated by American interests.

Industry Concentration and Brand Identification

The distilling industry is one of the most highly concentrated in Canada. The study by the Combines Commissioner for 1965 revealed that the top four firms had 84% of the market, and the top eight had 96%. In 1971 there were only 13 firms in the field and only twenty-two plants in operation. The industry is overwhelmingly dominated by two giants: Seagrams Co. Ltd. and Hiram Walker-Gooderham & Worts Ltd.

There are two reasons for the growth of concentration in this industry. First, there is a high degree of product differentiation supported by very extensive advertising. Both Seagrams and Hiram Walker are among the top fifty companies in Canada in advertising—in spite of the restrictions on advertising imposed by some of the provinces. All the other distilleries lag far behind in advertising. The two main companies have been able to establish a market and keep it.

It is also clear that the monopoly power of the two major firms has been aided by the fact that retail sales of alcoholic beverages in Canada are controlled by the provincial governments. The provincial Liquor Control Boards establish prices. The price differentials within each group of distilled spirits is very small. There is no opportunity for price competition.

In the United States, in contrast, alcoholic beverages are normally sold through private retail operations. Price competition on the local level is often fierce. Smaller regional companies have been able to survive because they offer lower prices made possible by the fact that they do not engage in the expensive process of national advertising. In 1972 the distributors of Canadian whiskey in the United States spent $10.7 million on advertising in magazines alone. Most of this was accounted for by the two Canadian giants.

The two dominant firms in Canada are quite different in their style of operation. Because they are among the most successful Canadian business enterprises, they merit additional comment. In 1971, Seagrams ranked ninth in sales among Canadian corporations and fourth in assets; Hiram Walker ranked sixteenth in sales and tenth in assets.

The Bronfman Empire

Ekiel and Minnie Bronfman left Bessarabia to come to Canada in 1889, settling near Wapella, Saskatchewan. They were never poor immigrants; they had been grain millers in the Old Country and they came with a supply of capital, a rabbi to teach the children, a maid, and a servant. Their early history on the prairies is documented in James H. Gray's popular book, *Booze*. The Bronfmans moved quickly into the hotel business with their base being the Balmoral Hotel in Yorkton, Saskatchewan. Other hotels were acquired in Emerson, Brandon, and Winnipeg, Manitoba; Port Arthur, Ontario; and Sheo, Leslie, and Saltcoats, Saskatchewan.

As Gray notes, the Yiddish translation of Bronfman is "whiskeyman," and it was not long before the enterprising family moved into this business, a natural outgrowth of the Western Hotel business. When prohibition was announced, the Bronfmans moved to Montreal, as Quebec was the only province which remained "wet." From there they operated a very profitable mail order booze business until it was banned by the federal government in 1917.

The Bronfman family as a whole epitomized the fabled entrepreneur. They were real "free enterprisers," always pushing to the limit. Using their ties to the Liberal Party, they obtained a permit from the Unionist Government in 1917 to import distilled spirits for "medicinal" purposes; the Canada Pure Drug wholesale company was established in Yorkton. In 1919 railroad carloads of medicinal Scotch whiskey arrived, around 300,000 cases. Later, straight alcohol

172

was imported in bulk and sold to others to be mixed. The distribution business was earning them at least $50,000 a month, but they knew more was to be made in manufacturing.

While Abe Bronfman always insisted that Rule One in the Book of Seagram is "make finer whiskies and make them taste better," this was not always the case. The original Yorkton brew consisted of 100 gallons of rye whiskey, 318 gallons of pure alcohol, and 382 gallons of distilled water. While the labels identified the ingredients as Scotch, Rye and Bourbon, it was all the same thing. As their "distilling" experience grew, caramel was added to give the rye colour. A base of dark-coloured Scotch was used (instead of rye) to provide a trace of the peat smoke taste. Caramel and blackstrap mollasses were added to straight alcohol and water to make rum.

The profits in this business were enormous. During a court case in 1922, Harry Bronfman admitted that the gross revenue from this operation was $500,000 a month for an average net of $391,000. The key to the whole operation was the export business to the United States, where the prohibition amendment to the U.S. Constitution had been ratified by the States in January 1920.

At first the Bronfmans decided to engage in rum running as part of their overall business operation. They established the Trans-Canada Transportation Company. A car full of booze, seized by the Saskatchewan Liquor Commission, brought a test case which established the right to transport by vehicle and not just rail. But it convinced the Bronfmans that they should steer clear of this end of the business; instead, they promoted the "come-and-get-it" system. The Bronfmans insured the operation: if their cars were confiscated by the authorities, they put up the double-duty bond required by customs for its release into the U.S. The system worked well. Unfortunately, one casualty was Harry Matoff, married to the oldest Bronfman sister, Laura. He was shotgunned by U.S. rum runners while making a sale.

In 1922 the export trade was to be ended, and there was a mad rush to get rid of booze in storage. The Bronfman's new brew was reduced to forty gallons of water, ten gallons of alcohol, and two gallons of malt whiskey. To this concoction were attached the labels on hand: "Dewar's," "Johnny Walker," "Black and White," and the well-known "no name" label. All were the same ingredient, but they sold for different prices. In the last ninety days of the bonanza it was estimated that they were doing $6,000 worth of business per day from their Regina company.

The Bronfmans, ever the enterprisers, took full advantage of their close ties to the Liberal Government in Saskatchewan, a government that was well-known for its system of patronage. When the Saskatchewan Liquor Commission seized beer being bootlegged, instead of dumping it, they would sell it for "export." Harry Bronfman bought it from the Commission for four dollars a barrel and sold it to other distributors for seventeen dollars; often they sold it back to Saskatchewan hotels for twenty-five dollars a barrel. There were many ways to make a profit.

The Bronfmans remained out of jail due to a combination of their cunningness, the corruption and incompetence of the government agents who were supposed to enforce legislation, their close political ties to the Liberal Governments in Ottawa and Saskatchewan, and the fact that their wealth could buy them a battery of competent and politically-connected lawyers.

However, all good things come to an end, as the saying goes. With the changes in 1922, the Bronfmans moved to Montreal and built their first legitimate distillery at Ville La Salle. They moved up from the Yorkton "boozorium" to a castle on Mount Royal next to all the powerful Anglo-Canadian financial elite. A new era was beginning for the family, interrupted only by the unpleasant hearings of the Royal Commission on Customs and Excise in 1926-1927, the "kidnapping" of Harry in 1919, and his trial in Saskatchewan by the new Tory government. The charge was bribing customs officials; the three best lawyers in the West got him acquitted.

Always a far sighted individual, Abe Bronfman, who emerged as the spark behind the new legitimate operation, realized that when the American states ratified the new amendment to the Constitution to repeal prohibition there would be a tremendous new market in that country. In 1928 he began to produce extra whiskey and stockpile it. When 1933 came, and the U.S. market opened, there were no distillers in operation in the U.S., and there was no aged high-quality whiskey available.

The Distiller's Corporation quickly moved into this market with "Seagrams V.O." and "Seagrams Seven Crown," establishing a reputation for high quality Canadian whiskey which exists down to the present. They purchased a distillery at Lawrenceville, Indiana (still their largest U.S. distillery) and entered what was to remain their major market. In 1976 the U.S. market accounted for 70% of all sales, Europe 11%, South America 11% and Canada 8%.

The history of the company is one of continuous expansion, the primary technique being the takeover of established companies with well-known brands. For the bootleggers, a reputation for high quality was most important. They also quickly realized that advertising and brand identification in the legitimate era was essential to success.

In Canada, the Bronfmans purchased the Joseph E. Seagram & Sons Company in 1928. Later they bought two distilleries in British Columbia and one at Beaupre, Quebec. Expanding overseas, they bought the Long Pond Estates in Jamaica, a sugar plantation and distillery producing rum; Robert Burnet Gin Co. in England; and Robert Brown and Chivas Brothers Scotch whiskey companies in Scotland.

In the United States, they now have twelve distilleries and maintain the original brand names of their acquired firms: Calvert, Four Roses, Kessler Distilling, and Hunter-Wilson Distilling. They moved into the wine business through the purchase of Browne Vintners, Paul Masson, and the establishment of Fromm & Sidiel, which is the sole distributor of Christian Brothers wines.

Established spirits, brandies, and wine manufacturers were acquired in France, Germany, Italy, Austria, Ireland; plants were established or acquired in Israel, Mexico, Costa Rica, Venezuela, Brazil, Argentina, New Zealand, and Spain. Today, Seagrams Corporation is the largest distiller in the world.

The biggest change in recent years has been the movement of the company from Montreal to New York City. In 1956 the thirty-eight storey Seagrams Building on Park Avenue was completed. The U.S. company was put in charge of all the company's operations except those in Canada, Israel, and Jamaica, which are retained at the Montreal branch plant. This meant that 90% of the company's business was now done out of New York. Stockholders reports are issued in U.S. dollars. Stock trades on the New York Stock Exchange.

Hiram Walker-Gooderham and Worts

Hiram Walker was born in Massachusetts, but moved to Detroit at an early period of his business career; he ran a grocery business there between 1838 and 1849. When he expanded into the liquor business, he was harrassed by Michigan prohibitionists. In 1858 the company expanded across the line and opened a grain mill and distillery in Canada. Walker was capitalizing on the reciprocity while maintaining and expanding his main enterprise in Detroit. In 1859 he moved to Canada and established Walkerville as his home.

However, the American Civil War greatly increased business opportunities in the U.S., and he moved back to Detroit in 1863. In fact, he set up a Republican newspaper which he operated in Detroit until 1881. Between 1882 and 1889 he developed the Lake Erie, Essex, and Detroit River Railroad which was hooked into the Grand Trunk. In 1890 the Walkerville Brewing Co. was organized, but most of his bottling was done in Detroit. His son, Hiram Walker II, took over when he died in 1899, and his grandson, Harrington E. Walker, became President in 1919.

175

By 1910 the Walkerville Distillery was the second largest in Canada and the largest manufacturer of whiskey. When prohibition came, they operated a "cash and carry" operation for American rum runners and were also in the "medicine" business. The Walker family's ties to the firm were ended in 1926 when the estate was sold to Harry Hatch and Associates for $14 million.

Harry Hatch worked for Corby Distillers. In 1923 he bought Gooderham & Worts of Toronto, one of the largest distillers in Canada. In 1927 the present firm was formed. H. Clifford Hatch succeeded his father as President of the firm in 1946. Like the Bronfmans, the Hatch family saw the opportunities in the U.S. following the repeal of prohibition. In July 1934 they began producing at their distillery at Peoria, Illinois; at the time, it was the largest in the world. In contrast to the Bronfmans, however, Hiram Walker has not expanded in the U.S. market by taking over existing firms; it is still operated as a centralized operation from this original plant.

Hiram Walker has been a much more conservative firm than Seagrams. It has not engaged in an extensive takeover programme nor has it been quick to diversify into other areas. In Canada, it bought out James A. Barclay and acquired a 50.1% interest in Corby's Distillers. In 1968 it bought Courvoisier, the well-established cognac firm; it also owns the Ballantine Scotch whiskey company. A major coup came in 1978 when Walker was able to buy 12% interest in Bacardi and obtain an option to purchase another 13%. Still family-owned, Bacardi rum, and particularly their white rum, was the fastest growing label in North America. But aside from this, Hiram Walker limits its other operations to importing wines and spirits.

But like Seagrams, it recognizes that the U.S. operation is the major market. In 1977, U.S. sales accounted for 57% of the total, 24% were from sales abroad, and only 17% of sales were in Canada. While the traditional head office is in Walkerville, the main operating office is across the river in Detroit. The company issues its annual reports in American dollars, trades its stock on the New York Stock Exchange, and its Canadian Board of Directors has traditionally included more Americans than Canadians, emphasizing established business connections in Detroit.

THE BREWING INDUSTRY

The brewing industry is one of the most monopolized industries in Canada. In the mid-1970s, the Big Three, John Labatt Ltd.,

Molson Industries Ltd., and Carling-O'Keefe Ltd. (formerly Canadian Breweries) had 97% of the national market. The rise of monopoly power and the disappearance of the regional, family-owned breweries is the story of the power of mass advertising, provincial government control of the sale of alcohol, and the failure of anti-combines action by the federal government.

In the 1950s, the regional breweries in Canada still had 20% of the national market for beer sales. As late as 1962 there were twenty independent breweries in operation across Canada. By 1976, there were only four left: Bison Brewing Ltd. in Newfoundland, Moosehead Breweries Ltd. in New Brunswick, Henninger brewery (Ontario) Ltd., a German branch plant which only began operations in Ontario in 1973, and the four breweries owned by Ben Ginter in Manitoba, Alberta, and British Columbia. In 1976, Ben Ginter's operation was in court receivership.

To a significant degree the process of concentration has been aided by the decision of the provincial governments to operate the retail end of the alcoholic beverages industries as a state monopoly. The most important factor here has been the decision of provincial liquor boards to maintain a uniform price for all beers. Small regional breweries, who do not have the benefits of national advertising, have had no chance to compete with the Big Three in the area of price. This is a major difference between Canada and the United States. In the American states, where retail sales are not controlled by government-owned monopolies, price competition is normal.

TABLE VIIIb

The Brewing Industry

Company	Ownership/Control	1971 Sales
John Labatt Ltd.	Canada/U.S.—Brascan	$426,757,000
Carling-O'Keefe Ltd.	South Africa—Rothman's	396,210,000
Molson Companies Ltd.	Canada—Molson Family	314,700,000
Moosehead Breweries Ltd.	Canada—Oland Family	19,200,000
Uncle Ben's Tartan Breweries Ltd.	Canada—Ben Ginter	5,000,000
Columbia Brewing Ltd.	Canada—H.W. Blakely*	3,837,000
Formosa Spring Brewing Co. Ltd.	U.S.—Phillip Morris**	3,400,000
Bison Brewing Co.	Canada—Newfoundland interests	N.A.

* Bought in 1974 by John Labatt
** Bought in 1974 by Molson

Another factor which has led to the demise of the local brewer in Canada and the United States is the development of uniformity of taste. This is in direct contrast to the United Kingdom and Europe, where the different breweries maintain traditional, distinctive flavours which are obvious to almost everyone. There was a time when there was a difference in flavour between breweries in both Canada and the United States. This has disappeared. In fact, most people can't tell the difference between pilsner and lager beer in North America.

With a product which is so uniform in quality and taste, sales promotion is the key factor in gaining and holding a share of the market. The shifts in market shares by the Big Three in Canada has largely been due to the success (of failure) of their marketing systems.

The major concern of the industry in the mid-1970s was the rather slow growth of the industry. Higher personal disposable income was leading to a drop in the brewers' share of the alcoholic beverages market. In 1966, beer held 58% of the total market; this had fallen to 51.3% in 1975.

The industry does not blame this on the ban on television advertising in some provinces. In Ontario, which has heavy beer advertising on TV, per capita consumption has not risen. As a spokesman for Carling-O'Keefe noted, "TV advertising tends to shift brand loyalties, rather than increase the total volume of beer sold." Once all the local brewers have been driven out of business, all that is left for the Big Three is competing for the beer drinkers' dollar through mass advertising and promotion. Price competition is ruled out by government control and the "mutual interests" of the three corporations.

The Rise of Canadian Breweries

The rise of Canadian Breweries to the largest brewery in the world is the story of the modern large corporation: success through the takeover of smaller business concerns. It is also the story of the business power and skill of one man: E(xcess) P(rofits) Taylor, as he has been called.

In 1923, E.P. Taylor graduated from university and joined McLeod, Young and Weir, an investment firm (his father was head of the office). Taylor was also named a director of Brading Breweries in Ottawa, owned by his grandfather. His early business venture was financed by Clark Jennison, an American promoter who obtained capital from British sources.

When Jennison and Taylor embarked on their takeover strategy, the Ontario brewing industry was just recovering from the 1916-1927

178

era of prohibition. There were thirty-six new business ventures, all struggling to make it in a highly competitive market. In direct contrast to the Bronfman family, Taylor was not an entrepreneur; he was a specialist in financial manipulation. Between 1920 and 1959 Canadian Breweries (so named in April 1937) took over thirty-seven companies. Many were simply shut down. When competitors resisted takeover offers, they were subject to predatory practices. In a few cases, Taylor bought up mortgages and then foreclosed.

In 1950 he moved west, buying Western Canada Breweries and Grants Breweries. In 1951 he acquired National Breweries in Quebec, which more or less shared the market in that province with Molson. In Ontario, his major competitors were bought out: The Carling Brewery, O'Keefe's, and Canada Bud Co. Canadian Breweries expanded into the U.S. through Carling Breweries Inc., which established six plants and rose to be the fifth largest American brewery by the mid-1950s. At this time E.P. Taylor had built a brewing empire which held 67% of the Ontario market, 50% of the Quebec market, and close to 50% of the entire Canadian market. It was at this time that the federal government stepped in with an investigation by the Restrictive Trade Practices Commission.

Regina v. Canadian Breweries Ltd.

The Report of the RTPC was issued on May 16, 1955. It traced the history of the takeovers and the methods used by Taylor. Company records showed that the takeovers were designed to reduce competition; the RTPC concluded that they had had this effect. In November 1957, the federal government finally took court action; a decision was served in February 1960.

The court case and the decision were landmark cases in Canadian anti-combines law and helped shape the future of the brewing industry. Canadian Breweries were charged under the Criminal Code with conspiring "to prevent or lessen unduly competition." The court did not dispute the fact that there had been a combine formed. Instead, the decision concentrated on the meaning of "unduly." Had the Crown offered sufficient "proof of the detriment or likely detriment to the interest of the public"?

"Unduly" was defined as giving the parties "the *power* to carry on their business virtually without competition." In such a case, there would be an *agreement* to unduly lessen competition. On the second point, the Court emphasized that under their interpretation of the Combines Act, combines as such are not illegal; only those which operate to the detriment of the public interest. In this case, the Court

179

ruled in favour of Canadian Breweries. Why?

There was no price competition. But the Court noted that this was because the provinces fixed prices. They were the controlling interest. If they wanted to promote price competition they could. Since they were responsible to the people, it was to be assumed that they were operating in the public interest when they set the levels of prices.

Furthermore, Canadian Breweries had not established a "monopoly" position. The Court noted that there remained in Ontario "two strong, aggressive competitors" in Molson and Labatt. Having 67% of the market was not evidence of monopoly power.

The Crown also tried to demonstrate that non-price competition had given the Big Three, and Canadian Breweries in particular, market power which created an effective barrier to entry by new firms. In 1959, Canadian Breweries spent $13.8 million on advertising. The Court admitted that there were "colossal sums" spent on advertising. But again the Court concluded that control of advertising in the alcoholic beverages field was a provincial jurisdiction. Some provinces had instituted controls, and their responsible authorities could restrict advertising if they so wished.

Another point raised by the Crown was the existence of "collateral agreements" between the Big Three. These formal company agreements eliminated traditional areas of non-price competition such as discounts, rebates, installation of servicing equipment, etc. The Court agreed with Canadian Breweries that these were merely "codes of ethics for the trade."

In conclusion, the Court noted that the combine had not diminished the supply of beer, nor was there a "substantial monopoly." The key question was, would the combine result in "the rise in prices which such monopoly might entail?" This was impossible where the provincial governments controlled prices. The questions of oligopoly, non-price competition, and economic and market power were outside the Court's interpretation of Canadian Combines legislation.

Following the 1960 court decision, the Big Three moved in quickly on the remaining regional breweries. In 1971, John Labatt took over Oland & Son of Halifax and Oland's Breweries Ltd. of St. John. The regional breweries traditionally had the largest share of the market in the Atlantic provinces, so Labatt kept the Oland's brand name. In 1974 Labatt bought Columbia Breweries at Creston, B.C. The addition of their 8% of the market gave Labatt about 55% of the B.C. brewing market.

In 1974, Molson bought Formosa Spring Breweries in Ontario, a relatively new brewery opened by Philip Morris. This gave Molson 38% of the Ontario market, and first place among the Big Three. Phillip Morris had bought Millers Brewery in the United States, one of the largest American brewers; they could see that there was little future for a small brewery in the highly concentrated Canadian market.

The Decline of Canadian Breweries

The Court decision of 1960 led to the complete domination of the brewing industry in Canada by the Big Three. The national share of the Canadian market was, in the future, to be determined by non-price competition among them. And there have been significant changes.

In the late 1950s, Canadian Breweries had about 50% of the national market, Molson 20% and Labatt 10%. By 1976, this had changed: Labatt was the leader with 37%, Molson had 33% and Canadian Breweries had only only 25%. What had happened?

In mid-1968, Rothmans of Pall Mall (Canada) Ltd., owned by Rembrandt Controlling Interests Ltd. of South Africa, bought 11% of the voting stock of Canadian Breweries. In May 1969, Phillip Morris, the American tobacco company, made a bid to acquire majority control from Taylor and his associates at Argus Corporation. Their price offering was too low, and stockholders did not meet the quota; the takeover fell through. However, in June 1969 Rothmans made a higher share offer and acquired the equivalent of 50.1% of all voting stock, giving them absolute control. The price was greatly inflated as the company was already beginning to lose its dominant position in the market; this decline continued into the mid-1970s.

Generally, there are two reasons advanced for the decline of Canadian Breweries in an industry characterized by high spending on advertising and promotion. First, Canadian Breweries had no national brand name and no identification like Molson and Labatt. In 1976 the shareholders agreed to change the name to Carling-O'Keefe in an attempt to gain national brand identification. Beyond this, their management and marketing effectiveness in general was clearly weaker than the other two breweries. In the 1960s, they misjudged the importance of advertising on national sports television programmes; in contrast, Molson obtained the rights to "Hockey Night in Canada" and Labatt gained control over beer advertising for the Canadian Football League. It was not until 1969, with the Montreal Expos, that Canadian Breweries got into this field.

Another factor has been the absence of corporate diversification. Of the Big Three, Canadian Breweries had been the only one to move into the large U.S. market. But in the 1960s and 1970s this branch of the company, once as important in sales as the Canadian market, also began to drop off. Corporate centralization was advancing in the U.S. as well. In 1974 U.S. sales were 43% of company totals. The company moved to strengthen its place in the U.S. market in 1975 when they merged with National Breweries of Maryland. This restored the Carling-National Co. to sixth place; but in the U.S. they still had only 4% of the total national market. In December 1977, Carling-O'Keefe of Toronto sold the U.S. operation to R and R Holdings Ltd., a company which is part of the Rothmans Group. This more or less intra-company transaction was expected to improve the standing of the Canadian operation.

The only major category of diversification of Carling-O'Keefe has been in the wine area. In 1972, they bought Gramercy Holdings, and in 1973 the wine operations in Canada owned by IMASCO. This gave Carling-O'Keefe 33% of the Canadian wine market and made them the industry leader. However, the wine industry is not very significant in the beverage industry, and wine sales only account for about 6% of company sales.

In contrast, John Labatt has expanded significantly in the food industry, which now provides 48% of company sales. For Molson Industries, brewing now accounts for only 48% of company sales. The remainder is outside the food and beverage area: office and educational products, home and office furniture, construction products, warehousing and distribution, retail stores (Saveway), Aikenhead Hardware, Beaver Lumber and Homes, and petroleum marketing equipment. Nevertheless, the brewing industry continues to provide a high share of company profits—70% of the total in 1975.

The Uncle Ben Story

One of the most interesting cases of the small brewer is that of Ben Ginter. From a working class background, he moved up the ladder when he began construction work in Northern B.C. By 1965 he had built up a small empire of fourteen companies, mainly on the profits made from building highways for the Bennett Social Credit Government. In 1962, he bought a small brewery at Prince George and pumped $1.5 million into renovations. Uncle Ben's Tartan Breweries moved into the B.C. market.

In 1971 he constructed a new brewery at Transcona, Manitoba and in 1972 another at Red Deer, Alberta. He also bought into the winery business in 1970, and he established soft drink manufacturing plants in Alberta and B.C. But in 1976 the Canadian Imperial Bank of Commerce foreclosed on a $3.5 million note; Uncle Ben's Industries was placed in receivership.

How did it happen? First, Ginter probably underestimated the power of the large soft drink companies. Trying to break into this highly differentiated market with his own brand was simply too difficult; he did not have a U.S. franchise. The soft drink factory in Vancouver was closed, and Ginter began building a new brewery at Richmond, B.C. Here he ran into labour difficulty: a jurisdictional dispute between two American unions, the United Brewery Workers and the Retail, Wholesale and Department Store Union.

Ginter offered to shift all his employees from the Vancouver soft drink plant to his new brewery. RWDSU, which represented the workers in the soft drink plant claimed union jurisdiction. The UBWU, which represented Ginter's employees at the Prince George brewery, claimed the Canadian Labour Congress had given them automatic jurisdiction over breweries.

The RWDSU, anxious to keep control over its workers' dues, set up picket lines and closed down construction of the Richmond brewery. In an amazing decision, the NDP-appointed provincial Labour Relations Board certified both unions! Nothing had been resolved. Shortly thereafter, the B.C. Federation of Labour declared all Uncle Ben's products "hot," costing the company around $30 million in lost sales in one year.

In the meantime, The Bank of Commerce came down on Ginter for for non-payment of the loan to build the new Richmond brewery. In order to secure the $3.5 million loan in June 1975, he had put up debentures covering *all* his operations, worth $40 million in assets. A Court-appointed receiver took over *all* his companies. His construction equipment was auctioned off at "fire sale" prices, for $2 million. At the end of 1976, The Bank of Commerce said he still owed $4.8 million! Why? The Court receiver kept the Prince George Brewery in operation; since it couldn't sell the "hot" product, they just dumped it. The receiver was costing Ben Ginter Industries $10.00 a case of beer. It is an incredible story.

What Ben Ginter's story does reveal is the close relationship between the chartered banks and the large corporations, and the difficult time that small businessmen have in obtaining financing. As an interesting contrast, we can cite the case of how the Canadian Imperial Bank of Commerce dealt with Laura Secord Candy Shops, as recounted by Peter Newman in *The Canadian Establishment*.

Laura Secord is a subsidiary of John Labatt Ltd., which in turn is controlled by Brascan. In the fall of 1974, Laura Secord was having serious financial difficulties. The company was insolvent. In the previous year it had lost $5.3 million. Its parent, John Labatt, had refused to guarantee any further credit for the firm.

The Brascan/Labatt conglomerate has traditionally had strong representation on the Board of Directors of the Commerce. In this case, it was J.E. Moore, a major stockholder and President of Brascan. They asked for and got $24 million in assistance, a "letter of comfort." No one raised any questions about the propriety of the loan. Not very many Ben Ginters get this kind of special treatment.

In March 1977, Ginter announced that he was trying to raise $7 million from U.S. sources to get his company back from the receiver. "There's no use trying Canadian banks," he said. "Once you get in trouble with one of them, you are in trouble with them all. They all have lunch together once a week."

Ben Ginter was a "small" entrepreneur. Very often small Canadian businessmen fail to comprehend the realities of monopoly capitalism in Canada and the degree to which markets are controlled in highly product-differentiated industries. Ginter is angry at the Big Three brewers, saying they worked to drive him out of business by predatory practices. He cites one good example. When he opened his brewery at Prince George, the Big Three jointly opened a bottle return depot right across the street from his construction company office. They refused to sell the empties to Ginter, trucking them down to Vancouver. Therefore, Ginter had to truck in empty bottles from Vancouver, 600 miles away.

In early 1978 Ginter launched a campaign to buy back control of his business. In January he raised $2.5 million to obtain control of the Alberta brewery. In April he bought back his winery for $1.5 million. But in May he lost the Prince George brewery to a group of local and Vancouver businessmen.

Our local entrepreneur shocked the Canadian business community by announcing in early 1977 that he planned to give away control of his company to the people who bought his beer and wine. For every person who turned in 200 bottle caps or labels from his wine, he would in return give them ten common shares in his company. This would at first be limited to 40% of his equity; but eventually, he was going to surrender controlling interest.

He told the press that "I'm giving out my assets this way instead of just selling shares because I don't want one of the big breweries like Labatt grabbing up 40% of my operation. They've already got too much of the beer business." A number of financial and government spokesmen denounced the proposal as a fraud and illegal. But Ginter replied that what he did with his own shares of stock was his own business. "There is no gimmick and there is no catch to it," he argued. "I just want the enjoyment of sharing my wealth with others before I die and have the government do the sharing for me."

184

THE WINE INDUSTRY

The wine industry began in Ontario in the 1870s. By 1934 there were fifty-one wineries operating in that province. From that time on, the system of pricing and listing adopted by the provincial liquor control boards has been a major factor in the rise of market concentration in these industries.

The Combines Investigation Report for 1965 found that the top four wineries in Canada had 71% of sales and the top eight had 95%. By the mid-1970s, there were only five major companies, and they accounted for around 95% of all sales in Canada. As with the other alcoholic beverage industries, concentration is very high.

TABLE VIIIc

The Wine Industry

Company	Ownership/Control	1971 Sales
Carling-O'Keefe Group	South Africa—Rothmans	$11,250,000
T.G. Bright & Co. Ltd.	Canada—Hatch Family	10,474,000
John Labatt Group	Canada/U.S.—Brascan	8,100,000
Andres Wine (Canada) Ltd.	Canada—Peller Family	4,832,000
Calona Wines Ltd.	U.S.—Standard Brands	4,300,000

The Big Five

The largest wine operation in Canada today is that of Carling-O'Keefe, majority owned by Rembrandt Controlling Interests Ltd. of South Africa. In 1972 Carling-O'Keefe (then known as Canadian Breweries) acquired 75% of Gramercy Holdings from Seagrams. This included Jordan Wines, Danforth Wines, and Villa Wines. In 1973, they acquired Growers Wine Co. and Chalet Wines from IMASCO. These different wineries were all consolidated under one subsidiary, Jordan Valley Wines.

Thus, by 1974 the South African concern had emerged as the largest single winery in Canada, with seven plants across the country. Their sales of $25.4 million gave them about 33% of the national market. In 1976, they announced that a new plant would be built at Surrey, B.C. to replace the old Growers Wine operation at Victoria. This B.C. firm is now known as Ste. Michelle Wines.

The second largest winery in Canada is T.G. Bright & Co., based at Niagara Falls. Founded in 1874, it was bought by Harry Clifford Hatch in 1933; it is still controlled by the Hatch family through an estate trust with W. Douglas Hatch as President. A second operating plant has been located at Lachine, Quebec: T.G. Bright (Quebec) Ltd. A third plant was opened at St. Hyacinthe, Quebec in 1973; it also was incorporated as a separate company, Les Vins La Salle Ltd. Bright's sales for 1971 were $10.4 million.

The third largest winery operation is also the result of takeover strategy by a large conglomerate. In 1972 John Labatt bought control of Chateau Cartier Wines, based in Toronto, with a subsidiary, Normandie Wines of Moncton, N.B. Later in that same year they acquired majority control of Chateau-Gai, with plants at Toronto, St. Catherines, and Niagara Falls. Finally in 1973 they bought Casabello Wines, a Penticton B.C. winery which specialized in high quality dry table wines. The Labatt group of wineries now is very close to Bright's in sales. Unfortunately, recent sales are hidden in consolidated reports.

The most rapidly expanding wine operation in Canada in recent years has been that of Andres Wine (Canada) Ltd which, in spite of its name, is a Canadian-owned and controlled company. Its base has been the plant in Winona, Ontario. In 1961 it opened a plant at Port Moody, B.C., and in 1970 purchased Beau Chatel Wines Ltd. from IMASCO. Other plants are located in Calgary and Truro, N.S. In 1975, it purchased Valley Rouge Wines near Winnipeg from the U.S. firm K-Tel International. Sales in 1971 were $4.8 million but have risen significantly since then. While it is a public company, it is controlled by the Peller family, located at Ancaster, Ontario.

The other major winery is Calona Wines, with plants at Kelowna, B.C. and St. Hyacinthe, Quebec. This winery, built by the well-known Capozzi family, was sold to the U.S. corporate giant, Standard Brands, in 1971.

Aside from these firms, there are only a handful of small wine companies: Uncle Ben's Winery, at Westbank, B.C.; London Winery, at London Ontario; Turner Wine Co., of Toronto; Barnes Wines of St. Catherines, owned by Reckitt & Colman Canada Ltd., a British firm; La Maison Secrestat Ltee., owned and operated by Seagrams of Montreal; and Les Vins Chantecler Ltees, also of Montreal, owned by Tate & Lyle of England. The latter two wineries specialize in manufacturing wine from imported concentrates.

Industry Trends and Problems

In the last ten years there has been a decided shift in Canadian tastes for wines, and this has created problems for both Canadian grape growers and wine manufacturers. Traditionally, Canadians preferred the higher alcoholic content wines, like sherry and port, which are relatively sweet. Then there was the boom in so-called "pop wines" in the early 1970s. The "pop wines" were little more than soda pop with a low alcoholic content. They were made from the traditional Canadian grapes of the labrusca rootstock: Concord, Niagara, Agawam, and Delaware. The industry believes that the "pop wines" created a new generation of wine drinkers.

Between 1969 and 1973, the share of the wine market held by the higher alcohol wines declined from 67% to 43%. The "pop wine" experiment peaked in 1974. As the income of this new generation of wine drinkers rose, they began shifting to drier table wines. And as they drank more table wine, they concluded that the wines made from the labrusca rootstock grapes, with their traditional "foxy" flavour, were not very appealing. This "foxy" character can be sublimated in the sweeter high-alcohol wines and the "pop" wines, but not in dry table wines. The result has been a tremendous upsurge in the consumption of imported wines.

In 1964, Canadian produced wines held 75.2% of the Canadian market. In 1973, this had fallen to 63.3%, and by 1977 it had fallen to 48.7%. In spite of the growth of wine consumption in Canada, between 1973 and 1976 sales of Canadian produced wine actually dropped from 15.9 million gallons to 15.2 million gallons. Between 1960 and 1973, the number of different imported wines listed at the government liquor stores rose from 989 to 2,405. This trend obviously has become a major concern of both the wine manufacturers and the Canadian grape growers. By 1976, the Canadian Wine Institute claimed that the wineries were operating at only 50% capacity and that government liquor stores were devoting even more shelf space to foreign wines.

The growers and the wine industry were also upset by the policies of the Trudeau Government. Canadian wines were not served in Canadian embassies and consulates abroad. Air Canada did not serve Canadian wines. The final insult came in 1976 when Otto Lang, Minister of Transport, authorized Air Canada to ship fifty cases of French Beaujolais wine to London, Ontario for English-Gunn Ltd., an English wine importer, for a promotional party. The shipment was free to the importer, under Air Canada's policy of promotional advertising.

Part of the import problem is caused by those countries which have

187

a policy of subsidizing the export of wine for the purpose of obtaining foreign exchange and supporting the continuation of a local industry. This gives them a distinct cost advantage over Canadian grape growers and wineries, which are not subsidized. This is particularly true of wines imported from Hungary and Bulgaria. According to industry reports, in 1976 one rather good popular Hungarian dry red wine outsold all the dry red wines from all the Ontario wineries. In that year the Canadian Wine Institute brought dumping charges against Hungarian wine. Their breakdown of Hungarian production costs found that the wine was being sold in Canada at less than cost—unless the Hungarian growers were receiving nothing for producing their grapes.

Grape growers in Canada cannot quickly change over their vineyards to the European varieties of grapes which are now preferred. Canadian vineyards are primarily planted to labrusca rootstock because the Canadian agricultural research department was certain that the European-style vinifera rootstock would not survive Canada's cold winters. When the grape industry began in British Columbia, this advice was imported from Ontario.

However, Casabello Wines in Penticton was not convinced of this. They planted vinifera grapes in the Okanagan in 1968. That first winter there was a bad freeze in the Okanagan. The viniferas survived: in fact, they did better than some of the hybrids that were being promoted at that time by the agricultural research experts.

Since this time, the wineries in B.C. and Ontario have been encouraging the planting of the vinifera grapes. However, conversion of vineyards to the new varieties is a very costly process, involving a loss of income at a time when grape growing is already a marginal industry. The Ontario Government has gone far in trying to save the growers by providing a cash grant of $1,500 an acre to remove labrusca grapes and replace them with vinifera varieties. And of course the wineries in Canada pay higher prices for the vinifera varieties.

But at the farm level there is still the general problem of the high cost of grape production. Land costs are much higher in Canada than in other grape producing areas, even the United States. Labour and all other farm input costs are higher. South African wines have a big market in Canada, but there is no way that Canadian farmers and winery employees can compete with their quasi-slave labour.

Ontario protects their industry by requiring the wineries to use only Ontario grown grapes; this protection is lifted when there is an insufficient local crop. B.C. regulations require the wineries to use Okanagan grapes if the sugar content is high enough to provide a normal wine. All the wineries would prefer to import their grapes and concentrate from the United States or Europe, where the costs of grapes is much lower, and the better quality grapes can be bought.

To get around these local restrictions, the wineries have opened plants on the prairies and in Quebec. Most of these wineries rely on imported concentrates. As a result, Ontario and B.C. provide shelf-space preference for local wines and discriminate against wines from the other provinces. The Parti Quebecois in Quebec has allowed small grocery stores to sell wine that is manufactured and bottled in Quebec. In 1976 the B.C. liquor control board refused to list any more of the cheaply made Alberta wines; in return, the Alberta Board refused to list any additional B.C. wines.

Like so many areas of agriculture, the problems of the industry arise from the absence of a consistent national food production policy. There is no well-thought-out integrated programme on tariffs, quotas, or other industry protections.

THE SOFT DRINK INDUSTRY

The soft drink industry is the most rapidly growing food and beverage industry in Canada. Between 1961 and 1971 its sales rose from $173 million to over $408 million. While the consumption of other beverages (in particular milk) has declined over the period, per capita soft drink consumption has skyrocketed.

The industry is unique among the food industries as it is based on a system of franchise ownership pioneered by the Coca Cola company in the United States. Thus, the Canadian Soft Drink Association proudly points out that 95% of the bottling companies are locally owned. Concentration figures published by the Combines Investigations Director shows that in 1965 the top four bottling companies had 41% of the market and the top eight firms had only 48% of the national market.

On the other hand, as far as brand names sales are concerned, there is an extremely high degree of concentration. In Canada, Coca Cola has 34% of the market, and Pepsi is second with 20%. Crush International is said to have 15% of the market, with Seven Up, Canada Dry, and Cott Beverages having another 15% of the market.

In the U.S. market, Coca Cola and PepsiCo have about 60% of total sales, with the next three largest companies, Dr. Pepper, Royal Crown Cola, and Seven Up, having another 16% of the market. The remainder is divided among 400 smaller manufacturers.

The two U.S. giants dominate the world market. In 1976, Coca

Cola had sales of $3,000 million and PepsiCo was not far behind with sales of $2,700 million.

The Franchise System

The key here is the franchise system. Local bottlers are given a franchise to manufacture, under licence, the nationally advertised brand. They pay a franchise fee, usually purchase their equipment from the firm, and they must buy the syrups from the company.

The local bottling company not only gets a licence to manufacture a nationally advertised brand, they are guaranteed a monopoly at the local level. All the franchise arrangements have exclusive territorial rights which go with a franchise. Thus, the company which bottles Coke in a designated area has no other local Coke manufacturers as competition. Furthermore, in many cases the local bottler may also obtain the local franchise for the competitive brands. This is often the case in smaller population centres.

In 1971 the U.S. Federal Trade Commission brought a complaint against the six largest soft drink manufacturers, charging that the franchise system is a technique for establishing local monopolies. There was Congressional involvement in this case, but in April 1978 the FTC concluded that Coca Cola and PepsiCo violated U.S. anti-trust law by restricting their bottlers to certain territories.

If there are major changes in the American system, which is duplicated in Canada, there could be repercussions here as well. The 1976 amendments to the Combines Investigation Act made the franchise practices of refusal to supply, exclusive dealing, tied selling, and market restrictions "subject to review."

In addition, the Foreign Investment Review Agency has questioned the termination provisions which exist in most franchise agreements. It gives the franchising firm (often American) power to takeover the locally owned (Canadian) operation, thus bypassing the FIRA provisions.

Furthermore, Revenue Canada is now investigating the system of paying royalties for licensing arrangements. They are planning to require franchising companies (many of which are American) to justify the amount and type of royalties paid.

In spite of the local monopoly provisions of the franchise system, local bottlers have been disappearing at a significant rate. Between 1963 and 1973, there was a 25% decline in the number of bottlers in the United States. Between 1961 and 1971 in Canada, about 20% of the local firms closed shop. The major companies also directly own many of the best bottling plants. Coca Cola directly owns twenty-five,

190

and franchises seventy-nine; Canada Dry owns four plants, in the prime markets, and franchises another thirty-five.

The franchise system has another major impact on Canada. Nominally, the industry is predominantly Canadian-owned, as most of the bottlers are locally owned. But domination and control is by the large American firms, and they effectively block the entry of new firms in the field.

The big soft drink manufacturers (including Crush International) use the franchise system on a world-wide basis. They do not have to put up capital to build local business; they just skim off the profits created by the mass advertising and promotion system. Thus, as the President of Coca Cola noted in 1973, the companies are relatively free from "the danger of expropriation." If they nationalize the soft drink firms, they are "nationalizing their own people."

Product Differentiation

Traditionally, success of the large firms in this field has been attributed to high amounts of advertising and well established brand names. Where most firms would consider allocating 10% of sales to advertising as excessive in recent years the two major firms, Coca Cola and PepsiCo, have been spending an incredible 25% of sales on advertising.

In 1976 Coca Cola spent $10 million on advertising in Canada. Generally, they outspend their nearest competitor, PepsiCo, two to one. The power of advertising was revealed in the 1976-1977 "cola war." In the Pepsi Challenge campaign, Pepsi in Canada spent $8 million. Coca Cola retaliated with an advertisement which claimed that many Pepsi drinkers preferred Fresca, their lesser-known citrus fruit drink. Pepsi claims that its share of the Canadian market increased by one-third; but sales of Coke also increased. It is widely agreed that sales of both cola drinks increased, and that both the two major brands increased their share of the total soft drink market during this advertising campaign.

While there are no figures available on how the big U.S. firms are doing in Canada, there are reported studies of profitability on their consolidated U.S. operations. The U.S. firms have been making sizeable returns on their investment. Between 1969 and 1974, the five leading U.S. soft drink firms averaged a 23% annual return on equity, a phenomenal profit. At the same time, the 2,900 U.S. local bottlers, operating under the franchise system, averaged a rate of return of only 7%. It is easy to see who benefits from the franchise system. During the same period, the top 500 U.S. manufacturing firms averaged a

191

12% annual return on equity.

Between the major franchising companies, there is very little price competition. It is widely recognized that there is a very high gross margin at the wholesale level, around 45-55% on the premium products. Because of this, small firms are enticed into the field, only to fall before the impact of mass advertising.

In Canada, the total soft drink market is divided roughly as follows: 60% of sales are in the marketing of colas (thus, the domination of Coca Cola and Pepsi). The ginger ales have 14% of the market, and another 16% goes to the so-called "green bottle" market headed by Seven Up. Finally, there is the alcoholic drink-mix market, dominated by Canada Dry, Schweppes, and the local private brands handled by supermarkets. They have about 10% of the market.

TABLE VIIId

The Soft Drink Industry

Company	Ownership/Control	1971 Sales
Coca Cola Ltd.	U.S.—Coca Cola	$110,213,000
Pepsi Cola Canada Ltd.	U.S.—PepsiCo	50,166,000
Crush International Ltd.	Canada—Neonex Int. Ltd.	35,909,000
Seven-Up Canada Ltd.	U.S.—Seven-Up*	13,653,000
Cott Beverages (Canada) Ltd.	U.S.—Cott Beverages	10,500,000
Canada Dry Ltd.	U.S.—Norton Simon	10,000,000
Pop Shoppes Ltd.	Canada—Venturetek	1,000,000

* In May 1978 the three founding families of Seven-Up sold controlling interest in the company to Philip Morris Inc. of New York.

Variations in the Canadian Market

Right after World War I, Coca Cola moved into Canada. Because of the franchise system and overflow advertising, they quickly gained the largest share of the Canadian market. Hires Root Beer, one of the early American favourites, followed closely thereafter.

Interestingly enough, Canada Dry Co. began in 1890 in Toronto. It was originally owned by John J. McLaughlin, whose family is best known for establishing the first General Motors operation in Canada. During prohibition, Canada Dry was highly touted as the perfect mix with bootlegged Canadian whiskey, and the #1 Canadian drink, "Rye and Ginger," grew out of that tradition.

In 1924 McLaughlin died, and the company was bought by P.D. Saylor, its Canadian representative in New York, and an American, J.M. Mathes. The American operation (as in the whiskey business) was the largest market, and it seemed only natural to transform the company into an American firm. Today Canada Dry is owned by the huge American conglomerate, Norton-Simon. Canada Dry claims to have 60% of the Canadian market for ginger ale. In 1974 they introduced a new drink, C-Plus Orange. Three years later, Canada Dry could claim that it has become the top selling orange drink in Canada.

A different story is to be found in the success of Crush International. This company was founded in the United States in 1916 as Orange Crush, and it developed a franchised chain of distributors. In 1921 it established its branch plant operation in Canada. However, in the 1940s the company experienced financial difficulties, and in August 1946 control was obtained by a group of Canadian businessmen. Ownership was diversified, with the largest block, about 23%, owned by the McConnell family of Montreal. In 1976, Neonex International, a Vancouver-based firm, acquired 41% of the outstanding voting stock, including the McConnell family holdings. Since that time Neonex, now a private firm owned by Jim Pattison, has increased its ownership of Crush stock to 54%. However, at this time Pattison has not exercised control over the existing management.

The company expanded by purchasing firms with well established brand names. In 1962 it acquired Hires Root Beer, the oldest soft drink in North America. In 1963 it purchased Pure Spring (Canada) Ltd. with trade names prominent in the Ottawa Valley. In 1965 it acquired the right to distribute Royal Crown Cola in Canada through its franchise system. There were other expansions through takeover in the United States. The Denis and Sussex brands, distributed in Quebec and the Maritimes, were purchased in 1972 and 1973. By 1977 it was claiming 14% of the Canadian market.

Crush International is a Canadian success story. In 1975, sales in Canada accounted for only 25% of the total. It was the only major soft drink franchise company operating in the United States owned by non-American interests. It had approximately 4% of the U.S. market. Crush also operates in sixty overseas countries, supplying them from its major manufacturing plant at Evanston, Illinois. Its success in a field already highly concentrated was due to the fact that it acquired well-established advertised brands and remained primarily a franchise operator, not a local bottling company.

TABLE VIIIe

Beverages
Per Capita Consumption

	(Gallons)		
Beverage	1968	1972	% Change
Soft Drinks	12.57	14.98	+ 19.0
Brews	14.76	17.84	+ 20.9
Spirits	1.08	1.44	+ 33.3
Wine	.66	1.04	+ 57.6

SOURCE: MacLean-Hunter Publications, *Food in Canada*, July 1973.

The Introduction of Price Competition

Surprising as it may be, Canadians have pioneered in a new form of soft drink distribution, and to date it has been very successful. The system began with the formation of Pop Shoppes at London, Ontario in 1969; it was then copied by Pic-a-Pop in Winnipeg in 1971. It is a system based solely on price competition.

The new soft drink manufacturers offer significant discounts over nationally advertised brands through the absence of high advertising costs and high cost distribution. Customers must travel to the store and put up a $3.00 deposit for a plastic case and twenty-four bottles; they then receive their selection of seventeen flavours of soft drinks. The savings in 1977 were about 25% compared to the cash price of the nationally advertised brands.

Sales by Pop Shoppes have grown at a phenomenal rate. In 1969, the first year of operation, they were $120,000; by 1973 sales had grown to $1.2 million; and by 1975 they had reached $13.5 million. A survey by *Chatelaine* in February 1976 showed that the Pop Shoppe varieties of orange, grapefruit, grape, root beer, and cream soda were first in sales, outselling such established brands as Orange Crush and Hires Root Beer.

As the company expanded, it adopted the traditional franchise system. By the end of 1977, Pop Shoppes had twenty-two factories and 440 depots in Canada. Other local firms have copied the Pop Shoppe formula but have remained primarily local operations.

The Pop Shoppe enterprise has proven to be very profitable. The company reported return on equity at 25% in 1974, 29% in 1975, and

34% in 1976. As they grew, they chose to move into the American market before their unique approach to marketing was pirated by other firms. To do so, they needed additional capital.

To finance this expansion, the owners borrowed from IMASCO; the British firm was granted 20% equity in the U.S. operation, plus an option to buy an additional 30% in 1978, which they accepted. The U.S. market has proven to be quite important. In 1977 the company reported that 41% of their profits and 35% of their sales came from this source.

However, it is doubtful that in the long run they will be able to gain a major share of the soft drink market. Most soft drinks are sold in retail stores, in fast food outlets, and through vending machines, all of which are dominated by the major firms' nationally advertised brands.

The beverage industries follow the pattern of the food industry in North America. There is the growth of the large firm and the concentration of sales in the hands of a few corporations in each industry. New firms which are successful are few and far between. Furthermore, the major firms in the distilling, brewing, winery, and soft drink industries are all conglomerates, expanding into other food and non-food areas.

The brewing industry in Canada is completely dominated by three firms, all conglomerates. The distilling industry is dominated by two large firms, most of whose sales are in the United States. The wine industry, originally family-owned, is being swallowed up by the large multinational firms. The soft drink industry is closest to a competitive industry, with the bottling firms locally-owned. However, the franchise system legitimizes a local monopoly system and ensures the domination of the industry by a handful of large firms, all but one of which are American-owned.

SOURCES

Association of Canadian Distillers. Various publications and briefs.

Barratt, Bob. "Ontario Wines," *Food in Canada*, XXXVI, No. 1, January 1976, pp. 20-23.

Beer, Wine and Spirits: Beverage Differences and Public Policy in Canada. Report of the Alcoholic Beverage Study Committee. Brewers Association of Canada, May 24, 1973.

Brewers Association of Canada. Various publications and briefs.

Canadian Soft Drink Association. Various Publications and Briefs.

Canadian Wine Institute. Various publications and briefs.

Denison, Merrill. *The Baby and the Stream: The Molson Story*. Toronto: McClelland & Stewart, 1955.

Gray, James H. *Booze.* Toronto: Macmillan of Canada Ltd., 1974.

Hightower, Jim. *Eat your Heart Out: How Food Profiteers Victimize the Consumer.* N.Y.: Crown Publishers, 1975.

Horst, Thomas. *At Home Abroad: A Study of the Domestic and Foreign Operations of the American Food-Processing Industry.* Cambridge, Mass.: Ballinger Publishing Co., 1974.

Jones, J.C.H. "Merger and Competition: The Brewing Case," *Canadian Journal of Economics,* XXXIII, November 1967, pp. 551-568.

Kahn, E.J. Jr. *The Big Drink: The Story of Coca-Cola.* N.Y.: Random House, 1960.

Marshall, Herbert, Frank Southard Jr., and Kenneth W. Taylor. *Canadian-American Industry.* Toronto: McClelland & Stewart edition, 1976.

Martin, Ron. "Soft Drink Industry," *Food in Canada,* XXXVI, No. 12, December 1976, pp. 26 *et seq.*

Mongoven, James F. "Advertising, the Franchise System and the Soft Drink Industry," *Anti-Trust and Economics Review, 1976.*

Newman, Peter C. *Flame of Power: The Story of Canada's Greatest Businessmen.* Toronto: McClelland & Stewart, 1959.

Newman, Peter C. *The Canadian Establishment.* Vol. 1. Toronto: McClelland & Stewart, 1975.

Park, Libbie and Frank Park. *Anatomy of Big Business.* Toronto: James Lewis & Samuel, 1973.

Patterson, R.A. *A Survey of Selected Segments of Canadian Agribusiness.* Study for the Federal Task Force on Agriculture, September 1969. Unpublished.

Rannie, William F. *Canadian Whiskey.* Lincoln, Ontario: William F. Rannie, 1976.

Restrictive Trade Practices Commission. *Report Concerning an Alleged Combine in the Manufacture, Distribution and Sales of Beer in Canada.* May 16, 1955.

Riley, John J. *A History of the American Soft Drink Industry.* N.Y.: Arno Press, 1972.

Rowe, Percy. *Wines of Canada.* Toronto: McGraw Hill of Canada, 1976.

Scanlon, Paul D. "FTC and Phase II: The McGovern Papers," *Anti-Trust Law and Economics Review,* V. No. 3, Spring 1972, pp. 33-36.

"The Queen V. Canadian Breweries Ltd.," in L.A. Skoech, ed., *Restrictive Trade Practices in Canada.* Toronto: McClelland & Stewart, 1956.

Wood, Ted and Mary. "C-Plus:A Lightly Carbonated Canadian Success Story," *Financial Post Magazine,* June 1976, pp. 5-8.

9. RETAILING FOOD

Since the end of World War II, there has been a rather dramatic change in the way food is distributed to consumers in North America. We have seen the rise of the supermarket and the virtual disappearance of the small "mom and pop" store, the development of the shopping centre, the growth of the large corporate chain stores, the expansion of the voluntary chains under the control of the large wholesalers, and the vertical integration of the corporate chains back into wholesaling and food manufacturing.

The rise of the supermarket was the first and perhaps most significant development. Over the years the size of the retail food store has risen steadily. In 1951, the average supermarket was around 4,500 square feet; by the 1960s the standard store was around 20,000 square feet. The size of the store increased in order to accommodate the proliferation of food and non-food items. At the end of World War II, the large retail food stores carried about 4,000 items. By the mid-1970s, the average urban supermarket carried between 8,000 and 10,000 items. (In 1975, National Grocers, one of the Weston Empire's large wholesalers, announced that it was going to reduce the number of items it handled from 27,000 to 16,000.) The typical supermarket today also carries a long line of non-food products, most of which are common household items.

Why has this change come about? Industry spokesmen and writers in the field agree that it is due to the rapid urbanization of North America and the development of the suburb around the city. With the rise in per capita income, people have been spending more on food, particularly the more highly processed food items which now fill the supermarkets. The expansion of automobile ownership has increased the attractiveness of the shopping centre with its large parking space and its large chain supermarket.

197

The industry argues that the large supermarket has brought economies of scale of operation, and with its wide choice of consumer goods, serves people's needs. This argument has been seriously challenged. But if the consumer is to be offered 10,000 food and non-food items in a single store, then the supermarket is the only way.

The rise of the supermarket, linked nationally through a horizontal and vertical corporate chain, is a natural development, and follows the pattern of general business concentration in advanced capitalist societies. This is also the era of sophisticated marketing. The manufactured items sold in supermarkets are widely advertised. Consumer demand has been created for many products. The supermarkets themselves engage in widespread advertising and promotions. Only large operations have the economic power to engage in this form of marketing.

Finally, the large supermarket, part of a large corporate chain, has economic power to bargain for manufactured goods at the wholesale level. The smaller voluntary chains do not have equivalent power, and the independent stores are in an even more disadvantageous position.

The Growth of the Chain Stores

In Canada today there are five major corporate chains: the empires created by George Weston, Dominion Stores, Canada Safeway, Steinberg's, and A & P of Canada. In addition to these there are a number of voluntary chains, the largest one being IGA Canada Ltd., which is in fact controlled by its two large wholesalers, M. Loeb and Oshawa Group. The growth of these chains is reflected in the following table which illustrates their share of the retail food industry in Canada:

	1951	1958	1963	1971	1975
Corporate chains	32.2%	44.0%	46.0%	54.1%	60.4%
Voluntary chains	5.0%	20.0%	36.7%	25.9%	25.7%
Independent stores	62.8%	36.0%	17.3%	20.0%	13.9%

The corporate chains (identified by Statistics Canada as any chain of four or more stores under single ownership) have steadily increased their share of the food market from 32% in 1951 to 60% in 1975. The share of the market held by the independent stores has fallen from 63% in 1951 to 14% in 1975. The small stores, in order to protect themselves against the predatory practices of the large corporate chains, joined many of the voluntary groups; as a result, there was an increase in the share of the market held by this type of operation. However, their share of the market peaked in 1963. The recent decline of the voluntary chains is primarily due to the fact that they do not have access to the new large shopping centres, which are generally prescribed for one of the large corporate chain stores. (In the 1970s, location has proven to be of utmost importance to the survival of a retail food store.)

The Canadian Business Service notes that while income has risen in Canada, food consumption has remained fairly stable as a percentage of personal expenditures. Under such a situation, there is competition for a relatively fixed amount of consumer spending. On an aggregate basis CBS concludes that the phenomenal growth of the food chain "is the result of the gradual displacement of other retail food outlets . . . Wherever a supermarket is opened, existing small grocery stores are either forced out of operation or continue to operate at a greatly reduced sales volume." Yet one of the interesting developments is that while the small "mom and pop" stores are going out of business, there is a rather significant rise in the corporate "convenience foods" stores on the local level, and they are making fairly high profits.

Who are the dominant corporate chains? Who owns and controls them? The following information is for 1975:

1. *Dominion Stores Ltd.* This is the largest chain by number of stores, with 387. Of these, 224 are in Ontario and 100 are in Quebec, where its sales are concentrated. It is controlled by Argus Corporation.
2. *Canada Safeway Ltd.* A wholly-owned subsidiary of the U.S. corporate giant, it operates 274 stores in Canada, concentrated in the four Western provinces. Recently they have decided to enter the Ontario market, where they had twenty-nine stores in 1975.
3. *Steinberg's Ltd.* Owned by the Steinberg family of Montreal, this chain operates 185 stores, 114 in Quebec and seventy in Ontario. This also includes Miracle Food Marts in Ontario.
4. *Loblaw's Ltd.* Most of the 166 Loblaw stores are in Ontario, with only a few on the prairies. However, Loblaw's is only part of the Weston empire, which includes retail chains in the United States, the United Kingdom and Ireland, and overseas. In Canada, it also includes forty-five O.K. Economy stores on the prairies, forty Super-Valu Stores in British Columbia, and thirty-one Shop Easy stores in Western Canada. In addition, Weston owns 40% of Sobeys in the Maritimes, the largest private retail chain in that area.

5. *A & P Canada Ltd.* This is a wholly-owned subsidiary of the American chain. It operates ninety-nine stores in Ontario and twenty in Quebec. In terms of sales, it is by far the smallest of the corporate chains.

The major route for expansion by the large chains has been the establishment of new stores in new locations, particularly shopping centres. But takeovers have also played a role in corporate expansion. The National Commission on Food Marketing in the United States concluded in 1966 that if the large U.S. chains had not absorbed local chains, then they probably would not have increased their total share of the national market.

The retail store situation in Canada is somewhat different. There is a much higher degree of concentration at both the national and the local level. The five large corporate chains have a far higher share of the market in Canada than in the United States. Takeovers of smaller chains have not been as significant in Canada as in the United States. Here it has been more the case of the new supermarket driving out the local businessman.

Nevertheless, there has been "merger" activity. And it has not ceased, for in Canada there has been no government action against this form of monopoly growth. Dominion expanded in Quebec by the purchase of twenty-five Thrift Stores in Montreal in 1955. In 1956, it entered the Maritimes in a major way through the takeover of thirty-eight Acadia Stores, concentrated in Nova Scotia. This allowed Dominion Stores to emerge as the only corporate challenge to Sobeys in the Maritimes.

Steinberg's has also expanded through takeover. In 1959 they bought the thirty-eight Grand Union stores in Ontario as well as Ottawa Fruit Supply, a wholesaling firm which serviced the voluntary chain of Clover Farm Stores. Steinberg's also moved into the Ontario market through the purchase of the Miracle Mart stores.

The Weston Empire has been built almost entirely on the takeover of existing companies. Corporate policy has dictated that they maintain their original names and independent operating status. That is why until 1966 no one really knew what George Weston Ltd. controlled; when the ownership chart was finally released, many people were surprised. In the retail area alone, Weston has expanded through the purchase of Kelly-Douglas, Shop Easy, and O.K. Economy. Many other stores are owned through the wholesaling companies. For example, the federal government ordered Weston to sell its 18% interest in M. Loeb; this was bought by Provigo. In turn, Sobey Stores owns 17% of Provigo, but Loblaw (Weston) owns 40% of Sobey Stores!

The Voluntary Chains

Most of the voluntary chains of independent stores in Canada began as branches of American counterparts. IGA Canada Ltd. was established in 1951, and Clover Farm Stores of Canada Ltd. in 1955. These are the two largest American voluntary chains. The other major national voluntary chain in Canada is Foodwide of Canada Ltd., which operates 563 Red & White Stores and 433 Lucky Dollar Stores. This is also one of the largest American voluntary operations.

As the supermarkets and corporate chains grew in the 1950s and the 1960s, the independent stores were forced to change in order to survive. The voluntary chains closed many of their small stores and concentrated on development of the medium-sized supermarket. At the same time they came under the control of the wholesale operations that were established to serve them.

In 1975 IGA Canada Ltd. operated 682 IGA stores and 719 Much More stores. The stores are effectively controlled by their large wholesale distributors: M. Loeb Ltd. (42.6%), Oshawa Group (42.6%), with the remainder held by Codville Co. of Winnipeg and H.Y. Louie Co. of Vancouver. In January 1973, M. Loeb took over Horne & Pitfield Foods Ltd., a major Alberta wholesaler which services independent stores.

The other voluntary chain is centred in Quebec and is controlled by Provigo. In 1975 it reportedly had 15% of the Montreal food market and close to 35% of the market in the rest of Quebec. Provigo owns retail stores and has associations with chains of convenience stores, volume discount stores, as well as conventional supermarkets. It has franchised relationships with 586 stores in Montreal and 527 in the rest of Quebec. In total, it services around 2,500 stores, including independents. The corporation has been controlled by the Provost and Couvrette families, but in the mid-1970s was under the corporate directorship of Antoine Turmel, also a large stockholder.

In July 1977 Provigo moved to take over M. Loeb. First, they purchased the 18.5% interest in M. Loeb from George Weston Ltd. Then they bought the 23.5% interest held by Caisse de Depot et placement du Quebec (the agency which invests Quebec Pension Plan money). They then made an offer to shareholders which the Loeb family interests could not match. By September Provigo owned 80% of the voting stock of M. Loeb, and one of the biggest wholesale mergers in Canada had passed with not even a blink from the federal Combines Investigation Branch.

In addition to the two major voluntary chains, a number of the major wholesalers operate franchise systems on the provincial level across Canada. In 1975 Kelly-Douglas sponsored about 680 stores in

B.C., mainly because of the weak presence of the Loeb-Oshawa group. On the prairies the Weston group again is the major competitor to Loeb-Oshawa, through Westfair Foods and Shelly Western. In Ontario, the Weston empire, through its local wholesaler, National Grocer, is the main competitor to Loeb-Oshawa. Loeb-Oshawa interests and Provigo control most of the voluntary chains in Quebec, although six smaller wholesalers have banded together in Alliance Trans-Kebec to try to hold their own. Independent stores have a much larger share of the retail market in Quebec than in the five provinces to the West. In the Atlantic provinces, the dominant force is Atlantic Wholesale, a subsidiary of Loblaw Companies Ltd. It runs three retail chains and services four voluntary chains and many independent stores.

The wholesalers try to provide the affiliated stores with some of the services and advantages that the large corporate chains make available to their individual stores: shared advertising, promotion, merchandising and management assistance, private labels, and cash and carry wholesale services for the smaller stores. The key to survival, however, is price discounts. The study done by Peter Dooley for the Royal Commission on Consumer Problems and Inflation (1968) found that 75% of the small stores never received volume discounts.

Price discrimination is a major factor in the retail food industry in Canada. Prices may differ on the same product, sold under similar conditions, to different purchasers. A wholesaler may offer his affiliates lower prices than the independents he serves. The affiliates may receive additional services from a wholesaler that the independents do not receive. Different purchasers may receive trade discounts, quantity discounts, cumulative discounts, or special discounts and allowances. The normal situation is differential treatment, depending on status and power. Under such a system, the independent grocer and the small grocer in a voluntary chain have a difficult time competing.

Market Concentration

As noted before, the clear trend in Canada is towards market concentration by the corporate chains, and the five largest chains are taking an increasing share of the national market. Lerner and Patil found that the five largest chains increased their share of the sales by corporate chains from 50.6% in 1930 to 97.4% in 1963. Their share of total grocery sales increased from 36.8% in 1956 to 44.8% in 1963. (These figures were taken from *Canadian Grocer*.)

Bruce Mallen, using slightly different figures and classification of store control, concludes that by 1970 the top four chains had about 44% of the national market, and the top six organizations, both corporate and voluntary chains, had about 55%. This reveals a much higher concentration on the national level in Canada than in the United States. According to the National Commission on Food Marketing, in 1963 the four largest U.S. chains had only 21% of the U.S. national market.

But such figures are grossly misleading, for the real (or relevant) food market is not the national level; indeed, it is not even the regional (or provincial) level; it is at the local level. For the consumer, the real market is the urban market, or the area in which he/she shops for food. It is at this level that we see the extent of monopoly control.

In the United States, the National Commission on Food Marketing found that the degree of concentration on the local level was much higher than it was on the national level. The larger chains tended to concentrate their stores in the urban markets, where they could realize economies of advertising. The top four firms on the local level, in 1963, averaged more than 50% of all grocery sales in "standard metropolitan statistical areas." In a number of cities, the share of the top four was between 65% and 70%.

Leon Garoian gives some illustrations of local chain concentration in the United States for 1963. Whereas A & P had 11.4% of national sales, they averaged 15.6% in markets where they operated. Others are as follows: Safeway, 5% of national and 22% of local markets; Kroger, 4.4% of national and 15.7% of local; Winn-Dixie, 1.4% of national and 22.9% of local; Weingarten, .3% of national and 14.4% of local; and Jewel Tea, 1% of national and 24.6% of local.

Bruce Mallen's study concentrates on retail food sales in thirty-two large urban centres in Canada; these account for around two-thirds of all food sales in the country. In 1973, the four large corporate chains had 64% of this market. On a regional basis, the four corporate giants held 54% of the large urban markets in Quebec, 62% in Ontario, 70% in British Columbia, 73% in the Atlantic provinces, and 84% on the prairies. The concentration ratios are raised even higher if the large voluntary chains are included.

On the local level, Mallen's study for the thirty-two urban centres found that concentration by the Big Four ranged from a low of 23% in Lake St. John to a high of 98% in Thunder Bay. The median for all centres was 69.6%. By any standard, this is a high rate of oligopolistic control.

It is also possible to illustrate the trend towards greater local market concentration by comparing the findings of Mallen in 1973 with those of Peter Dooley for 1966. They are as follows:

Share of Top Four Corporations

	1966	1973
Winnipeg	48.7	80.6
Regina	69.6	87.7
Saskatoon	75.7	83.2
Calgary	67.2	76.2
Edmonton	64.1	92.9

Clearly there is a steadily increasing trend towards oligopoly and monopoly power in food retailing in Canada. By 1973 on the prairies, all the major urban areas fell under Bain's classification of "very highly concentrated oligopoly."

The other major factor in assessing the impact of market concentration is the fact that the large retail chains do not operate in all Canadian urban or regional markets. Company strategies have been to stake out an area of total market. In British Columbia, Canada Safeway is the major power, with ninety-three of the total of 211 supermarkets. The next largest chain is Super-Valu, with forty stores owned directly and another forty-six leased. But Safeway is the recognized price leader. Dominion tried to move in but was driven out in an advertising war.

The prairies are also under the control of Canada Safeway. In 1975, the industry leader had 152 of 244 supermarkets in this region. The only significant competition to Safeway comes from nineteen Loblaw supermarkets and forty-five smaller O.K. Economy stores, both part of the Weston chain. In 1976, the Weston Empire sold its Loblaw stores on the prairies to Super-Valu (the B.C. subsidiary), which in turn began to lease them out in Alberta. This was done because Loblaw was never able to break into the market controlled by Canada Safeway.

In 1975, sales for all chains amounted to $187.9 million, and for all other stores $151.4 million. On the prairies, Canada Safeway has about 50% of all retail food sales, with only slightly less in British Columbia. A & P and Dominion Stores tried to move into Alberta, but were driven out in an advertising war by Safeway. The West is clearly Safeway country.

It is widely recognized that the most competitive retail market in Canada is in the metropolitan Toronto area. Here the two leaders, Dominion and Loblaw, vie for market leadership. On a province-wide basis, Dominion leads with 224 stores, followed by 147 Loblaw stores. A & P has ninety-nine stores, Steinberg's has seventy, many of which are the Miracle Mart stores. The Loeb-Oshawa wholesalers operate an additional 267 IGA stores.

The study for the Ontario Special Committee on Farm Income found that in 1966 Dominion had 18.4% of the Ontario market, Loblaw 18.2%, IGA 13.4%, A & P 8.2%, and Steinberg's 4.2%. The independents affiliated to National Grocers (Weston) had an additional 13.6% of the Ontario market.

Since that time there has been the highly publicized 1970 price war in Ontario. Dominion Stores began the war in August in an attempt to gain a larger share of the existing market. The other chains had to follow to try to keep their share. The large voluntary chain, IGA, was pressed by the wholesalers to meet the cut prices to hold its share of the market. Prices dropped by 4% in 1970, but by March 1971 they were back to their previous level. Between December 1970 and October 1972 they rose by 15%. In the meantime, the share of the market held by the corporate chains increased substantially. Executives for Dominion Stores proudly told their stockholders that their share of all food sales in Canada rose from 10.1% in 1970 to 14.6% after the price war ended.

The trend in Ontario sales to corporate domination did not end with the price war. By 1975, the chains had 73.1% of all food sales in that province, the highest of any province in Canada. Sales by unaffiliated independents had fallen to 9.8%.

In Quebec, the chain stores have the smallest share of any market in Canada, "only" 43.6% in 1975. Steinberg's has traditionally been the leader in this province; in 1975, they had 114 supermarkets. However, Dominion has moved into Quebec in recent years, and with 100 stores provides a strong challenge to the traditional leader. In 1975 they started a price war which did not last very long. However, as mentioned earlier, the distinctive feature of the Quebec retail food market is the rise of the voluntary group around Provigo. In 1975, the affiliated voluntary group held 38.9% of the Quebec market, much higher than the average of 25.7% held by the voluntary chains on a national basis.

In the Atlantic Provinces, the industry leader has been Sobey's stores, with Dominion stores the only corporate competitor. In these scattered, small town and city markets, the unaffiliated independents had 30.9% of the market in 1975, compared to a national average of only 13.9%. The structure of the market offers no incentive to the large chain operations.

Price Leadership

Price competition is simply not a characteristic of the retail food industry in North America. Occasionally, there will be "price wars," as in Ontario in 1970 and in Quebec in 1975. But these are usually short-lived and designed simply to re-arrange shares of local markets.

The Royal Commission on Price Spreads of Food Products (1959) concluded that ". . . as between supermarkets, whether operated by the same chain or not, there is little variation in the total cost of a basket of food products in any given area." In 1971 the Consumers Association of Canada did a survey of a given food basket in the Toronto area and found that there was less than sixty cents difference between the prices of the six big chains.

In March 1974 I conducted a survey of ninety-four processed food items which appeared in all four of the major supermarkets in Saskatoon (Canada Safeway, Loblaws, Saskatoon Co-op, and Dominion).These covered nationally advertised brands in processed meats, poultry, dairy products, canned and frozen vegetables, canned fruits and juices, jams, soups, breakfast cereals, biscuits, confectioneries, and miscellaneous foods.The total cost of the ninety-four items ranged from $87.29 in Dominion to $89.83 in Loblaws. As a general rule, prices of all products were uniform. Where there was a difference, it was invariably in only one store and appeared to be a pricing "mistake" rather than a "loss leader" or advertised special. The manager of one of the supermarkets told me he had store employees checking prices in the other major supermarkets in the general shopping area. Ted Earl, an advertising consultant, reminded the 1973 convention of the Canadian Grocery Distributors Institute: "Your competitors aren't your enemies, but your consumers are."

Under existing Canadian Combines legislation, collusion to fix prices is illegal but price leadership is not. As Lerner and Patil note, "even in the absence of outright collusion, firms may agree tacitly to avoid price competition although still engaging in various forms of non-price competition. Price competition among the 'big five' appears to be almost non-existent."

In his study of the retail food industry on the prairies for the Royal Commission on Consumer Problems and Inflation (1968), Peter Dooley did a questionnaire survey of the stores on the prairies. Of those who replied, 77% admitted that they recognized Canada Safeway as the price leader. But it is more than local market power that establishes a firm as the price leader.

The study by the U.S. Federal Trade Commission of the food marketing industry (1960) found that in any local market there is a generally recognized "market leader" which sets the level of prices. A study done by the Wharton School of Business at the University of Pennsylvania found that A & P was the recognized price leader in the local Philadelphia markets. This may not seem surprising, as A & P is the largest U.S. food chain. However, in this case American Stores actually had a larger share of the Philadelphia market. The study concluded that "A & P's nationwide strength was repeatedly cited as a factor explaining its ability to serve as price leader."

This does not necessarily mean that price leadership is uniform on an urban basis. There normally is "zone pricing" in larger urban markets. As the 1966 study by the National Commission on Food Marketing described it, the stores recognize certain territories of a city as a particular zone. Very often this is a result of social and economic market analysis, as well as an assessment of the degree of market competition distinguished by the number of stores and floor space relative to population. A single chain would have a different pricing system for each zone.

Zone pricing is standard American chain store practice, and therefore exists in Canada as well. A study of Edmonton done by Hawkins, Warrack and Patterson in 1968 found that area pricing was recognized by all the leading firms. Prices differed between stores of the same chain, with the highest difference being on staple items.

In 1972 a group at Simon Fraser University headed by Gary Rush conducted a similar study in Vancouver. They found that price leadership was the norm, but that the leader depended on the strength of the particular chain in each zone. For example, in Delta, where Super-Valu had the most stores, they were the recognized price leader; in New Westminster, Safeway, with the largest number of stores, was the price leader.

In recent years charges have been made that the supermarkets maintain higher prices in lower income areas. Generally, studies find this to be true. In 1966, the U.S. Bureau of Labour Statistics conducted a survey in six cities for the National Commission on Food marketing. They found that prices were in fact higher in the low income areas for a number of reasons:

1. There were few large chains, with no chain competition;
2. There were more independent stores, which charged higher prices;
3. The stores generally carried smaller packages, with higher unit prices;
4. The stores were "less orderly and less clean";
5. The meat and produce was not as fresh; and
6. They were "high cost market" zones.

This did not satisfy many people who were familiar with supermarket practices in large urban centres. The Agribusiness Accountability Group in Washington, D.C. conducted its own study. They found that chain stores charged more in slum areas than in the suburbs, where there was more competition. They found that the large chains often transferred older produce and meat from the suburban stores to their slum zone stores.

As a result of this report and other public pressures, the U.S. Federal Trade Commission conducted a special study of retail store practices in Washington and San Francisco. Safeway and the other chain stores were found guilty of overpricing advertised specials and very often of not having the advertised specials in low income zone stores. The FTC did not accuse the chains of a deliberate practice of higher pricing in low income zone stores, but found that in reality the poor did pay higher prices. Low priced specials were often not available, and poor people did not have the ability to drive to the larger supermarkets where prices were lower.

Jennifer Cross is much more skeptical of the studies by the U.S. federal government. All of them were preceded by wide publicity on where they were to be taken. Bureau of Labour Statistics actually informed the stores ahead of time that their survey team was coming. In contrast, she cites a dozen independent surveys which all revealed price discrimination in poor "zones." These were all done anonymously, unannounced. The President of the National Association of Food Chains admitted that zones were normal, but argued that they were based on a warehouse distribution and transportation system.

Monopolistic Practices

This does not mean that there is no competition between the chain stores for customers. There is. But it normally takes the form of non-price competition. Some of the major techniques are as follows.

1. **Predatory Pricing**. This is the practice of lowering some prices in a specific area in order to gain a foothold in a market, or to drive a competitor out of business. A few examples will illustrate the scope of this activity.

In 1954-1955, Safeway undertook to capture 50% of the market in Dallas and El Paso. Complaints by their competitors led to an investigation and action by the U.S. Federal Trade Commission. The FTC found that 10% of the items being sold by Safeway were selling below cost. The losses in this area were offset by higher profits in other areas, where they had established themselves as the price leader. Predatory pricing of this nature is illegal in the U.S., and Safeway signed a consent decree promising not to do it in these two markets.

On a more restricted level, Walter Stewart recounts how Canada

Safeway drove Charlie Murphy, a small grocer, out of business in Calgary. The American chain offered lower prices at the store nearest his Ranch Discount supermarket. These low prices would be advertised locally through leaflets distributed in the surrounding neighbourhood. Only at this store could one find these advertised specials. It took two years, but Canada Safeway finally drove Charlie Murphy out. Partly as a result of this case, the Combines Commissioner took action against Canada Safeway in Alberta. In an out-of-Court settlement, Safeway agreed not to lower prices only near a competitor; special discounts would have to be offered on a city-wide basis.

Another example occurred in Toronto in January 1977. Darrigo's Supermarkets opened a new large supermarket in Toronto's west end. The family has a small chain of five stores in Toronto. The new store was an attempt to reach beyond their traditional Italian-speaking market. Dominion Stores had four supermarkets in the area of the new store. Through flyers distributed n the neighbourhood, Dominion advertised special low prices for the four stores near the new Darrigo Supermarket. The advertised specials were not available in Dominion's other stores in the city. While predatory pricing is technically illegal under the Combines Investigation Act, the authorities in Ottawa have been extremely reluctant to take any action in this area.

2. Loss Leader Selling. All the large supermarket chains advertise weekly "specials" in an attempt to attract customers to their stores. This should not be confused with price competition. Normally, a chain supermarket will advertise only twenty to fifty items a week, and over the year between 100 and 200 items. This is out of a total of between 8,000 and 10,000 items. While the stores may lose money on these items, they make it up through higher prices on the other items in the store. This type of advertising extends to non-food items as well.

For many years, small retailers have protested loss leader selling. The Restrictive Trade Practices Commission conducted a separate investigation into loss leader selling in 1955; they concluded that it was a powerful tool of the large chains. However, the federal government decided not to take any action on the report.

In November 1976, the Retail Merchants Association of Canada presented a brief to the Department of Consumer and Corporate Affairs urging that loss leader practices be banned in the new "competition" legislation. The loss leader practices were driving small businesses to bankruptcy. They noted that the chain could take losses on certain items, and they could be made up by volume discounts, advertising allowances, and other subsidies provided by the suppliers. Fresh farm products and bread were most often sold as loss leaders.

In January 1977 the Ontario Egg Producers Marketing Board strongly objected to the five major Ontario chains using eggs as advertised loss leaders. Whereas large Grade A eggs were normally selling at around ninety-two cents a dozen (which was a very low price), the chains were selling them for seventy-two cents a dozen. The Marketing Board said that the loss leader selling of fresh farm products "distorts the market and gives consumers a false sense of value." Then when prices are returned to normal, consumers denounce farmers and marketing boards.

3. Location Barriers. One of the major explanations for the increasing domination of the large chains in Canada is the development of the shopping centre. In one Canadian survey in 1973, cited by Bruce Mallen in his study for the Food Prices Review Board, convenient location and good parking were the two most frequently mentioned reasons for shopping at a particular food store. Lower price was placed far down the list. A recent American study found 52% bought at a particular food store because of location; only 13% said that price was an important factor.

In both the United States and Canada, the large chain stores, which widely advertise, have a preferred status at shopping centres. In the United States, builders require a AAA rating for a food store and net worth of $1 million. According to the National Commission on Food Marketing, in 1965 52% of all new supermarkets were controlled by the chain stores.

In Canada, shopping centre domination is even more pronounced, reflecting the greater power of the chains. Between 1961 and 1972, the number of shopping centres in Canada doubled. Of the 744 in operation in 1972, 558 had food stores owned by the corporate chains; only 186 were represented by "independents," and most of these were affiliated with voluntary chains. In the largest shopping centres, almost all the food stores were owned by the four major chains. Only in the smaller shopping centres, often in the smaller towns, did the independents have a chance of becoming the central food store. As Mallen notes, "the shopping centre is a hand-maiden to economic concentration."

It is normal for the shopping centre owners to wish to have a major chain to attract shoppers. But the chains have also insisted on having exclusive food distribution in shopping centres. As the Combines Commission noted in the case against Canada Safeway in 1973, in Alberta the American giant agreed to enter shopping centres only if the contract for leasing space included a "restrictive clause" that prohibited the owners of the shopping centre from providing space to other food stores.

The chain stores have concentrated in large urban centres, close to large populations, to take advantage of volume advertising. The main problem now is lack of good new locations. As a result, all the chains are shutting down small stores, opening new larger ones, or adding to existing stores.

The new stores being built in 1977 by the chains were very large, between 32,000 and 45,000 square feet. In the mid-1970s, the larger stores, generally with better locations, have proven to be more economical. They have reduced fixed overhead costs, added more specialty services, and have generated more sales per square foot. The large stores usually have bakeries, large frozen food and meat displays, and drug stores.

Steinberg's is planning to open seven stores with areas between 50,000 and 70,000 square feet in Ontario in 1978 and 1979. They found that the larger stores had a faster turnover of merchandise, and they were able to include larger areas for general merchandise. These non-food items had higher margins and could support the lower margins in some food areas.

This trend has not only been hard on the independents, but has been a matter of great concern for the voluntary chains. For example, in 1977 Oshawa Group Ltd. reported to stockholders that their returns were dropping because the retail food stores they were servicing were experiencing a decline in sales due to the growth of the five big corporate chains. IGA Canada Ltd. announced that their share of the Canadian market had dropped by 2% to only 6.9% in 1976. Donald Tiggert of Burns Fry Ltd. commented that the expansion of store size in favoured locations meant that the chains "will have to take market shares from independent operators to maintain sales levels."

4. Advertising. The large chains have a distinct advantage over all other grocery stores in the area of advertising. First, the chains concentrate in urban centres, and as the number of stores expands in a given advertising market, the cost per store declines. Second, as their total volume of advertising expands, the chains receive discounts from newspapers which are not available to smaller operations.

The volume of advertising by retail food stores has steadily increased in the period since the end of World War II. The Royal Commission on Price Spreads of Food Products (1959) found that in 1949 advertising costs represented only .46 cents of each sales dollar by the corporate chains. This rose to .88 cents by 1957. By 1966 this had risen to 1.0 cents on each sales dollar.

The technical staff study on food retailing done for the National

Commission on Food Marketing in the United States in 1966 documented the advantages of the large chain over the small retailer. Chains with more than 20% of the local market had advertising costs which were between only one-quarter and one-third those of the stores with 5% of the market or less.

The Royal Commission on Consumer Problems and Inflation (1968) concluded that advertising by the chains was the major barrier to entry on the prairies. They estimated that "every new competitor which entered the market would have a cost disadvantage of 4 to 5 cents on sales." Saturation advertising by Canada Safeway drove Dominion Stores and A & P out of Alberta. It was also the reason why Dominion sold their six stores in the lower mainland in British Columbia. Canada Safeway's policy of concentrating stores in the larger urban centres assured an advertising advantage and the dominant share of the market. According to the Combines Commissioner's orders to Canada Safeway in Alberta, they were not supposed to engage in "market saturating advertising" between 1974 and 1978.

The highest degree of retail market concentration is on the prairies, where Canada Safeway has about 50% of total food sales. Peter Dooley's inquiry found that in the five major cities on the prairies, the corporate chains spent 1.65 cents of each sales dollar for advertising, compared to the national average of 1.0 cents on the sales dollar. The non-chain stores spent .55 cents on the sales dollar, compared to the national average of .47 cents. On the prairies, it was found that high concentration went hand-in-hand with high advertising costs, high gross markups, overstoring, and higher-than-average profits.

The Power of Vertical Integration

The corporate chains have a tremendous advantage over their competitors through the market power which arises from vertical integration, back through wholesaling into manufacturing of food and even primary production. At the other end, a number of the chains have diversified into institutional, catering, and restaurant sales of prepared foods.

One of the first areas of diversification was into wholesaling. The Royal Commission on Price Spreads of Food Products (1959) found that there were three major trends in Canada: (1) movement of the large corporate chains into the area of direct ownership of wholesale firms; (2) the association of locally-owned "independent" stores with voluntary wholesale chains, which had grown in market power; and (3) the decline of the independent stores, which did not have the advantages of market power associated with wholesale ownership.

Similar trends have been noted in the United States. The U.S. Federal Trade Commission's study in 1960 concluded that direct ownership of wholesale concerns was "very important" to the success of the chains in the United States. A similar conclusion was reached in 1966 by the National Commission on Food Marketing. Direct ownership of wholesale firms added efficiencies and guaranteed distribution.

In Canada, the Weston Empire is the strongest in this area, with direct ownership of a number of wholesale firms operating from coast to coast. The largest include Kelly Douglas, Westfair Foods, National Grocers, and the Atlantic Wholesalers. Canada Safeway purchased McDonald's Consolidated, which serves as its wholesale distributor. Dominion Stores does not have a separate wholesale firm, but operates large distribution centres from which it services its stores in Ontario, Quebec, and Nova Scotia. Steinberg's does not have a wholesale operation, but has concentrated its operations in Ontario and Quebec, where there are many independent wholesalers. Furthermore, it has benefited from Ivanhoe Corporation, its real estate subsidiary, which develops shopping centres and provides Steinberg's stores with rental space at preferred rates. The fifth chain, A & P of Canada, does not operate a wholesale operation in Canada; this has often been cited as a reason for its poorer market performance.

There are a considerable number of independent wholesalers operating in the large urban centres in Ontario and Quebec, but in the rest of Canada there are only a few major concerns. In these markets, vertical ownership is very important. The wholesale level is also another level where profits can be made. Bruce Mallen cites a survey by the Canadian Imperial Bank of Commerce for 1974 which found that the profit on net worth after taxes was higher in the wholesale trade than in retail food stores, department stores, or for total retail trade. The IGA wholesalers (M. Loeb and Oshawa Group) and Provigo have also done very well, compared to the retail food stores.

The market power of chains is greatly enhanced by vertical integration. In fact, Murray Hawkins of the University of Alberta has argued that "procurement power" is growing in importance; while horizontal share of market is an important guide, it is "a diminishing factor" in judging the power of the retail chains. He proposes a new index to measure market power, which would include the degree to which the retail food store is able to utilize private label sales; benefits arising from formula pricing associated with standing orders; and the degree to which the store relies on only a small number of suppliers.

Looking at grocery retailing in the United States, Leon Garoian finds that vertical integration is most important to the profit performance of the retail food industry. He argues that the high degree of concentration in grocery manufacturing in the United States encouraged vertical integration by the chains back into food manufacturing.

All the chains widely use private labelling of various food products. Manufacturers package their products under the house brand labels of the chain store (both corporate and voluntary). This reduces advertising and selling costs on these items. Private brands normally bring higher profits to the retail store. The Technical Study on food retailing done by the U.S. National Commission on Food Marketing in 1966 found that the average gross markup on advertised brands was 22.4%, and that of the private brands was 24.8%. This is a major reason why the stores will allocate substantial shelf space for their private label brands.

Vertical integration, and the availability of manufacturers to provide private brand labelling, has given the chains a strong bargaining weapon when dealing with brokers or salesmen representing both the small food manufacturers and the large food corporations selling nationally advertised products. In recent years the chain stores have been able to extract substantial "fees" from distributors in the form of co-operative advertising, which are a form of purchasing shelf space. The independent stores and small manufacturing firms simply do not have equivalent market power.

All of the large chains are not only in the business of expanding the line of private labels, but they are also increasingly involved in food manufacturing. The prototype here is the Weston chain, which is involved in the manufacture of almost every basic food item, distributed through its wholesale operations to thousands of retail stores across Canada. In fact, recent profit problems experienced by Weston may be associated with management confusion due to its wide-ranging diversification.

All the other major chains are also in food manufacturing. While this is not true of A & P in Canada, they are involved in direct manufacturing in the U.S. on a large scale, and they do import private brand labels when it is to their advantage. Steinberg's has its own bakery, Phenix Mills, as well as Cartier Sugar, Steinberg Foods, and a food services operation. In 1977 Steinberg's reported that private label accounted for 25% of their total sales volume. Dominion Stores has its own dairy and farms, controls General Bakery, and has close co-operative and financial links with York Farms division of Canada Packers. Canada Safeway has its own dairy and poultry operations (Lucerne Foods) and manufactures through its subsidiary, Empress Foods.

214

As an example of this power, we can look at Canada Safeway's operation in Alberta, as described by Walter Stewart. Murphy's Ranch Discount supermarket had a contract to buy canned goods from Broder's cannery in Southern Alberta, and they received a volume discount on a substantial order. However, Canada Safeway bought the cannery, and the discount disappeared overnight.

On the other end, Canada Safeway generally refuses to buy products manufactured by one of its wholesale-retail competitors. This was documented in the Combines Commissioner's case against Canada Safeway in 1973. It wouldn't even sell toilet paper made by E.B. Eddy Co., which was owned by the Weston empire.

These are just a few examples to illustrate the central fact: vertical integration is available only to the large chains. It greatly increases their monopoly power, particularly in relation to independents and voluntary groups. Its development, along with conglomerate growth, has been outside the scope of traditional anti-combine legislation in both Canada and the United States. Furthermore, there is no indication that the governments of either are interested in curbing this concentration of economic power.

Overstoring

It is widely recognized by independent economists as well as by spokesmen within the retail food industry in Canada that one of the most serious problems is overstoring: there are simply too many stores for the existing population. Or, in some cases, there is too much floor capacity for the existing population. The result of this is poor economic performance in areas where there is some degree of competition; on the other hand, in areas where there is a regular price leader, the gross margins are increased and the inefficiencies are passed on to the consumer through higher prices.

One of the difficulties in assessing the efficiency of the grocery store in Canada is determining what constitutes full utilization. About one-half of the costs of a store are fixed costs, which remain the same whether or not the store is open for use. In the United States, supermarkets are now regularly open seven days a week, normally every night of the week, and often twenty-four hours a day. This has resulted in the virtual disappearance of the "mom and pop" retail stores and in their replacement by the chain convenience store, like Seven-11, which hires employees at regular hours, and which also has higher prices.

In Canada, store hours vary from province to province, and judgements on efficiency have to take local store hours into consideration. But there is no doubt that government decisions to greatly restrict store opening hours in Canada have led to inefficient utilization of capital. For consumers, it undoubtedly has meant higher-than-necessary prices. The strict closing hours may also be a factor in overstoring.

One new chain with a difference is Knob Hill Farms in the Toronto area. Their marketing strategy is based on volume turnover in very large stores which stress bulk quantities at low prices. Their four stores are open Monday through Friday, 9 a.m. to midnight, and 8 a.m. to midnight on Saturday. Steve Stavre feels that the long hours are essential to making a profit when selling with a lower gross margin.

Partly as a result of the Knob Hill Farms experience, plus keener competition for the Metro Toronto customer, Steinberg's and Dominion have also shifted to longer hours in this market.

In December 1976, the *Canadian Grocer* noted that the major problem of many retail grocery stores in Canada was underutilization of capacity. In 1975, average sales for all stores were $3.2 million per year, or a weekly average sales per square foot of $5.95 (this is the standard of measurement commonly used by the industry). The retail stores which lost money in 1975 averaged $2.3 million in sales, or $4.13 per square foot. In June 1975, *Canadian Grocer* quoted an executive from a chain store who claimed that "a chain can't consider a location that won't produce a minimum of $100,000 a week, and more is needed." That would mean annual sales of more than $5 million, which would be a bare minimum performance for a store of 20,000 square feet. However, in the late 1970s, the chains were opening stores in the urban centres which averaged between 32,000 and 55,000 square feet.

A study done by Donald Tiggert, a food retailing analyst with Burns Fry Ltd. of Toronto, on supermarket performance in the Toronto area in 1976, found a wide range of performance between the top four chains (A & P does not make figures available on their Canadian operations). In the Toronto area in 1976, Dominion Stores sales averaged $5.46 per square foot, Steinberg's $4.71, Canada Safeway $4.08, and Loblaw $3.90. Thus, by 1975 standards, Loblaw and Canada Safeway both lost money in the Toronto area. It should be remembered that the Toronto area is considered to be the most competitive in Canada with generally the lowest retail prices.

The prairies offer a distinct contrast to the Toronto area, for Canada Safeway is the recognized price leader with about 50% of total sales. Peter Dooley's study for the Royal Commission on Consumer Problems and Inflation (1968) focused on this situation. He found that there was about twice as much floor space on the prairies as in the United States for the same size population. Using the American average as a base, he concluded that there were twice as many stores on the prairies as the population required, and this was costing the consumers an additional 4% per year on their grocery bill.

The standard used for comparison may not in fact reflect actual efficient usage, as overstoring is also considered to be a major problem in the U.S. retail grocery industry. It should be quite obvious to anyone that retail food stores in Canada are all being underutilized. They are crowded during certain peak shopping periods: on Saturday, evenings, and to a lesser extent near the end of each week day. The majority of the time there are more employees in the ordinary supermarkets than there are customers.

Bruce Mallen and M. Haberman did a study of optimal store size in 1975. They concluded that the optimal store size was 14,245 square feet, with a utilization rate of $11.25 in sales per square feet per week. As the stores increase in size, costs increase more than sales. They concluded that "diseconomies of size . . . are setting in at a level which is substantially below the size of most supermarkets that have been built recently or are being planned for tomorrow."

Why do we have too many stores? This question was asked of the managers of chain stores by Peter Dooley in his survey of the prairie industry. If a store had a prime location, with high sales/capacity relationship, its profits would also be quite high. This would invite in a competitor. To block such entry, the existing chain either expands its store or builds another store. This is deemed preferable to loss of market share (and potential profits) to a competing chain. Overstoring is a technique for maintaining market share and domination by the large firms.

Bruce Mallen's study for the Food Prices Review Board found a general correlation between high market concentration and overstoring in 1973. He also found that the excess capacity that is a general problem "is the result of excess stores rather than excess space within stores." This may change as the corporate chains are shifting from smaller stores to larger stores and expanding existing stores.

In the urban centres with the highest degree of concentration of the market, the average population was 9,799 per store. In the medium-concentrated markets, population averaged 12,788 per store. In the areas (like Toronto) with the lowest level of concentration, there were 14,296 people per store. Thus, in the urban markets in 1973 with the highest degree of concentration, Mallen found there were 55% more stores per unit of population than in the competitive markets.

Spokesmen for the retail food industry say that their profits are low, and they cannot be blamed for high food prices. The Food Prices

217

Review Board backed them up, proclaiming that supermarket profits are not too high. But that is not good enough. We know that there is a tremendous markup between the price of food at the farm gate and at the retail store. Profits are low because of the gross inefficiencies of the Canadian retail food operation. And consumers are paying much more for food than they would need to pay—if there were an efficient distribution system.

Profits at the Retail Level

Costs of operating a retail store are divided between fixed costs (rent, property, taxes, heating, lighting, refrigeration, as well as some labour) and operating costs (most salaries and wages, advertising and promotion). Peter Dooley estimates that fixed costs are about 50% of total costs. There are variable costs which rise as additional labour is utilized—up to a certain point. Capital costs for starting a store are not great. The prairie Royal Commission estimated them at around one-tenth of annual sales. The capital required to open a store is not considered a significant barrier to entry.

The size of store does not appear to be a significant factor in costs of operation. Bruce Mallen notes that all the studies seem to conclude that economies due to physical scale of operation are "relatively insignificant." The U.S. National Commission on Food Marketing's special study on the food retailing industry found that physical costs rarely were more than 2% of sales in the difference between the large and the small store. The key factor was utilization of capacity. The U.S. study concluded that there was no reason for building very large stores. On the other hand, as Peter Dooley and others have pointed out, there are very high costs involved in the luxury supermarkets with the large parking lots.

While there do not seem to be figures on shifts in store costs in Canada, the 1966 U.S. study, *Food Retailing, Organization and Competition*, provides figures for changing costs between 1954 and 1963:

Cost Item	% Change
Gross Margin	13.97
Total operating expenses	18.34
Store labour	5.46
Advertising	2.30
Promotion	31.03
Rent & real estate	43.40

218

Heat, light & power	47.92
All others	1.74

As can be seen from the above, the largest increases have been in fixed costs and promotion. The study also found that productivity was increasing: for stores with sales of over $1 million, sales per employee rose from $37,214 in 1948 to $55,356 in 1963.

The concern of many who have looked seriously at trends in the food retailing industry is that pricing patterns will follow those of manufacturing industries in general: as the industry becomes more concentrated, and market control is reached, price leadership becomes the norm. As in the oligopolistic manufacturing industries, prices will be set as a percentage markup over costs. We have noted the industry inefficiencies which have cost consumers dearly. How have industry profits stood up during this period of over-expansion of stores?

First, it is important to distinguish between profit as a percentage of sales and profit as a return on investment. The industry likes to cite profit as a return on sales, for it sounds lower and presents a better public image. But as the U.S. Federal Trade Commission pointed out long ago, a one cent return on sales may be a very high profit in terms of return on investment. The most useful standard is return on investment (or equity) after taxes.

The Royal Commission on Price Spreads of Food Products (1959) found that between 1949 and 1957, the five large corporate chains realized an average return on investment of 17.1%. During that same period, the return on equity for all manufacturing was 10.7%; for all retail trade, 9.8%; for food processing,8.4%; and for wholesale food distribution, 7.7%. Profits for the large chains were almost double those of retail trade in general. This abnormally high return on investment stimulated the construction of stores.

The same thing was happening in the United States. The National Commission on Food Marketing (1966) concluded that profits were higher than for other industries in the post-war period, and this resulted in the construction of too many supermarkets. High profits attracted investment. In its staff study on food marketing done in 1961, the U.S. Federal Trade Commission concluded that "average returns after income taxes on net assets of large food chains have been greater than that of a sample of nonfood chains in every year since 1949, and the margin of difference has been widening."

The Canadian Business Service notes, "Canadian food chains have generally enjoyed somewhat higher profit margins than those in the United States where keen competition exerted an increasingly depressing effect on net earnings." But if we are to believe the spokesmen for the retail food industry in recent years, they are going through a virtual depression.

Lerner and Patil have stressed the growth of the corporate chains and the increasing share of the market that they control. In 1964, they found that the four largest chains in Canada were returning 15.8% on equity. By normal standards, that is a very good return. The Food Prices Review Board surveyed sixteen major food wholesalers and retailers for the period between 1964 and 1974. They argued that their return on shareholders' equity was 10.6% over this period, but they did not publish any figures to support their claim.

TABLE IXa

Retail-Wholesale Food Distributors

Company	Ownership/Control	1971 Sales
Loblaw-Weston Ltd.	Canada—Weston Family*	$2,558,752,000**
Canada Safeway Ltd.	U.S.—Safeway	845,527,000
Steinberg's Ltd.	Canada—Steinberg Family	786,407,000
Dominion Stores Ltd.	Canada—Argus Corp.	768,600,000
IGA Canada Ltd.	Canada—Retailers	550,000,000
Oshawa Group Ltd.	Canada—Wolfe Family	469,771,000
M. Loeb Ltd.	Canada—Loeb Family/Weston***	434,222,000
A & P Canada Ltd.	U.S.—A & P	251,817,000
Provigo Ltd.	Canada—Courette/Provost	209,035,000
Federated Co-operatives Ltd.	Canada—Member Co-ops	117,000,000
Sobey Stores Ltd.	Canada—Sobey Family/Weston	92,813,000

*Whether the Weston chain should be considered to be Canadian-owned is debatable. W. Garfield Weston, the present head of the clan, lives permanently in England, where he was even a Member of Parliament between 1939-1945. His son, Galen, assumed control of the Canadian operations in 1972. He was born in Britain and prior to 1972 lived in Ireland. In 1973 it was reported that he spent about one-half his time in Canada, at a newly purchased Rosedale home. They spend much of their time at their estate in County Wicklow, outside of Dublin.

** Corporate figures for this year are consolidated to include all retail and wholesale figures by subsidiaries, including Loblaws Inc. (U.S.), National Tea (U.S.), as well as some of the manufacturing firms not directly owned by George Weston Ltd. They do not include most of the food manufacturing firms or Associated British Foods Ltd., which consolidates overseas sales.

*** Bought by Provigo in 1977.

The size of the chain operation may also make a difference. The food chains in Canada are very large compared to those in the United States, and it appears that there are diseconomies of scale.

In the United States in 1972, A & P, the largest U.S. retail chain, and the only chain which really operates on a national scale, reported losses. Safeway, the second largest chain, which emphasizes a policy of concentration in local markets, had a return of 15% on equity. Kroger, which had engaged in a price war with A & P, reported a return of 5.2% on investment. Jewel Companies, the fourth largest, reported 12.5% return; Lucky Stores, 19.7%; Winn-Dixie, 19%; and Giant Foods, 17%. The medium sized firms, which were more regional in operation, had the highest return on investment.

In Canada, the degree of concentration of the market seems to be the more important factor. Dooley's study for the Prairie Royal Commission is most revealing, for this is the area of highest concentration of power. Furthermore, the other stores recognize and follow Canada Safeway as the price leader.

Between 1960 and 1964, the supermarket chains averaged a 16% return on equity for their Canadian operations. In the five cities studied by Dooley for the Royal Commission, the return to the chains for the same period was 28.1%. In the U.S., the return for chains on a national basis was 13.8% for the same period.

The advantages of price leadership by Canada Safeway also carried over to the smaller stores. Dooley reported that the 1966 profits of the unincorporated stores was 21% above the Canadian average for the same category of stores. Prairie profits in 1966 were between 200% and 300% above U.S. profits! The Royal Commission on Consumer Problems and Inflation concluded that "the excess profits which are earned on the prairies are due to monopoly power."

In this context, and given the political position of the Food Prices Review Board, Bruce Mallen's study for 1973 is also interesting. He evaluated the data on store gross profits and net operating income in the various cities he surveyed. He concluded that "there *is* a definite moderate positive correlation between profits of the giants, especially net operating income, and concentration."

In November 1975 *The Financial Post* reported on the performance of the large retail chains for the fiscal year ending in 1975. Most of the chains averaged a 13% return on shareholder equity. In spite of an advertising war in Quebec, Dominion Stores and Provigo Inc. reported returns of about 20% on equity. It seems that even in "bad times," the corporate chains were not doing too badly.

In 1977 Kelly-Douglas & Co. reported earnings of $8.2 million for the previous year and predicted this would reach $10 million. Their parent firm, Loblaw, argued that this was because British Columbia had a high population growth and "price competition is normally less intense than in Ontario."

The other major chains in Canada have also reported fairly good

221

results in the 1970s. Weston reported a 17% return on equity in 1973; this dropped to a low of 7% in 1975 but was back up to 13% in 1977. Dominion reported a low of 13.3% in 1974 and a high of 20.8% in 1976.

Provigo, a wholesaler for independents and voluntary chains, reported returns on equity ranging between 3.7% in 1973 and 5.9% in 1975. Oshawa Group Ltd., with 75% of its sales in its food wholesale business, reported returns on investment from a low of 4% in 1977 to a high of 13% in 1975.

Another method of measuring performance is pre-tax profit margin on sales; the overall goal here is to reach a return of 2%. For 1977 *The Financial Post* reported that Canada Safeway Ltd. "enjoys a comfortable 4% profit margin due to limited competition in the West." The nearest chain was Dominion, with a 1.8% margin. Steinberg's was reported to be very close to Dominion with Loblaw trailing at 1.3%. The return for Safeway in the United States for 1977 was 1.27%.

Despite the public relations efforts by the large corporate chains, consumers seem to have their own views on who is responsible for high food prices in Canada. In May 1977 two federal departments, Agriculture Canada and Environment Canada, released an independent survey conducted by a Toronto research firm on the general subject. The firm conducted in-depth interviews with 923 people across Canada. Those interviewed singled out retailers as mainly responsible for food price increases. The others, listed in descending order of guilt, were wholesalers, processors, increased costs of production, higher transportation costs, marketing boards, and at the bottom, farmers.

It is all too evident that how we market food in Canada is determined by trends and new developments in the United States. In planning developments, it is assumed that the Canadian market is a mirror image of the United States. One recent example will serve to illustrate that this situation is not changing.

In 1973 the U.S. food retailing industry announced that it was going to install the computerized checkout system. It was argued that this would reduce checkout time, reduce noise in the stores, and allow the supermarkets to reduce labour costs. The idea was quickly supported by the large food manufacturers. All products would be coded when packaged, and the computers would read the codes at the checkout counter.

The code (which is familiar to all Canadians) was drawn up in March 1973 at a secret meeting of representatives from Del Monte, General Foods, Greenbelt Co-op Stores, H.J. Heinz, Procter & Gamble, Red Owl Stores, Safeway Stores, and Winn-Dixie Stores.

The code tells what the product is and who made it; the price is set by the local store and the computer matches it to the code. In 1974 all the big U.S. chains began to install the computers; it was estimated that by 1980 conversion of the large supermarkets would be virtually completed.

Consumer groups in the U.S. (and later in Canada) expressed concern over the change. Prices no longer appear on the individual products, only on the shelves. This makes price comparison more difficult, particularly when the customer tries to match his print-out list with the products at home in the kitchen.

Steinberg's introduced the change at a store in Montreal, and customers were not happy. In 1977, it was extended to a few Miracle Mart stores in Toronto. It was then adopted as an experiment by Loblaw. In B.C., Safeway and Super-Valu introduced the change in a couple of stores in 1978. But the industry predicted only 10 stores would be utilizing the system by the end of the year. They all feared customer resistance.

In California, a law was passed requiring pricing on individual items—a response to popular demand. In British Columbia, the computers enabled the store to charge new prices for old stock, reaping additional profits. The lines at the cash register have not speeded up; they actually seemed to have slowed down, due to scanning problems. Furthermore, the stores are pocketing the savings in labour; the prices in the stores with computerized scanners are not lower than the prices in the chain's other stores. Once again, Canadians are welcoming another American marketing innovation, this one by Sperry-Univac and IBM.

The general trends in the industry are plain to see, and they have not changed since the end of World War II. The large corporate chains are increasing their share of the market every year—at the expense of the voluntary chains and the independent grocers. Markets are becoming more highly concentrated each year. Price leadership is the norm in almost all areas of Canada. At the same time, overstoring continues to cause major industry inefficiencies. Canadians are paying significantly more for food than they would if they had an efficient wholesale and retail distribution system.

SOURCES

Canadian Business Service. *The Food Chain Industry*. Toronto: Canadian Business Service, May 4, 1971.

Cann, K.E., and L.C. Rayner. "Marketing Costs of Food in Canada, 1949-1964," *Canadian Farm Economics,* I, No. 4, October 1966.

Combines Commissioner. *Annual Reports*, 1973 and 1974. Ottawa: The Queen's Printer, 1973 and 1974.

Cross, Jennifer. *The Supermarket Trap*. Bloomington, Ind.: Indiana University Press, 1970.

Cubberley, David and John Keyes. "The Weston Conglomerate," *The Last Post,* V, No. 1, October 1975, pp. 18-29.

Dooley, Peter C. *Retail Oligopoly: An Empirical Study of the Grocery Trade on the Prairies*. Saskatoon: Modern Press, 1968.

Food Prices Review Board. *Retail Food Stores Survey*. Ottawa: Food Prices Review Board, November 1973.

Garoian, Leon. "Grocery Retailing," in John R. Moore and Richard G. Walsh, eds., *Market Structure of Agricultural Industries*. Ames, Iowa: Iowa State University Press, 1966, pp. 3-37.

Gonick, Cy and Fred Gudmundson. "Food, Glorious Food," *Canadian Dimension,* IX, Nos. 7 & 8, 1973, pp. 26-46.

Hawkins, Murray H. "Aggregate Competitive Behaviour in the Food Industry," *Canadian Journal of Agricultural Economics,* XVI, No. 2, 1968, pp. 13-19.

Hawkins, M.H., A.A. Warrack, and A.A. Patteson, "Intracity Retail Price Behaviour and the Impact of Price Inquiries," *Canadian Journal of Agricultural Economics,* XVI, No. 3, 1968, pp. 131-141.

Lerner, Arthur, and T.S. Patil. "Changes in the Marketing Structure of Grocery Retailing," *Canadian Journal of Agricultural Economics*, XII, No. 1, 1965, pp. 20-35.

Mallen, Bruce. "A Preliminary Paper on the Levels, Causes and Effects of Economic Concentration in the Canadian Retail Food Trade: A study of Supermarket power." Food Prices Review Board, unpublished, February 1976.

Morgan, H.E. "Concentration in Food Retailing: Criteria and Causes," *Journal of Farm Economics,* XCVIII, No. 3, Part II, August 1966, pp. 122-136.

National Commission on Food Marketing, *Food from Farmer to Consumer*. Washington D.C.: U.S. Government Printing Office, June 1966.

National Commission on Food Marketing, *Food Retailing, Organization and Competition*. Technical Study No. 7. Washington, D.C.: U.S. Government Printing Office, June 1966.

Padberg, Daniel I. *Economics of Food Retailing*. Ithica, N.Y.: Cornell University Press, 1968.

Partley, G., O. Famure, M. Faminow and Murray H. Hawkins. "A Critical Review of the Mallen Report," *Canadian Journal of Agricultural Economics,* XXIV, No. 3, 1977, pp.40-49

Restrictive Trade Practices Commission. *Loss Leader Selling*. Ottawa: Department of Justice, 1954.

Report Transmitting a Study of Certain Discriminatory Pricing Practices in the Grocery Trade made by the Director of Investigation and Research. Ottawa: Department of Justice, 1958.

Robbins, William. *The American Food Scandal*. N.Y.: William Morrow & Co., 1974.

Royal Commission on Consumer Problems and Inflation. *Final Report*. Regina: The Queen's Printer, 1968.

Royal Commission on Prices, *Report*. Ottawa. The King's Printer, 1949.

Royal Commission on Price Spreads of Food Products. *Final Report*. II Retailing, III General Studies. Ottawa: The Queen's Printer, 1959.

Rush, Gary B. *Supermarket Storybook: The Food Chain Expose*. Vancouver: Department of Sociology, Simon Fraser University, 1972.

Stewart, Walter. *Hard to Swallow*. Toronto: MacMillan of Canada, 1974.

U.S. Federal Trade Commission. *Economic Inquiry into Food Marketing*. Part I. Concentration and Integration in Retailing. Washington, D.C.: U.S. Government Printing Office, January 1960.

Ward, Bob. *Food for Thought: A Study of Skyrocketing Food Prices*. Don Mills, Ontario: Ontario Federation of Labour, 1973.

Weijs, J.H., William Janssen, and Diane Kennedy. *Wholesaling and Retailing of Food in Ontario*. Staff Study No. 14, Ontario Committee on Farm Income, 1969.

10. THE QUALITY OF FOOD

Over the past thirty years there has been a rather significant shift in the way North America is producing, processing, distributing, and eating food. Economists look at these changes from the perspective of how well scarce resources are utilized. Sociologists are concerned about the effects on the social environment in which we live. Ecologists are concerned with the total effect of these changes on our environment. But all of us should be personally concerned about the effect of these changes on the food we eat. Is our general health improving? Are we receiving a good, balanced nutritional diet? Certainly, with the scientific advances that have been made over the last thirty years, our health and well being should be dramatically improving. If they aren't, then there is reason to question the entire food production system.

The facts are disturbing. Our life expectancy is falling in relation to other countries. In the early 1970s there were ten other countries where individuals had longer life expectancies than Canadians. Our infant mortality rate is actually increasing, particularly in relation to other countries. What lengthening there has been in our life span over the past fifty years is due primarily to the drop in infant mortality. Beyond the age of fifteen, there has been little difference in lifespan.

The medical and scientific professions have done a very good job of controlling infectious diseases like influenza, bronchitis, pneumonia, tuberculosis, typhoid, smallpox, and infant diseases. The mortality rate from these diseases has dropped from around 150 per 100,000 in 1931 to almost zero in 1971.

But on the other hand, there has been a significant increase in deaths due to cancer, heart disease, and strokes. A U.S. Presidential

Commission in 1964 found that these three diseases accounted for 70% of all American deaths. In Canada in 1971, the three diseases accounted for around two-thirds of all deaths. Deaths due to diseases of the circulatory system have risen from 190 per 100,000 in 1931 to around 375 per 100,000 in 1971. Deaths due to cancer have also been rising, but not as dramatically.

But it is not only these three diseases that are of concern. There has been an increase in diverticulosis, diabetes, gall stones, gout, high blood pressure, urinary stones, and senility.

In 1970, the U.S Surgeon General reported that nearly 6% of all live births include "significant birth defects"; this is a rise over the past. One in seven pregnancies (outside of abortion) fail to produce a living child. The National Foundation—March of Dimes has concluded that 80% of these birth defects are due to environmental factors.

Children's obesity has become a serious problem. Hyperactivity, or hyperkinetic children, has become almost a national crisis. Some medical authorities are now claiming that 10% of North American children have this new disorder.

Measuring the general ill health of the overall population is more difficult, but it is now being attempted. Absenteeism in industry, health conditions of people in poverty areas, and the impact of environmental pollution are being studied. The last survey done in Canada was in 1951, the Canada Sickness Survey. Its report was distressing. In 1965 the Department of Health and Welfare in Canada estimated that there were more than four million chronically disabled in Canada, about 20% of the population. One-half of these were suffering from mental and emotional disorders. Monique Begin, federal Minister of Health, reported to the National Food Strategy Conference in February 1978 that her department's statistics show that 50% of Canadian adults are overweight, and 24% have lost some of their teeth.

At the same time, this degeneration of the overall well being of the Canadian population has been paralleled by vast expenditures on scientific research and medical treatment. Only the United States, spends a higher percentage of their gross national product on health care, and they have the second worst mortality rate among the advanced capitalist countries.

In the 1965-1966 fiscal year, Canadians spent $2.2 billion on health. By 1975-1976, this had risen to $9.17 billion. Health and welfare costs rose from 11% of the GNP in 1965-1966 to 16% in 1975-1976. Spending on hospitalization is 4.5 times what it was ten years ago. The tremendous drain on the federal budget for health costs was the major reason why the Trudeau Government changed the traditional 50-50 cost-sharing agreement with the provinces. As the economists in

TABLE Xa

Number of Patient-Days and Cost per Patient-Day for Nutrition-Related Diseases, Canada

Disease Classification	Number of Patient-Days, 1971	Total Cost, 1975
Heart Diseases	3,739,713	$405,310,000
Respiratory diseases	2,645,769	286,748,000
Cerebralvascular diseases	2,216,752	240,252,000
Diseases of the musculo-skeletal system	1,743,874	189,001,000
Hypertension and arteriosclerosis	1,256,014	136,127,000
Cholelithiasis	1,028,084	111,424,000
Diabetes	889,550	96,409,000
Cancer of the digestive organs	681,800	73,893,000
Ulcers of the stomach and duodenum	675,241	73,183,000
Diseases of the skin, including cancer	624,882	67,725,000
Diseases of the Prostate	565,533	61,292,000
Diseases of the blood, including cancer	533,151	57,783,000
Endocrine, nutritional, and metabolic diseases	155,990	16,906,000
TOTAL, Nutrition-related diseases	16,756,353	$1,816,053,000
TOTAL, All Diseases, Canada	41,288,313	$4,474,827,000

Percentage of total diseases that are nutrition-related: 40.58%

SOURCE: R.G. Wirick, "A Preliminary Paper on Some Food Policy Aspects of Nutrition and Health," Food Prices Review Board, unpublished, June 1976, Table 2-4, pp.40.

228

Ottawa point out, the federal government has been experiencing "ever-diminishing health returns" from its tax dollar expenditure. Why is it that our general health is declining when we spend more and more on research and health care?

The Decline of Nutrition

Without a doubt, a considerable part of our problem lies in the modern life style in North America. People are jammed into very large urban centres where they are exposed to all sorts of environmental pollutions and stress. These factors, the product of unplanned capitalist development, where the profit motive has been the determining factor, should not be underestimated. But the rise of ill health is also due to the decline in nutrition.

Public concern over nutrition levels in North America rose after the publication of studies done by the U.S. Department of Agriculture in the mid-1960s. In 1955 the USDA found that 60% of Americans surveyed were consuming enough good basic foods to give them a balanced nutritional intake. By 1965 they reported that this had fallen to only 50%.

The percentage of American families with "poor diets" had risen from 15% to 21% in this ten-year period. A "poor diet" was defined as containing less than two-thirds of the recommended daily allowance for one or more basic nutrients. These guidelines, set by the Food and Nutrition Board of the National Academy of Sciences, were minimal; they are not considered adequate for persons "depleted by disease, traumatic stresses, or prior dietary inadequacies."

The USDA survey found that there was a definite decline in the quality of food being consumed by Americans in all economic brackets. Indices published by the U.S. Department of Health, Education, and Welfare showed that malnutrition could be found at every level of American society. But of course, nutrient deficiencies were more pronounced among those in the lower income brackets.

In 1966 the *Journal of Nutrition Education* began a study of the nutritional level of Americans, and its results were released in 1969. It expressed shock that "nutrient inadequacies" were found in all income groups, in all regions of the United States. Nearly all children under one year of age had an iron intake that was below the Recommended Dietary Allowance. They found that infants in high income families were actually less well nourished than those in lower income groups. The study concluded that "dietary habits of the American public have become worse, especially since 1960."

Partly as a result of this growing concern, the U.S. Congress began an investigation of its own, holding hearings over several years. In 1971 a U.S. National Nutrition Survey revealed appalling shortcomings in the diet of the average American. Anemia was widespread. Vitamin A and calcium deficiencies were widespread.

Against this background, the Canadian government launched its own survey of the nutritional level in this country; the Nutrition Canada study was released in 1973. To no one's surprise, it was found that Canadians eat the same general diet as Americans and suffer the same effects. Most Canadians consume far too much protein. However, this was not true of all groups of people. Between 15%-25% of Canadian girls and men and women in advanced age groups, where incomes are generally low, did not eat enough protein.

The most disturbing finding was the inadequate intake of basic vitamins and minerals in the diets of our young people. Over 50% of all boys and girls had a range of 50%-70% deficiency in iron. Around 20% of this group were deficient in calcium and vitamin D. Vitamin C deficiencies were noted in all groups, and in particular special groups like Amerindians and Inuit people. Girls in particular showed below-normal intake of vitamin A.

R.G. Wirick, in his study for the Food Prices Review Board, notes that the North American nutrition studies have been "almost exclusively orientated to the less controversial nutritional issues, such as vitamin and mineral deficiencies." They have deliberately avoided coming to grips with the *changes in diet* which have produced their deficiencies. They have also avoided a discussion of the rise of ill health, and its relationship to diet in general.

Changes in our Diet

The decline in nutritional levels in North America, and the rise of certain diet-oriented diseases to near epidemic levels, is a reflection of change in our overall diet and in how food is produced and processed. We are eating more than twice as much beef, veal, and pork than is required; our poultry consumption is almost three times what is needed. At the turn of the century, North Americans consumed about 100 lbs. of meat per year; consumption in Canada in 1973 was around 200 lbs., and in the U.S., 245 lbs. This is about 5 times as much meat as is consumed by the Japanese. North American consumption of fish dropped during this period.

The excess consumption of meat has been accompanied by the increased consumption of saturated animal fats. Most heart specialists have linked overconsumption of saturated fats with the dramatic increases in cardiovascular disorders. North Americans are also generally inactive physically, which compounds the problem. Over the last twenty years, Canadians have increased their fat consumption from 34% to 41% of their total calorie intake.

In contrast, the Japanese have the lowest death rate in the world from heart attack, in spite of the fact that they live under extreme stress. They are also far below the world averages for cancer. This is generally attributed to the fact that they consume protein primarily through fish and poultry, use vegetable oils, eat a wide variety of vegetables and fruits, and eat almost no processed foods. They consume very little red meat, and until the American invasion after World War II, almost no sugar. This is not hereditary, for when Japanese moved to North America and assumed our eating habits, they experienced the same disorders.

Mormons in Utah, who don't drink or smoke, have a cancer rate that is about 40% lower than the U.S. population as a whole. Seventh Day Adventists, who live on a lacto-ovo vegetarian diet, and who neither smoke nor drink, have a cancer rate that is half that of the American average.

Since World War II, Canadians and Americans have significantly reduced their consumption of dairy products while rapidly increasing their consumption of soft drinks. In 1973, Canadians consumed only 65% of the nutritional requirements of milk as recommended by Agriculture Canada. Egg consumption has also dropped by 18% since World War II.

In this period, consumption of fruits and vegetables has risen slightly. However, there has been a decline in the consumption of fresh fruits and vegetables in both the United States and Canada. In 1973, Agriculture Canada concluded that Canadians consumed fewer vegetables than were required to meet normal nutritional requirements.

Cereal grain consumption has declined on a steady basis. This is generally attributed to the rise in personal disposable income. The main problem is the fact that most cereal is consumed in its refined form, particularly wheat and rice. The refining process removes most of the basic nutrients as well as the food fibre or roughage now recognized as necessary to the digestive process.

Perhaps the most serious change has been the dramatic increase in sugar consumption. The average North American now consumes around 120 lbs. per year, most of this in the form of processed foods. Sugar consumption has been directly linked to the rise in many of the increasing diseases, not to mention dental problems. As Emanuel Cheraskin notes, refined sugar is not only valueless in terms of nutrients, it is a chemical menace; it lacks the B vitamins and minerals necessary for its assimilation. Our present generation of children is becoming hooked on sugar at a very early age, mainly through the consumption of soft drinks, candies, gum, and other processed foods.

In Norway during World War II food rationing greatly reduced the consumption of sugar and refined carbohydrates. At the same time, a national food policy increased the consumption of potatoes, vegetables, milk, and bread. Dental decay dropped on a progressive basis, only to rise again when rationing was lifted and sugar was once again available.

Dr. Zak Sabry, who was a co-ordinator for the Nutrition Canada Study, and Ross Hume Hall, a biochemist at McMaster University, have both discussed the effects in Great Britain during World War II when the government was forced to institute a rationing system based on nutritional value. Rationing included forcing the flour millers to retain a larger percentage of the bran in the wheat used in making bread. The death rate declined, as did the incidence of disease in general. After the war, when rationing was lifted, millers returned to making pure white "enriched" bread. The incidence of disease, and the death rate, rose once again.

The Feeding of Infants

It is now generally recognized that the shift from breast feeding of children to bottle feeding has been detrimental to the health of the baby and the mother. Furthermore, with the early introduction of prepared solid foods, today's children are started on an unhealthy diet which carries over to the growing period.

At this time it is reported that less than 20% of North American babies are breast fed. The introduction of substitutes based on cow's milk is a relatively new phenomenon in the history of man, dating back only around fifty years. The major problem associated with the change in the advanced Western countries is the rise of infantile obesity. This is due to calorie overdosage in children who are bottle fed; breast feeding is regulated by the infant's natural appetite and thirst.

Substitute formulas prepared by the large food and chemical corporations try to approximate human milk, stressing the three main properties: protein, fat, and lactose. However, it is now recognized that each species has a natural milk which is designed by nature to ensure optimal growth, development, and survival.

A great deal of research in this area has been done by Derrick and Patrice Jelliffe of the School of Public Health at UCLA. As they point out, human milk has "the abundant supply of nutrients most needed for the rapid growth and development of the central nervous system,

232

including the brain." Many of these nutrients are not found in the manufacturer's substitutes.

But there are other important qualities of human milk that are not present in the substitutes. Mother's milk contains immunological properties which protect babies from early diseases, particularly marasmus and the associated infective diarrhea. Thus, gastrointestinal disorders are widespread among bottle-fed babies.

In addition, North American babies are placed on a solid food diet as early as one month after birth. There are two periods of development during which fat cells will rapidly multiply. These are during the first year of growth and during puberty. Thus, solid foods and overfeeding during these crucial growth periods predispose our youth to a life of obesity.

The pressure to shift babies quickly onto a diet of solid foods arises largely from the advertising of Gerber, Heinz and Beech-Nut, the firms which totally dominate the baby food industry in North America. The early shift to prepared solid foods not only contributes to the problem of obesity, but is directly linked to the rise of allergies, sugar addiction, dental problems, hypertension, and cardiovascular diseases.

Modern prepared baby foods have traditionally contained sugar and salt. Until 1969 they also included monosodium glutamate (MSG), in spite of the fact that research had demonstrated that this chemical was dangerous to infant nervous systems and caused irreversible brain damage in infant test animals. The addition of all three ingredients was designed to please the taste of parents.

Research has shown salt to be directly linked to hypertension. Sugar is one of the most destructive foods in existence. Many researchers believe that sugar is more significant than fats in the cause of cardiovascular disease, which has reached epidemic proportions in North America. Is it wise to be feeding these substances to infants and young children?

Processing Foods

A major reason for the decline in the nutritional level of food eaten in North America is the steady increase in the percentage of processed foods that we eat. While the food manufacturers like to advertise that their products are "fortified" with vitamins, only some vitamins and no minerals are replaced.

The most serious problem posed by unnecessary processing involves cereal grains, particularly wheat and rice, the staple diet of most people in the world. Bread, once considered the "staff of life" in

233

North America, is still a very important item in everyone's diet, particularly in that of the lower income brackets. Ross Hume Hall, a biochemist at McMaster University, has traced the decline and fall of bread making in the Anglo-Saxon world. In the 1840s the modern system of mechanized milling of flour was introduced into Great Britain, and with it the infamous white bread. White flour has almost all of the wheat germ and grain removed in the milling process, and as a result almost all of the vitamins and minerals.

With this milling technique, white bread, butter, jam, and tea became the standard diet of the British working class. The general physical condition of the large majority deteriorated seriously; their physical size fell, and they experienced general deterioration of health. Along with this, British workers developed what has often been described as "sugar sickness." Because of plantation colonialism, the British have been major consumers of sugar and sugar products like candies, jams, and desserts.

Today the white bread we eat is "enriched" with some vitamins, but most of the nutrients are removed, including important trace minerals. Basic nutrients such as Vitamin E, folic acid, and pyridoxine are reduced substantially in the milling process and are not replaced. The same loss of nutrients takes place when rice is milled and bleached; nothing is replaced in this case. Furthermore, there is a long list of unhealthy chemical additives which are now included in the baking process designed to make the bread soft and able to stand on the shelf without growing mold for weeks on end.

When the outer husk is removed in the milling process, there is the loss of fibre, which is now recognized as most important to the digestive process. The milling process has been identified as the main cause of the rise of cancer of the colon. In 1975, there were 10,000 new cases of cancer of the colon in Canada. Ironically, many medical people are recommending that we supplement our diets by eating bran at breakfast.

Dr. Emanuel Cheraskin, Chairman of the Department of Oral Medicine of the University of Alabama, has pointed out that the outside shell of the cereal is discarded and used as animal feed. In actual fact, farm animals fed on milling by-products are receiving a better diet than North Americans who are left eating the remaining endosperm, which is "mostly plain starch and poor quality protein."

A second staple in our diet has traditionally been potatoes. The potato is a good source of Vitamin C, contains several of the required minerals, some protein, and eight amino acids. For the Irish, the potato prevented the development of scurvy. The sweet potato, which has almost disappeared from North America, was also an excellent source of Vitamin A. In recent years there has been a significant drop in fresh

234

potatoes and a steady increase in the amount of processed potatoes consumed in Canada, particularly in the form of snack foods and frozen french fries. The high temperature used in processing these potatoes (particularly french frying) destroys the Vitamin C. Furthermore, these processed potatoes include great volumes of fats which we certainly do not need.

Baking a potato retains the highest level of nutrition. As the processing is increased, its nutrient value declines. By the time the potato is reduced to "Pringles" or instant mashed potatoes, it has virtually no food value. But the end product represents high profits for firms like McCain's, Carnation, and Procter & Gamble.

Unfortunately, the general nutrient level of all basic foods is reduced through processing. Freezing destroys Vitamin A. Vitamin C and other nutrients are destroyed when fruits and vegetables are heated to high temperatures in the canning process. This is undoubtedly one of the main reasons for the decline in vitamin levels in contemporary diets. The U.S. Department of Agriculture reports that in the 1925-1929 period the average American ate 414 lbs. of fresh fruits and vegetables per year. By 1971, this had dropped to 239 lbs., and consumption of processed fruits and vegetables had risen from eighty-four lbs. to 293 lbs. The same trends hold true for Canada.

Milk is often referred to as "nature's most perfect food." It provides more of the essential nutrients and minerals than any other natural food. In recent years, this basic food has come under attack by those who feel that its fat content is too high or that it may be indigestible for many people. Dr. Roger J. Williams points out that about 10% of Caucasian adults cannot digest sweet milk. The same is true for about 70% of Negro adults and a large percentage of Oriental adults. They lack the enzyme lactase which splits milk sugar and makes it digestible.

Yet we find non-white cultures where milk is the basic diet. In these societies, fermented milk (which is low in lactose) is consumed. Dr. Emanual Cheraskin points out that the microorganisms that ferment milk into yogurt and buttermilk also contribute to the body's manufacture of essential vitamins in the intestinal tract.

For North Americans with a problem of overweight, skimmed or low-fat milk is recommended. Because most of us have desk-pushbutton jobs, and we have replaced physical activity with television, there has to be a change in diet. However, it appears that low-fat milk is much preferable to the common beverage substitutes: soft drinks, coffee, tea, and alcoholic beverages.

But to push a point to an extreme, we might look at what the pasteurization process does to milk. Everyone accepts the necessity of this process to control tuberculosis and undulant fever.

235

This was essential in the days before modern sanitary conditions. But today, cows can be tested and vaccinated against disease. They then give Certified Raw Milk, a product which the processing industry does not want to see expanded.

It is now becoming recognized that the pasteurization process does more than ruin the taste of milk. The American nutritionist Carlton Fredericks points out that the process lowers the Vitamin C content, reduces Vitamin B1 and B2, and results in an appreciable loss of calcium. Studies by Arthur Harman and Leslie Dryden of the U.S. Department of Agriculture Research Service conclude that pasteurization leads to a 20% loss of Vitamin C, a 25% loss of thiamine (B1), a 10% loss of biotin, and a 10% loss of B12. Other researchers say that there is also a loss of 15% of the Vitamin E.

Pasteurization also eliminates the anti-stiffness factor which is similar to the adrenal hormone which prevents arthritis among animals. The anti-anemia and anti-ulcer factors are also destroyed. As the National Farmers Union points out, raw milk contains a natural germicide which holds back the multiplication of bacteria; thus, at room temperature, raw milk will actually keep longer than pasteurized milk. The heating process destroys this natural germicide as well as more than a dozen basic enzymes.

Processed Foods and Profits

There is another aspect to the processing phenomenon. We know that the more highly processed foods provide the food corporations with higher profits. In many cases, this is because the corporations can substitute cheaper ingredients for the basic foods. Thus the decline in nutrition, quality, taste, and value is often a deliberate act by the processing corporations. For example, consumer groups have regularly attacked the process of watering hams and poultry, and cutting canned fruit juices with water. These are minor examples within the broad spectrum of food manufacturing.

An example of replacing basic ingredients with cheap substitutes would be the frankfurter, long a staple meat item in the basic diet of lower income people in North America. The U.S. Department of Agriculture reports that between 1937 and 1968 the protein content of the frankfurter declined from 19.6% to 11.8%. Over the same period, the fat content rose from 18.6% to 31.2%. Another 56% is water.

In 1972, Neal Holt of the Crop Sciences Department of the University of Saskatchewan found that the average frankfurter sold in Saskatoon contained 12.2% protein and 30% fat, indicating that Canadian meat packers were following in the footsteps of their

236

American pace setters.

Processed cheese is another example. Kraft's Velveeta is one of the biggest sellers in the cheese market. Processing enabled the large cheese manufacturers like Kraft to use what was previously unsaleable cheese. The low quality hard and moldy cheeses are ground up, heated, and mixed with salt, water, and an emulsifier. This mixture is then poured into packages. It is no wonder that the end product is so low in food value that it will not grow a mold; it just turns hard and dries up. But it is very profitable.

The trend in the industry is towards more production of "convenience foods." We are told that this is what the consumer wants, so that he or she can prepare dinner in fifteen minutes instead of the usual thirty. There is also the false claim that the ready-prepared foods are every bit as nutritious and good tasting as the home-cooked meal.

Breakfast cereals, as we all know, have come under constant criticism for lack of food value. The roasted and puffed-up flakes that are served today, even with the vitamin "enrichment," are certainly no substitute for the basic nutritional goodness of old-fashioned rolled oats. But we know that the profits in the instant breakfast cereal business are phenomenal.

The most commonly used prepared dinners are a "rip-off" in terms of quality, nutrition, what you get for the money, and of course, taste. A study done at Rutgers University found that there was no Vitamin C in the popular chicken pot pies, despite the presence of vegetables. Most of the pie is watered gravy, with very little meat, and not very much in the line of vegetables.

In February 1973, the Consumers Association of Canada (CAC) did an analysis of canned beef stews. The meat content varied from 7% to 17%, with potatoes ranging from 35% down to 14%. The survey indicated that the best buys were actually in the products of the smaller firms; the more highly advertised national brands had a lower content of meat. Because of the wide variation in content, the CAC asked the federal government to institute regulations requiring a minimum content of basic ingredients.

The general deceptiveness of the "heat and serve" convenience food manufacturers is detailed by Sidney Margolis, one of the first of the contemporary consumer muckrakers. As he notes, all the corporations grossly exaggerate the contents of their package in pictures on the outside of the package. For example, Swanson "Turkey Dinners" features a picture of three "rather thick slices of turkey." When the contents were analysed, he found "one thin slice and some very small pieces under that." More significantly, Margolis (and many others) have noted that consumers pay around twice as

237

much for this prepared food item as they would if they had prepared the same sized portion at home. The cost is indeed high.

Another example of how the corporations profit on these highly manufactured food items is demonstrated by looking at Lipton's "Beef Stroganoff." The U.S. Department of Agriculture requires Beef Stroganoff to contain 45% beef, the rest being noodles, sour cream, and "garnish." Lipton's packages the ingredients in three sub-packages: one contains noodles, one "garnish," and the third beef, sour cream, and soybean protein meal. This last package is 45% meat, but the total beef content is only 20%. Soybean meal is about one-ninth the cost of beef. Thus Lipton's realizes high profits by using a cheap beef-substitute.

To cut down on our cholesterol level, we are urged by Standard Brands to substitute "Egg Beaters" for real eggs. A study at the University of Illinois found that rats fed "Egg Beaters" weighed only one half as much as rats fed regular eggs after three weeks, and those on the Standard Brands' diet all died in the fourth week. For this we are asked to pay much more than regular eggs.

In 1969 the President of PepsiCo withdrew from a White House Conference on Nutrition after Conference Director Jean Mayer attacked fat-fried snacks like "Frito-Lay," saying "Fried worms would be better. At least you'd get some protein."

My two prizes, however, go to the soda pop industry. First, to the U.S. National Soft Drink Association for reminding us that "soda pop is a great source of water"! Secondly, a prize to Coca Cola for their advertisement, "Fanta, Fanta, just a bottle of fun." That, at least, is honest. There is no claim for food value for the sugar, chemicals, and water.

The controversy over saccharin in 1977 brought attention to the role of so-called "diet foods" in North America. For the most part, these foods are simply substituting sweetener for sugar. The product invariably costs more. For example, in May 1977, a nine oz. jar of "diet" raspberry jam cost seventy-nine cents in Toronto supermarkets; an equivalent sugar-based raspberry jam cost sixty-three cents. Consumers were paying 20% more for an item which actually should have cost less, for saccharin was cheaper than sugar.

This is all just part of the "consumer as the enemy" attitude of the food corporations reflected in their determination to deceive. "Diet food" is pushed on people with serious health problems. But in fact, as the Toronto Nutrition Committee showed in their 1976 survey of 252 "diet foods," many have the same calorie content as the products they were supposed to replace. More important is the fact that saccharin-sweetened foods are generally not good for anyone's health. The highest selling "diet foods" are junk foods like soda pop, candies, and cookies. The correct alternative is to cut out sweetened foods and return to a good diet of basic foods. But there is no profit for the food processors in that approach.

The ultimate in "diet food" is now being developed in the research and development laboratories of a number of the large food firms: indigestible food. They are attempting to construct foods which will pass through the human digestive system without being digested. The other item being worked on is the development of a chemical that will stop the natural digestive process for particular foods such as starches and meat fats. This is the ultimate diet food. North American gluttons will be able to eat all the junk food and sweets they want without fear of gaining weight. The sale of processed foods will rise significantly.

One person working on this is Dr. George Bray, a professor of medicine at the University of California in Los Angeles. One example he cites is the cellulose-based foods, which are digestible by animals but not by people. Cellulose would be used in the manufacture of much of these artificial "foods."

To end this section, I think it most appropriate to quote the Vice-President in charge of research for General Foods:

> [We] are moving into a world of designed consumer foods. Natural farm produce such as milk, potatoes, and grains are no longer just complete foods to be eaten as part of a meal. They have become ever-expanding sources of raw materials to be utilized as building blocks for new [and] more diverse . . . synthetic foods.

Cancer and the Environment

There is growing concern over the fact that cancer has been increasing in the twentieth century. In 1900, only 8% of the deaths in North America were attributed to heart diseases and 4% to cancer. Now these two diseases claim the majority of lives. Leukemia is also on the rise.

There is growing acceptance of the view that cancer is primarily caused by environmental factors; hence, the disease is ultimately preventable. In 1965 the World Health Organization estimated that 50% of all cancer was linked to the environment. A study in 1972 by the Stanford Research Institute set the figure at about 80%. In July 1976, the U.S. National Cancer Institute estimated that 61% of cancer in women was directly due to diet.

When we talk about environmental causes of cancer, this must include the foods we eat. In this area we are concerned about the basic diet as well as the chemical carcinogens which are in our foods, either by accident or by design.

Cancer of the liver, esophagus, colon, and stomach have been directly related to diet. These cancers were responsible for 25% of all Canadian cancer deaths in 1970. The drop in stomach cancer in North America in recent years has now been attributed to the increased consumption of Vitamin C.

The major contributing factors in diet-related cancers are increased consumption of fat, protein, and sugar, plus a decline in the consumption of fibre and other roughage. In this brief overview, it might be more relevant to look at health problems caused by the introduction of harmful ingredients in the foods that we eat by the food production and processing industries.

Inadvertent Food Additives

It is now estimated that 80% or more of the meat and eggs we consume comes from animals and birds fed antibiotics added regularly to their feed by manufacturers and mixers. Antibiotics were first used to control disease in our modern factory farms, but they were later found also to act as a growth stimulant.

In both the United States and Canada, increased residues of antibiotics are being found in meats, eggs, and even milk products. Medical authorities are expressing concern, as these residues are resulting in allergic reactions in many people.

But there is a much greater threat in the evidence that drug resistant strains of bacteria are being developed by this practice. In October 1976, the Quebec Order of Pharmacists and the Quebec Order of Veterinarians demanded a halt to the sale of all meat and milk in Canada which contained "toxins" such as steroids and antibiotics.

In December 1976, a group of federal meat inspectors submitted a report to the Department of Agriculture warning that the level of antibiotics in beef was becoming excessive and could threaten public health. Several papers on this subject were presented at the 1977 Council of the Canadian Medical Association.

A second area of concern is the increase in heavy metal residues in animals, particularly lead, copper, mercury, cadmium, and zinc. Residues in recent testing have been below the maximum tolerance level set by the Food and Drug Act, but some were very close to the permissible level, particularly copper.

One heavy metal that is commonly found in animal foods is arsenic, which is a known carcinogen in humans. At one time it was widely used as a pesticide, but it is now banned for use on crops. However, it is used as a growth hormone in feeds for chickens and hogs, particularly in the United States.

Tests by the U.S. Department of Agriculture found that a high percentage of chickens had arsenic residues. When Super-Valu imported broilers from Missouri into B.C. in 1977, the B.C. Poultry Marketing Board charged that U.S. standards permit higher levels of arsenic residues in chickens than do Canadian regulations.

With the publication of Rachel Carson's *Silent Spring* in 1962, the public became aware of many of the problems associated with widespread use of pesticides, particularly the chlorinated hydrocarbon insecticides (the DDT family). It should also be remembered that Carson was roundly denounced by a host of scientists and experts, as well as by the spokesmen from the chemical industry. Personnel in the various government Agriculture departments were extremely critical. Yet events have proved her right.

While DDT has been banned in Canada, many of the other chlorinated hydrocarbon insecticides are still being used. And we know that residues from all of them are regularly appearing in our food. Everyone in North America already has chlorinated hydrocarbons stored in their fats.

The main concern is that this family of insecticides is strongly suspected of being a carcinogen. But while they are being banned in Canada and the United States, they are still heavily used in the Third World countries which provide much of our food imports.

In 1977 the World Health Organization reported that there are at least 500,000 pesticide poisonings each year. They report that there is great misuse in the underdeveloped countries, where regulations are very lax. For example, in Central America it is normal to spray DDT on cotton thirty to forty times during the three-month growing season. U.S. and Canadian law permits the chemical companies to manufacture and export pesticides which are banned in North America.

Some fungicides used in Canada are cause for concern. The U.S. Food and Drug Administration reported in 1976 that carbamate fungicides break down naturally into ethylene thiourea (ETU) which causes cancer of the thyroid gland in laboratory experiments. Traces of the fungicide remain on fruits and vegetables sold in our stores. In that same year, the U.S. Department of Health reported that the EDBC fungicides, used widely in Canada, formed ETU when present in foods being cooked. They are used extensively on fruits and vegetables, and some residues remain on the produce we buy in the stores.

In the last few years there has been a noticeable buildup of residues of the phenoxy herbicides in our foods. The most dangerous, 2, 4, 5-T, has been banned from farm use, but is still widely used as a

241

"non-selective" herbicide by all levels of government, hydro corporations, railways, and forest services. In one study in Alberta in 1971, 2,4,5-T residues were found in samples of vegetable oils, margarines, and chicken livers.

One of the other phenoxy herbicides, 2,4-D, is widely used on cereal grains in North America. Studies are showing that residues are building up on the prairies in the water and the soil, and are often present in the air. In 1976 the U.S. Food and Drug Administration dropped their "no tolerance" rating for 2,4-D residues for many foods and set some arbitrary levels which are now considered "safe." This was necessary to deal with the reality of the residues. All of the phenoxy herbicides are powerful teratogens (cause miscarriages, still-births and birth defects), and several studies on laboratory animals suggest that they are also carcinogenic.

Food Additives

Over the past few years there has been a proliferation of books on the subject of food additives and their effect on human health. The most widely read appear in the list of sources at the end of this chapter. It is simply beyond the scope of this introductory chapter to in any way cover this vast subject. All that can be done is to mention the major concerns raised by those writing on this subject.

In 1977 there were around 3,000 different food additives being used in the processing of food in Canada and the United States. The consensus seems to be that the average person in North America, following the average diet, consumes about five pounds of food additives per year.

The use of food additives has increased dramatically over the past few decades, following the rapid expansion of processed foods. For example, the U.S. Food and Drug Administration has reported that the use of coal tar dyes alone has increased from 251,000 lbs. in 1940 to over 3,735,000 lbs. in 1970. Ninety-five per cent of this production ends up in foods.

Economically, the production of food additives is a substantial industry. Since 1955 sales have tripled. As Table Xb illustrates, by 1977 sales in the United States alone have approached $1 billion. All of the major U.S. chemical corporations have a stake in this business, including Monsanto, Pfizer, Union Carbide, Abbott, Allied Chemicals, Atlan, Miles, Dupont, Dow, and others. These are the same companies which distribute the additives in Canada.

Why has there been such a tremendous expansion of the use of food additives? There are several reasons. The primary reason is their

242

contribution to increased profits. The more highly processed foods, which require more additives, bring in the highest profits. In addition, food additives help to cover up poor manufacturing quality and the use of lower quality ingredients. For example, flavour enhancers permit the company to reduce the amount of the natural ingredients. "Enrichment" is cheaper than using ingredients with higher nutritional value. Saccharin was used because it was cheaper than sugar. Thickening agents and stabilizers are used to cover poor ingredients, as in the case of ice cream.

TABLE Xb

Current and Estimated Food Additives Markets (1971-1980)

Class	Millions of $		
	1971	1975	1980
Acidulants	55.84	69.92	98.19
Antioxidants	12.73	15.55	19.82
Preservatives	10.64	12.58	16.06
Colours	16.77	19.37	27.38
Flavour and flavour enhancers	254.00	326.90	476.40
Enzymes	21.63	27.84	40.84
Stabilizers, etc.	98.80	128.40	151.30
Nutritive agents	61.11	91.40	146.60
Surfactants	53.71	62.05	71.64
Miscellaneous	50.74	56.18	60.58
TOTALS	635.97	800.19	1108.81

SOURCE: American Institute of Chemical Engineers, cited in Jim Hightower, *Eat Your Heart Out*. N.Y.: Crown Publishers, 1975, Table IV-Z, p. 86.

The most widely used additives are there simply for cosmetic purposes. This is particularly true of artificial colouring. The industry argues that natural colours are "unstable" and will often pale or change colour when exposed to sunlight or when held over long periods of time. They argue that the consumer wants bright, differently coloured products (like jams and jellies) in clear bottles, rather than the colour of the natural product. Petroleum waxes are added to many fruits and vegetables to increase their shiny appearance.

Sodium nitrate and nitrite are used to preserve processed meats, but the main reason they are used is that they retain a bright red colour in the meat. Our government and the industry continue to use these preservatives even though it is known that when cooked they combine to form nitrosamines, a carcinogen. These preservatives have been banned in other Western countries; others have demonstrated that meats can be preserved without the use of these dangerous substances.

The antioxidants BHT and BHA are added to vegetable oils to prevent spoilage. These additives are highly suspect, and are banned in a number of Western countries. We know that high quality manufacturing eliminates the need to use these dangerous additives. Yet our industry and government allow their continued use in Canada.

It is important to remember that there is no automatic distinction between natural and artificially manufactured food additives. Some of the artificially produced additives are normal in the human diet; some are even beneficial, such as citric acid and lecithin. Caffeine is a natural product, but it is toxic to humans; in high doses of coffee, tea and colas it can produce human birth defects.

It is also true that most food additives are found in chemical form in foods that we eat. But it does not automatically follow that they are therefore safe as used by manufacturers. There is the question of the quantity used. Are the chemical additives normally consumed by human beings? Is the amount consumed normal to the ecological balance of the human body? How do they act in combination with other additives and environmental pollutants?

In Canada, the federal Health Protection Branch sets standards for food additives. This agency must contend with several serious problems. First, the U.S. Food and Drug Administration and the U.S. Environmental Protection Agency, with much larger budgets and research staffs, cannot give adequate advance screening for the several thousand new chemicals which flood the market each year. How can the HPB do its job? In practice, it has generally just gone along with American decisions.

The other major problem is the fact that Canada is a northern extension of the American market. Most processed foods in Canada are manufactured by the large American food corporations. Politically, the federal government does not feel that it can impose different or more stringent regulations on these companies than does the U.S. government. It is a captive of continentalism.

Therefore, regulation of food additives in Canada has in practice followed the major shifts in the U.S. system. Prior to 1958, the corporations could use any food additive they thought was safe; it was up to the government to prove it unsafe. In that year the Delaney Amendment was added to the U.S. Food and Drug Act. The burden of proof was then shifted to the manufacturer to show "proof of a reasonable certainty that no harm will result from the proposed use of an additive." Canada adopted similar procedures.

However, the U.S. Delaney Amendment banned all food additives and pollutants which cause cancer in tests on laboratory animals. The Canadian government does not have such a regulation.

When the Delaney Amendment was passed, the U.S. government had to deal with the fact that there were hundreds of food additives already being used. It created the "generally recognized as safe" (or GRAS) list through a process that has been severely criticized. It involved no research. A number of the GRAS additives have subsequently been banned, after testing showed they were dangerous to public health. The Canadian government did not require manufacturers to submit research experiments on food additives that were already in use.

Inadequate Testing and Control

There are three standard tests for food additives. The acute-toxicity test determines how much of a chemical is required over a twenty-four hour period to kill 50% of the test animals. The "safe dosage level" is then multiplied by a factor of ten to account for the fact that humans are on the average ten times more sensitive to chemicals than laboratory rats. It is then multiplied by ten again to add a "safety margin." This is how safe dosage levels are arrived at by federal authorities.

Equally important is the subacute test, which usually lasts between ninety days and six months, to determine how much animals can tolerate under repeated dosages for longer periods of time. But the most important tests are the chronic feeding studies, conducted over the entire lifetime of the animal. These are the studies which can show if a chemical is a carcinogen. To be effective, they must be carried out on a series of different animals. Dr. Jacqueline Verrett, one of the top researchers of the U.S. Food and Drug Administration, points out that "few of the food additives we eat today have ever been subjected to lifetime feeding studies."

Dr. Verrett lists a number of major concerns about the system of approving food additives for the United States; they apply equally in the case of Canada:

1. The federal government agencies do not have adequate budgets or facilities to do a good job of checking on food additives.

2. Almost all testing is done by the chemical manufacturer. All the regulatory agencies do is review the tests. The investigations of the U.S.

FDA reveal that in most cases all the government did was review the summaries; they did not even examine the basic research. Many of the scientists who do the research (i.e., who are on the manufacturers' payrolls) can hardly be described as independent; much of the research is inadequate and faulty.

3. Both Canada and the United States federal agencies reject research done by other countries. This is particularly true of research done in the socialist bloc countries.

4. As mentioned before, very few additives are tested for carcinogenicity in lifetime chronic tests. There is no testing required for mutagenesis; the official excuse is that the tests are not reliable.

5. There is no requirement that previously registered additives be tested for possible chronic effects. Many that have been shown to be harmful are being kept in use because of industry pressure. In many cases, the federal agencies must weigh positive tests against negative ones; usually, they rule for the corporations, as in the case of MSG where four negative tests "washed out" thirteen positive tests.

6. It must be recognized that there can be no tolerance levels set for chemicals which cause chronic disorders. Individual susceptibility varies as much as 1,000-fold due to a variety of factors such as age, hormonal status, diet and nutritional status, genetic factors, different metabolic rates for chemicals, exposure to other environmental contaminants, etc.

7. We do not know what the long term cumulative effects will be. What will be the effects of the interaction of hundreds of food additives? How will these chemicals interact with other environmental pollutants? Is there a synergistic effect? How many are co-carcinogenic when in contact with the many other chemicals ingested into our body? We just don't know. Both Dr. Jacqueline Verrett of the U.S. Food and Drug Administration and Prof. David Suzuki of the University of British Columbia warn that this may be the carcinogenic generation. We are all laboratory rats.

8. There is inadequate labelling on processed foods. Despite pressures by consumer groups, the food corporations have had their way, and food labels today are incomplete. In Canada, all that is required is "artificial colouring" and "artificial flavouring." And "standardized products" like butter, margarine, flour, cheese, jams and vegetable oils, all of which contain numerous additives, have no ingredient labelling at all.

The extent to which the regulatory agencies are captives of the large food corporations is illustrated by the decision of the U.S. government to establish an additional research laboratory at Pine Bluff, Arkansas, and to carry out "mega-mouse" experiments using known carcinogens. The purpose of these tests, using 50,000 to

100,000 rats fed a known carcinogen at low doses over a lifetime, is to try to establish a threshold level or "no effect level" for known carcinogens. The food and chemical industry has been pushing for this for years. First, the approach ignores the fact that there are many carcinogens in the environment (everyone is exposed to them) and that carcinogenic effects are cumulative and irreversible. But secondly, Dr. Verrett attacks this programme on practical grounds. Instead of spending $300 million on this useless experiment, we could be testing 4,000 chemicals each on 500 mice, and by so doing we could filter out our strongest environmental carcinogens. This example illustrates where government priorities lie.

The fact is that the food corporations, who are in the business of making money, have repeatedly proven that they are willing to overlook dangers to human beings in their pursuit of profit.

Finally, we should not underestimate the role that food additives play in market control. Having products that will sit on the shelf for months without deteriorating is a major advantage to the large food corporations. They are able to distribute their products on a nation-wide basis from centralized locations. This is an important weapon in their war on the local food processors and the producers and distributors of fresh foods. Food additives have obviously been a major factor in the growth of horizontal market concentration.

The Disappearance of Taste

One of the by-products of corporate-style production of food is the disappearance of good old-fashioned taste. When basic foods are considered simply raw materials to be put through extensive processing, to which are added a seemingly endless string of chemicals, how could it be otherwise?

But the problem of taste goes back beyond the factory, to the production of the basic food itself. The socio-economic system under which we live promotes the development of corporate farming, even when it is operated by a single family. Large farming under our system, which emphasizes contract farming with food processing corporations, demands uniformity of product.

Remember all the different varieties of apples and soft fruits that used to be on the market? Fewer and fewer varieties are produced every year. The supermarkets don't want to bother handling a wide variety. Furthermore, with all the middlemen in the system, and the extensive handling and packaging of fruits and vegetables, varieties are being pushed because of their durability rather than their taste or nutritional value.

Red Delicious apples now sell in the supermarket all year round, thanks to controlled atmosphere storage. They are by far the biggest seller in North America, pushing most of the other varieties off the shelf. This apple was developed because it does not bruise easily and stores for a long time. The fact that it has a very poor taste and texture is immaterial. People are beginning to believe that the Red Delicious is the way apples always tasted, or are supposed to taste. Furthermore, apples are graded according to colour, not taste or nutritional quality. The emphasis on redness promotes the use of growth hormones simply for cosmetic purposes. The farmer has no control over this. The standards are set by the food industry and their partners in the government.

The tomato is another good example. University geneticists worked long hours to develop a tough tomato which could be mechanically harvested; now they are making them square, uniform in size, so that they can fit into the small boxes. They are picked green, boxed, placed in a room and sprayed with ethylene gas to make them uniformly "pink." Again, the fact that they are tasteless seems to make no difference. Consumers are encouraged to coat them with salad dressing. As one U.S. Department of Agriculture spokesman told Susan Demarko of the Agribusiness Accountability Project, "your children will never know the difference." They will never have tasted a real tomato.

The emphasis in producing new varieties of fruits and vegetables is on durability; if they can be mechanically harvested, they quickly take over the market. The carrots we buy in the store are largely one variety, developed to resist breaking by mechanical harvesters. Agriculture colleges have developed hard-headed lettuce, cantaloupe, asparagus, avocados and strawberries for mechanical harvesting. All have a very poor taste. Most of the time the customer can only buy Iceberg head lettuce in the store. Not only does it have almost no taste, it has only one-ninth the Vitamin A of leaf lettuce.

For farmers, the emphasis must be on quantity, not quality. They are paid to produce, and the more they produce from a particular area of land, the more they have a chance of breaking the cost-price squeeze. This applies to all forms of agriculture. Growers pour water and fertilizers on their fruits and vegetables to gain weight. Consumers pay more for the water and get less taste. As John and Karen Hess point out, this even affects the milk industry. The Jersey and Guernsey cows have disappeared from the pasture. They produced very rich milk. They have been replaced by the Holstein, which produces more milk with a lower butter level. Canada imports butter.

Does most of the cheese you eat taste bland? The wide variety of cheeses produced from local milk by the small factories have given way to the standardized product, including artificial colouring. To protect us against natural bacteria which bring taste to cheese, large corporations have convinced the government that all cheese should be pasteurized.

The Fast Food Phenomenon

One of the most notable developments in North America has been the rapid growth of the fast food outlets. Howard Johnson's pioneered in this area, but McDonald's now symbolizes the fact that more and more meals are being eaten out, not at the local restaurant, but at the specialized fast food outlet. More than anything else, McDonald's Restaurants symbolize the new tasteless America.

John and Karen Hess point out that when *Time Magazine* celebrated McDonald's Restaurants in 1973, Vance Packard commented that "this is what our country is all about—blandness and standardization." As one American novelist pointed out, whereas eating is considered a pleasure in most countries, this is not true in the United States. "Eating is just something done in response to advertising." The fast food explosion in Canada is a good example of how American corporate culture quickly moves in, and through mass advertising, takes over.

In 1976, the "Big Mac" gave the customer a beef patty at the rate of $4.00 a pound. Profit is the name of the game. Dr. Michael Jacobson, in his book *Nutrition Scoreboard,* gives a McDonald's meat patty eighteen points and Alpo dog food thirty. McDonald's "milkshakes" contain no milk; instead there is synthetic milk based on sodium caseinate, vegetable fat, emulsifiers, buffers, protein, stabilizers, body agents, sweeteners, artificial flavourings and colourings, and preservatives.

Frozen french fries are becoming standard items in the household kitchen as well as a basic component of the fast food operation. It is possible to reheat them, deep fry them, and make them crisp on the outside. But they will still be mushy and tasteless on the inside. *Food Processing* magazine claims that frozen french fries offer the largest profit margins for the fast food outlet next to soft drinks. In 1975, a serving cost five cents; the customer paid twenty cents.

Jim Hightower notes that fish caught for McDonald's "Filet O' Fish" sandwiches are treated on factory ships to remain white and to be odourless and tasteless. At the fish mill at Gloucester, Massachusetts, the fish, frozen in blocks, are sawed, thawed, breaded and refrozen, and shipped to the restaurants where they are deep fried. The result "tastes crisp." A sales manager argues that "we sell more fish now that it doesn't taste like fish."

The decline in nutrition in North America may in large part be due to the increase in food consumption out of home, in the fast food franchised chains. There are a lot of calories in the beef-patty burger, frozen french fries, and the chemical milk shake. But it is certainly not a balanced diet: it lacks basic vitamins and minerals. Dr. Jean Mayer, a Harvard nutritionist, has argued that a regular diet of McDonald's-style eating could bring back scurvy.

That Americans and Canadians are increasingly consuming less nutritious food should not come as a surprise. The food industry is emphasizing highly processed "convenience foods," fast foods purchased outside the home, and "snack foods" for children. Our schools provide very little in the area of nutritional education. The cafeterias serve the same corporate foods. For our society as a whole, knowledge of nutrition seems almost non-existent.

Dr. Abram Hoffer has pointed out that physicians who graduate from Canadian medical colleges know precious little about nutrition. Just recently the University of Toronto created a Department of Nutrition, the first in Canada. The Colleges of Home Economics and Food Science at our universities seem to have been created after a model provided by the large food corporations. Their graduates believe in highly processed technological foods.

But our doctors and home economists cannot be blamed for their lack of knowledge about basic nutrition. Individual Canadians cannot be blamed. The best intentions in the world could not counteract the massive advertising campaigns by the large food corporations.

The growth of malnutrition, diet-related diseases, poor eating habits, and the disappearance of taste is directly related to the structure of the food industry in North America. We are programmed to eat the way we do. As long as food is provided according to the profit motive, and consumption patterns are determined by mass advertising, this will be the case. In the face of this economic power, our regulatory agencies face an impossible task.

SOURCES

Abelson, Philip H., ed. *Food: Politics, Economics, Nutrition and Research.* Washington, D.C.: American Association for the Advancement of Science 1975.

Allaby, Michael, and Floyd Allen. *Robots Behind the Plow: Modern Farming and the Need for an Organic Alternative.* Emmaus, Pa.: Rodale Press, 1974.

Berg, Alan, and R. Muscat. *The Nutrition Factor: Its Role in National Development.* Washington, D.C.: Brookings Institute, 1973.

Bookchin, Murray, *Our Synthetic Environment*. N.Y.: Harper Colophon Books, 1974.

Carson, Rachel. *Silent Spring*. N.Y.: Houghton Mifflin Co., 1962.

Cheraskin, E., and W.M. Ringsdorf, Jr. *Psychodietetics*. Toronto: Bantam Books, 1974.

Frazier, Claude. *Coping with Food Allergy*. N.Y.: Quadrangle Books, 1974.

Graham, Frank Jr. *Since Silent Spring*. N.Y.: Houghton Mifflin, 1970.

Hall, Ross Hume. *Food for Nought: The Decline in Nutrition*. N.Y.: Vintage Books, 1974.

Hess, John L., and Karen Hess. *The Taste of America*. N.Y.: Grossman Publishers, 1977.

Hesch, Rick, Robin Karpin, and Carol Pearlstone. "The Safety for Humans of Beef and Pork in Canada." Unpublished manuscript, 1973.

Hightower, Jim. *Eat Your Heart Out: How Food Profiteers Victimize the Consumer*. N.Y.: Crown Publishers, 1975.

Hunter, Beatrice Trum. *Consumer Beware! Your Food and What's Been Done to It*. N.Y.: Simon and Schuster, 1971.

Hunter, Beatrice Trum. *Fact Book on Food Additives and Your Health*. New Cannan, Conn.: Keats Publishing Co., 1972.

Jelliffe, Derrick B., and E.F. Patrice Jelliffe. "Human Milk, Nutrition and the World Resources Crisis," in Philip H. Abelson, ed., *Food: Politics, Economics, Nutrition and Research*. Washington, D.C.: American Association for the Advancement of Science, 1975, pp. 65-69.

Jacobson, Michael. *Eater's Digest: The Consumer's Factbook of Food Additives*. Garden City, N.Y.: Doubleday Anchor Books, 1972.

Jacobson, Michael. *Nutrition Scoreboard*. Washington, D.C.: Center for Science in the Public Interest, July 1973.

Karamchandani, D.T. "Changes in Food Expenditure Patterns, 1969-1974," *Canadian Farm Economics*, XI, No. 5, October 1976, pp. 16-29.

Lappe, Francis Moore. *Diet for a Small Planet*. N.Y.: Ballantine Books, 1971.

Lerza, Catherine, and Michael Jacobson. *Food for People Not Profit*. N.Y.: Ballantine Books, 1975.

Lucas, Jack. *Our Polluted Food: A Survey of the Risks*. N.Y.: John Wiley and Sons, 1974.

Margolis, Sidney. *The Great American Food Hoax*. N.Y.: Dell Publishing Co., 1971.

Marine, Gene, and Judith Van Allen. *Food Pollution: The Violation of Our Inner Ecology*. N.Y.: Holt, Rinehart & Winston, 1972.

National Farmers Union. *Nature Feeds Us*. Saskatoon: Modern Press, 1976.

Nutrition Canada National Survey. *Nutrition: A National Priority*. Ottawa: Information Canada, 1973.

Robbins, William. *The American Food Scandal*. N.Y.: William Morrow & Co., 1974.

Schumacher, E.F. *Small is Beautiful*. London: Abacus Books, 1974.

Turner, James S. *The Chemical Feast*. N.Y.: Grossman Publishers, 1970.

United States. Department of Health, Education, and Welfare. *1868-70 Ten-State Nutrition Survey*. Washington, D.C.: U.S. Government Printing Office, 1972.

Verrett, Jacqueline, and Jean Carper. *Eating May be Hazardous to Your Health*. Garden City, N.Y.: Doubleday Anchor Books, 1975.

Wellford, Harrison. "Behind the Meat Counter," *Atlantic Monthly,* October 1972, pp. 86-90.

Wellford, Harrison. *Sowing the Wind*, N.Y.: Bantam Books, 1973.

Williams, Roger J. *Nutrition Against Disease*. N.Y.: Bantam Books, 1973.

Wirick, R.G. "A Preliminary Paper on Some Food Policy Aspects of Nutrition and Health." Ottawa: Food Prices Review Board, Reference Paper No. 8, unpublished, 1976.

Zwerdling, Daniel. "Drugs in the Meat Industry," *Ramparts*, XI, No. 12, June 1973, pp. 37-41.

11. CONCLUSION

Most of us are aware that Eugene Whelan, the federal Minister of Agriculture, repeatedly reminds us that Canadians on the average spend far less of their personal disposable income on food than do the vast majority of people in the world. Therefore, food prices should not bother us. But they do.

While the Consumers Association of Canada feels that farm incomes are too high, and that marketing boards protect "inefficient" farm operations at the expense of the consumer, farm organizations are always complaining about the cost-price squeeze.

Grocery products manufacturers, as well as wholesalers and retailers, are forever protesting the wages they have to pay. They argue that high wages are the major reason for high food prices. How valid are all these complaints?

Are Food Prices Too High?

On the average, there is no doubt that Canadians spend little of their take home pay on food compared to other countries. Table XIa reveals that in 1972 the average Canadian family spent only 17% of disposable income on food. Only Americans do better. In 1976, the average spent on food eaten at home was only 13%. This is a far cry from the 50% to 70% spent on food in many underdeveloped countries. It is much better than most European countries. Furthermore, as Table XIb reveals, the amount we spend on food has been declining over the years. For this reason, Statistics Canada has decided to reduce the food factor in the proposed new Consumer Price Index.

TABLE XIa

Expenditures for Food as a Percentage of Disposable Income

Country	1963	1972
United States	18.9	15.4
CANADA	20.5	17.5
The Netherlands	26.2	22.0
France	34.9	23.4
Belgium	29.9	24.1
West Germany	30.4	24.2
Luxembourg	32.2	25.2
Japan	32.3	26.0
Sweden	28.8	27.1
Austria	37.8	28.6
United Kingdom	34.1	29.8
Greece	42.5	32.6
Finland	46.5	33.6
Italy	39.9	33.6
Ireland	46.5	37.8

SOURCE: Working Paper #1, Committee for Agriculture, OECD. Reprinted in *Canadian Farm Economics*, Vol. 10, No. 5, p. 10.

However, averages can be quite misleading. We don't live in an egalitarian, socialist society. There are gross inequalities of wealth and income in Canada, as in all the capitalist countries. There is no such thing as a "rich world" and a "hungry world." The wealthiest capitalist countries all have a segment of the population that is living in poverty, suffering from an inadequate diet. Furthermore, in even the poorest capitalist countries of the underdeveloped world there is a segment of the population that is well off and certainly not hungry.

In Canada there is a sizeable section of the population that is living in poverty and that finds it difficult to acquire a nutritionally adequate diet. How poverty is defined is a matter of dispute. In 1968, the Economic Council of Canada declared that poverty existed when an individual or a family had to spend 70% or more of its income on the basic necessities of life: food, clothing, and shelter. This put poverty at a subsistence level.

A second definition was offered by Ian Adams and his colleagues, who worked as the staff for the Special Senate Committee on Poverty. They argued that poverty was relative to a society's general standard of living. They drew the poverty line at one-half the average standard of living of all Canadians, and adjusted figures for size of family. They concluded that in 1969, 21% of the population were living below their "Relative Poverty Line." Another 14% were living below the "Near Poverty Line," people whose income was only two-thirds of the Canadian average.

TABLE XIb

Personal Expenditures on Goods and Services in Canada (Percentages)

Category	1952	1962	1972
Food and Non-Alcoholic Beverages	20.3	18.1	15.6
Alcohol and Tobacco	6.9	6.8	6.6
Clothing and Footwear	9.3	8.7	8.4
Gross Rent, Fuel and Power	15.1	18.7	20.4
Furnishings, Household Equip. and Serv.	11.2	10.3	10.8
Medical Care and Health Serv.	5.4	4.4	3.1
Transportation and Communications	12.3	14.1	15.6
Recreation, Educ. and Entertainment	5.9	6.3	8.9
Personal Goods and Services	13.6	12.6	10.6

SOURCE: Statistics Canada, *Perspective Canada*. Ottawa: Information Canada, 1974, Table 8.3, p. 182.

Many people mistakenly believe that the extensive social welfare system in Canada has gone far towards reducing inequalities. This is not the case. Statistics Canada reports that in 1975 the poorest 20% in Canada were receiving only 6.1% of total income, down slightly from 6.5% in 1965, and up only slightly from 4.4% in 1951. On the other hand, the richest 20% of the population received 46.9% of all income in 1975, up slightly from 45.2% in 1965 and up from 42.8% in 1951.

This conclusion was supported by a study done by Professor W. Irwin Gillespie for the C.D. Howe Institute, published in April 1978. He found that the social insurance system in Canada didn't protect the poor from inflation, but benefitted the highest income and/or the lower-middle income families.

In March 1973, the National Council of Welfare released a report on food and malnutrition among the poor in Canada. They noted that the Special Senate Committee on Poverty concluded that 25% of Canadians were living below the poverty line. In these cases, food was the largest portion of the family's total spending. But the poor in

Canada are not only those on welfare and unemployment; 63% of those below the poverty line are "the working poor," people with jobs who had inadequate or barely adequate income.

The low income people in Canada suffer from malnutrition and are more susceptible to various diseases and disorders. The National Council of Welfare cited a 1971 survey of 3,500 children in Montreal. City health officials found more than half of the children physically sick, 10% required immediate hospitalization, and "poor kids' diseases" like anemia, rickets, impetigo, and upper respiratory infection were "widespread." The health officials attributed the poor health to inadequate diets.

In December 1971 a survey was made of people in Toronto living on welfare. After making the required outlays for housing, essential personal expenses, clothing and emergencies, welfare recipients were left with only fifty cents per day per person to spend on food, or seventeen cents a meal! In other areas of Canada, where the cost of housing was lower, welfare recipients were allocated between twenty-eight and thirty-three cents per person per meal.

But when there is a sudden increase in the price of food, it is more than just the poor who are effected. When the price of food rose in an unusual manner in 1973-1974, this upset the budgets of all Canadians except those in the upper income brackets. The fact that the increases were almost entirely due to international markets and weather factors was no consolation.

In reality, most Canadians spend far more than 15.6% of their take home pay on food. Actual spending was documented by Statistics Canada in their 1974 Family Food Expenditure Survey, which covered 5,000 families living in fourteen urban centres across Canada.

For a family of four in 1974 whose income was under $6,000, the average spent on food was 28%. For those in the lowest income brackets, 40% to 50% was spent on food. A family of four had to have an income of around $18,000 a year in order to get their food expenditure down to 15% of their take home pay.

For a substantial (but diminishing) segment of the population, food costs are not really that crucial to their existence. They do not worry about price. And they throw away enormous amounts of food. For several years, a group of anthropologists at the University of Arizona have been studying the living habits of 1,200 families in Tucson by carefully examining what they throw out in their garbage. They estimate that each year the 400,000 people in Tucson throw away more than 10,000 tons of edible food, valued at around $12 million.

Lack of nutrition is not limited to the poor, however. The nutrition studies done in Canada and the United States have documented the decline in nutritional level of food consumed by all income groups.

We also know that in spite of the fact that we spend more per capita on health care than any other country in the world, and in spite of the great advances in medicine and science, the general health of Canadians is declining. All Canadians, regardless of class or economic status, are victims of the corporate culture of food production and consumption.

Are Wages Responsible for High Food Costs?

Most of us are aware of the repeated claims by the spokesmen for the food and beverage industry in Canada that "high wage demands" are responsible for prices which are considered high by consumers. Nevertheless, average wages in the food and beverage industry in Canada have historically been below the average earned by all workers in manufacturing. There are two factors that account for this.

In 1971, about 71% of all employees in manufacturing in Canada were covered by contracts negotiated by trade unions; in the food and beverage industry, only 54% of employees were covered by negotiated contracts. Where trade unions exist, wages are generally higher.

The other factor is the relatively high percentage of women workers, and the fact that in Canada (and in the United States) there is an historic pattern of paying women less than men, even for equal work. In 1969, women workers accounted for 22.9% of workers in all manufacturing; they were 26.9% of the work force in the food and beverage industry, and their weekly wages averaged 47% less than their male counterparts.

Furthermore, within the industry itself, wages vary greatly. In 1971 the average hourly wage was $3.55 in the red meat processing industry (17.6% women workers), the only segment of the food and beverage industry where wages were above the average for all manufacturing, which was $2.95 per hour. In fish processing (38.6% women workers) the average hourly wage was $2.00; in fruit and vegetable processing (44.6% women workers), $2.45; and in confectionery manufacturing (59.2% women workers), $2.49.

Under the leadership of Beryl Plumptre and Jean Luc Pepin, the Food Prices Review Board established a reputation as a propaganda organ for the corporate sector of the food industry in Canada. Yet even this group had to admit that increases in wages in the food and beverage industry between 1968 and 1972 were only "a small fraction of the price increases recorded for these industries." They also found that in the food processing and distribution industries, the non-wage items in the collective agreements tended to lag two to six years behind manufacturing as a whole.

The other major area of employment in the food industry is at the retail level. As in the manufacturing sector, wages vary widely according to province and region, as well as to degree of unionization. However, the industry averages for 1970, as published by Statistics Canada, do not reveal that wages in this area are out of line with other sectors of the economy. The retail stores hire a substantial proportion of part-time workers, and their wages tend to be substantially below those of full-time workers. Male workers tend to be higher paid (by a considerable rate) and are more likely to be the full-time workers. For part-time or casual workers, there is less discrepancy in wages between men and women.

In 1970, the average hourly wage for full-time, part-time, and casual employees in retail trade in general was $2.45 an hour; for food stores, it was $2.69. The average hourly wage for the similar group in department stores was $2.33. The difference can be attributed to the extent of trade union involvement. In the retail food industry, a very high proportion of workers are unionized; in department stores, unions are almost non-existent.

Finally, a word must be added regarding the other wage-earning sector of the food industry: farm labour. As the statistics reveal, hired farm labour has been rapidly disappearing in Canada with mechanization. Yet "hired hands" are still important, particularly during harvest seasons. As a general rule, farm workers are in the lowest income area of working Canadians. Most get little more than the minimum wage, cannot obtain full-time work, and are not provided with the basic protections of provincial labour legislation.

Trade unions are almost non-existent in this area in Canada. This is undoubtedly due to the fact that corporate-style farming is not as advanced in Canada as it is in the United States, where large pools of migrant workers are the norm. How long this will be the case is a matter of speculation. The Federal Task Force on Agriculture predicted in their 1990 model for Canadian agriculture that there will be a "drastic reduction in farm population," and with the rise of corporate farming, there will be "a high and rising proportion of farm workers becoming employees working for salaries and wages." Under such a development (which they support) "farm employee unions may emerge and become a factor in the bargaining process."

The Farming Sector

If we are to believe the pronouncements of the Food Prices Review Board, farmers are the only people getting rich under our system of production and distribution of food. But over the years there has been a rapid flight of farmers from the land. In 1951, farmers represented 21% of the labour force; by 1971, they had fallen to 6%. Over this twenty year period, the number of farms in Canada declined by 70%. In most cases farmers do not leave the land of their own free will; they are driven off by economic pressures. Young people find they do not have the capital to get on the land or else conclude that it is too much work for too little return.

Most people have heard of the "cost-price squeeze." How does it work? Between 1946 and 1967, the average annual increase in the cost of all non-agricultural goods and services was between 7% and 8%. During this same period, the average annual increase in the price of agricultural and fishing products was only 2%.

As a result of this, farmers are squeezed off the land, or must find off-farm work. According to the 1971 census, 50% of all farmers in Canada had off-farm work, and the wages earned accounted for 40% of their total income. In 1950, off-farm work accounted for only 10% of total farm income.

While the professional economists insist that farmers must operate in a "free enterprise" system where they compete against each other and against imports from low wage countries, the Canadian farmer faces monopoly power in all his major farm supply inputs. The farm machinery industry operates as an informal cartel, as the Barber Royal Commission documented. The petroleum industry is one of the oldest cartels. All of the fertilizer industries (nitrogen, phosphate and potash) have long histories of combines and international cartels. Pesticides are manufactured by the large multi-national chemical companies, where national combines and international cartels have existed since the inter-war period. The motor vehicle industry is highly monopolized, with a recognized system of price leadership. The banks are a government supported monopoly in Canada.

At the other end, the farmer must sell in a market controlled by fewer and fewer corporate chains of wholesalers and retailers. The efforts by Canadian farmers to create co-operatives, state enterprises, and marketing boards have always been opposed and fought by these interests. That is why farmers are so quick to denounce those economists who insist that they alone should operate in a state of free competition while everyone else operates according to an entirely different system.

Because of the cost-price squeeze, net income for farmers has always been relatively low. Net income for all farmers in Canada peaked in 1951, but this level was not reached again until 1966. When international grain prices fell, so did net income; when prices dropped in 1976, so did net income. The decline in the rate of inflation in 1976 was almost entirely due to a drop in farm income.

National figures on farm income can be greatly misleading. There is a tendency in Canada to look at national figures and assume that these trends are typical, regardless of the commodity produced, or where the farmer lives. When prairie grain farmers do well, everyone assumes that all farmers are well off. This is very often not the case, as in the period between 1972 and 1974 when producers who used feed as a major farm input were having disastrous years.

Grain farmers, whose prices are set largely by international factors, have typically had boom and bust periods. But over the long haul, neither they nor other farmers have been getting rich at the expense of the public. The grain farmer received less than two cents for that loaf of bread sold in the supermarket in the mid-1970s.

The year 1966 was a good year for grain farmers. Yet in that year 55% of the 420,000 farm families in Canada had net incomes of under $5,000. Using the definition of poverty set by the Economic Council of Canada, in 1966 about 150,000 farm families were living at or below the poverty level. Statistics Canada reports that in 1971 across Canada, only 15.9% of all families were living at a "low income" level, which they set at less than $4,000 for a family of five. Yet in that year 43.5% of farm families were placed in this "low income" bracket, by far the highest of any class of working people.

It is true, of course, that farm families have certain advantages that are not available to urban wage earners or people on fixed incomes. They have the tax advantages that the Canadian capitalist system gives to businesses but are not available to those on wages and salaries. They have the land to grow much of their own food. Thus, there is undoubtedly some truth to the common belief that farm families can live on lower cash incomes.

A few economists have recently attempted to determine the real income of farm families by placing a value on these "hidden" advantages. By including off-farm income, rental value of the house, and capital gains in property, Don McClatchy and Catherine Campbell concluded that total farm income on the average is roughly equal to that of industrial workers.

Another study was done by George Brinkman and Jack Gellner of the School of Agricultural Economics at Guelph. They found that commercial farmers in Ontario (with gross sales of more than $50,000 per year) had a net income that was roughly equal to that of self-employed businessmen. As farm sales dropped, so did their ratio of income compared to that of small businessmen.

Farmers are quick to point out two problems with such studies. First, capital gains are included; these are not part of a farm family's income until they sell out or retire, when the capital gain serves as their pension. In the Brinkman-Gellner study, capital gains represented

35% of the farm's total returns over the period studied.

The other items not included in most of these assessments are the hours of labour by the farmer (compared to the urban worker), and the unpaid family labour on the farm. For most farmers, the farm wife is now the "hired man," often putting in the equivalent of the farmer in hours of farm labour, and then, of course, also running the house.

But even if it is conceded that the average commercial farm in Canada has an income equal to that of the industrial worker, it should be evident that farmers have not been getting rich at the expense of the consumer.

Farmers' Efforts to Protect Their Interests

In Canada, farmers have tried to save themselves from the persistent cost-price squeeze largely through the formation of co-operatives, marketing boards and farm organizations. On the local level, co-operatives have certainly helped to curb some of the worst abuses of the private enterprise system. But co-ops have certainly not proven to be the answer. Where they have become successful (as in the wheat pools on the prairies or the milk co-operatives in Quebec) they have become large, bureaucratic organizations. Farmers find them beyond their control or even influence. All too often the large co-operatives work together with the large monopoly corporations, finding that they have more in common with big business than they do with their owners, the farmers.

The other approach has been the creation of producer-directed marketing boards. There are well over 100 of these in Canada. However, only in a few areas do they have any control over the production or prices: milk, eggs, poultry, and flue-cured tobacco. In all other cases, the marketing boards serve only as central selling agencies.

Marketing boards are certainly no threat to private corporate control of the food industry. Even where they are effective, they guarantee the processing firms a steady supply of the basic food product. In no case does a marketing board cut into the share of the consumer's dollar that goes to the processors, wholesalers, and retailers.

Nevertheless, the Consumers Association of Canada, and a number of "free enterprise" college professors, have claimed that marketing boards result in abnormally high costs to consumers, at least in those areas where there is some form of production or price control. It is curious that much of this criticism comes from college professors, whose incomes average more than twice that of farmers, who are

261

protected from competition for their jobs by tenure and the old boy system, and who are protected against low-wage imports from other countries.

In recent years we have heard endless complaints about the Canadian Egg Marketing Agency. When it was established in 1973, there was an increase of 44% in egg prices. Since then there have been yearly changes, up and down; in February 1978 egg prices were up 86% over 1971. Yet this compares to a 92% increase in all food prices in the Consumer Price Index.

On the other hand, we should not underestimate the importance of marketing boards to farmers as selling agencies. Farm work is a full-time job, to say the least, and only a few farmers are large enough to be able to hire a highly qualified man to do their work while they run off trying to sell their product.

Marketing boards also provide the farmer with a better chance to obtain a reasonable price. One has only to look at the reasons why farmers created them in the first place. In most cases, boards were the result of a long struggle against brokers and wholesalers who exploited farmers in many different ways. Without central selling agencies, there would still be thousands of farmers each trying to sell his product individually in a highly oligopolized market—a grossly unequal power situation. One has only to read the history of the organization of the Tree Fruits Marketing Board in British Columbia to understand how the system of "free enterprise for farmers only" works. Even after the growers had formed their own co-operative packing houses, the wholesalers would play one off against the other to drive down prices. Wholesalers were even turning in claims for "damaged fruit" before they had received it. The central selling agency had to be established in an attempt to improve the fruit growers' bargaining power.

Finally, marketing boards allow farmers to distribute their products more evenly over a longer period of time and to reach markets that were otherwise closed. In the fruit and vegetable industries, farmer pooling has permitted the construction of large cold-storage units that would be beyond the reach of individual farmers or co-operative packing houses. Consumers benefit by having locally grown produce, which always sells for a lower price, over a longer period of time.

But even where marketing boards have been able to control supply of produce and price, the farmers have not been able to increase their standard of living significantly. Dairy, poultry, and egg farmers may have a large equity built up in their operation, but their net income is low compared to other farmers. Even the Food Prices Review Board had to conclude that "the part of the agricultural economy experiencing one of the smallest relative gains in net income was dairying, which is more regulated and subsidized than any other agricultural sector.''

The reasons are simple. In all cases, the marketing board is selling in a highly concentrated market, with only a few major buyers. It is very dependent on a few large wholesale corporations. It is also faced with an almost completely open border which allows the importation of fresh and processed foods from lower wage areas. And it is also a fact that the chain supermarkets most often use fresh or non-processed foods as loss leaders. Under such circumstances, marketing boards simply can't set prices.

As well there is the fact that there are absolutely no controls over the prices of farm inputs. These monopolized industries are in the nice position of being able to simply raise prices when they feel like it. When farm prices go up, the price of farm inputs usually goes up even more. Thus, when prices rise at the farm gate, there is certainly no guarantee that net income will rise correspondingly.

Finally, the farmers have tried to solve their problems through the formation of farm organizations and by taking direct political action. For Canadian farmers, this may be part of their problem. They have followed the American pattern of farm organization rather than that of the United Kingdom or continental Europe. Thus, Canadian farmers are split into seemingly hundreds of independent commodity groups, operating on a provincial basis. Divide and conquer works well in this situation.

In contrast, all farmers in the U.K. belong to one organization, the National Farmers Union, and this gives them far greater political and economic power. The farmers within the European Common Market have long been organized into farmers unions and have been able to obtain a net income roughly equal to that of industrial workers. Indeed, Rene Dumont, writing in 1969 supporting the extension of American-style mechanized farming, complains about the power of the European farmers to force governments to ''prevent decreases in peasant income.'' He finds that prices have become ''political prices,'' fixed by ''bitter negotiations between the government and the farmers unions.''

The Marketing Sector

While the Canadian farmer has been producing more food at what can only be considered reasonable prices, a larger and larger proportion of the consumer's food dollar has been going to the ''marketing'' sector of the food and beverage industry. As Table XIc illustrates, between 1949 and 1973 the farm share of the consumer's dollar fell from 60% to 37%.

TABLE XIc

Food Costs: From Farmer to Consumer

Year	Retail Value ($ Millions)	Farm Receipts ($ Millions)	Marketing Costs ($ Millions)	Farm Value as % of Total
1949	2,064	1,243	821	60
1955	3,029	1,499	1,530	49
1960	4,191	1,765	2,426	42
1965	5,224	2,295	2,929	44
1970	7,000	2,775	4,225	40
1971	7,600	2,800	4,800	37
1973	11,300	4,200	7,100	37

SOURCE: Department of Agriculture, Economic Research Branch.

The trends in the food and beverage industry in Canada are quite evident. There is a steady growth in concentration in all of the individual food manufacturing industries. The mortality rate of the small firm in all areas continues to be high. The level of concentration varies according to industry; the determining factor appears to be the real market. Industries which have a relatively low level of concentration on a national basis (e.g., milk, bakery goods, poultry, feed, and soft drinks) have a high degree of concentration on the regional or local level.

At the same time, the 1960s and 1970s have produced the large conglomerate firm. Traditional measurements of market concentration simply cannot deal with this development. The economic (and political) power of a very small number of food firms is greatly enhanced by the expansion of the firm into many different areas of the food industry. No longer is it possible to identify the large firms with a single product. Against this development, the small, regional, single-product firm has a diminishing chance for survival.

The other major development is the expansion of vertical integration. This is now a normal characteristic of both food processing and food distributing firms. Again, vertical integration is limited to the large firms and provides them with a measure of economic power which is simply not available to the small firm.

In the retail and wholesale area, there has been a steady growth of market domination by the large corporate chains. The independent grocers are rapidly disappearing; their services are being replaced by the corporate chains of "convenience" stores. Even the independents

264

which are associated with the voluntary chains are in a weakening position, steadily losing their share of the market to the corporate chains.

Clearly, this is the era of the large food corporation, operating as a conglomerate. There is no such thing as "price competition" as it is described in the traditional neo-classical economics textbooks used in our colleges and universities.

Studies in Canada and the United States reveal that there is a close correlation between the existence of oligopoly, monopolistic practices by the large firms, high spending on advertising and product differentiation, and higher profits. The evidence demonstrates that the large firms in the oligopolistic markets are earning higher than average profits. In this case, classical liberal economic theory has proven true: the absence of "price competition" leads to exploitation of farmers, workers and consumers in the market place.

At the same time, we should recognize that what is happening in this area in Canada is a normal development under the capitalist system of production. Geographic centralization is occurring in all the capitalist economies. The fall of the small firm before the onslaught of the giant corporation is happening everywhere. In no advanced capitalist state does the government act as a protector of the farmer and the consumer against the rise of monopolistic corporations. In fact, the record everywhere is clear: governments in the capitalist economy act as partners to the large corporations.

It is a normal process under the capitalist system of production for firms to concentrate on the increased use of capital as an input, leading to a reduction in the use of labour. In Canada, when governments provide "incentives" to industry to invest, or expand, this invariably results in increased use of technology and machinery and less use of labour. As recounted in a classic illustration before, this is precisely what happened under the incentives programmes in the processed cheese industry in Ontario.

Geographic centralization of population is also an inevitable development of capitalism, where planning is done by the corporations on the basis of maximizing profits. The trends are very clear in Canada. But this makes local, decentralized, regional enterprises "inefficient" and accelerates the centralizing process. Only in a planned economy, where values other than maximization of profits are used, could such a trend be held back or reversed.

The other major focus of this survey has been the role of the U.S. firm in the Canadian food economy. The large and growing firms in the food processing industry in Canada are primarily foreign-owned firms, and most of these are American. There are fewer than ten Canadian firms which have the size and economic power to compete successfully with the large foreign-owned food and beverage corporations. The Canadian firms are almost invariably the smaller firms, regionally based, with lower profit rates, and persistent economic difficulties.

I don't think it is out of place to re-emphasize the fact that Canada is not an independent country in the matter of production, manufacturing, distribution, or even eating of food. We follow the American example. This is partly due to the existence of our "colonial mentality" which leads too many Canadians to believe that whatever the U.S. does must be best, or better than anything Candians might do on their own. But more accurately it is a reflection of the fact that Canada is a political, economic, and cultural dependency of the United States.

It was no accident that the American food corporations moved first into Canada. This country has always been a mere extension of the American market. The large food firms, emphasizing highly advertised products, had the advantage of a market already familiar with their brands. The marketing advantage to the American firm due to overflow advertising cannot be overestimated. This factor creates marketing difficulties for even the largest of Canadian food manufacturers.

The Cheap Food Policy

Farmers are always talking about the "cheap food policy." For consumers, this is hard to understand, for food never seems cheap. But as farm spokesmen repeatedly point out, food at the farm gate has not risen anywhere near as fast as other consumer commodities. Even when it has passed through the processing and distribution system, food is a good buy, relative to other commodities.

The "cheap food policy" has been followed by successive federal governments since the 1930s. Food prices in Canada are kept at a low level (relative to food prices in other countries, and to other commodities) so that Canadians will have more income to spend on other consumer commodities.

This has been achieved by two means. First, there have been a minimum number of direct subsidies to farmers. While the public knows that the Canadian farmer receives a number of subsidies, they are less than those in any other advanced capitalist country, even the United States which is considered to be the epitome of the "free market" economy. There is no system of parity pricing, setting farm prices to match increases in prices in general. For years this was a demand by farmers attempting to combat the cost-price squeeze. It has recently been revived by the new Canadian Agriculture Movement.

The second technique is to all but eliminate tariffs and quotas on imported fresh and processed foods. Farm prices in Canada are depressed due to the availability of low priced imports from countries where there is greater exploitation of labour (like South Africa, Mexico, Taiwan, and South Korea) or else greater government support for agricultural exports through direct subsidies (as in the case of fruit from Australia).

The Costs of the Present System

The costs to consumers from the present system are high. First, there are the excessive prices we must pay due to the oligopolistic nature of the food industry and its inefficiencies. The cost of monopoly power is difficult to measure.

In 1972, the economic staff of the U.S. Federal Trade Commission examined thirteen food industries which had a high degree of oligopoly. They estimated that the lack of price competition in these industries cost American consumers an additional $2.1 billion for food in 1971. The U.S. Senate Anti-trust and Monopoly Subcommittee, under the direction of Senator Philip Hart, estimated that the cost to the American consumer may be as high as forty cents on the dollar. Professor Charles Mueller, one of the best known American experts on monopoly, wrote in 1970 that this forty cent figure "may well turn out to be on the low side if a program of serious reform is ever actually undertaken and the real extent of the over-pricing in these industries is exposed to the light of day." Undoubtedly the same judgements can be applied to the Canadian industry, which is more highly monopolized.

Most Canadians have high enough incomes to afford even inflated prices for food. But all Canadians suffer from the quality of food that we eat, as reflected in the growing rate of illness due to poor diet. We are all victims of the fact that our governments do such an inadequate job of policing the food industry to ensure the quality of food. Every day we are ingesting accidental and deliberate food additives which are known to produce long-term illnesses. The fact that so little is spent on controlling the quality of food we eat is a reflection of the reality that our governments do not really protect *our* interests, but are dominated by the corporate ideology which has a stranglehold on our country.

The Consumers Association of Canada and other interests have regularly supported the cheap food policy. The basic idea behind this policy is that we should not bother to produce food when it can be bought cheaper in other countries. The fact that food from less developed countries is "cheap" due to super-exploitation of local people by the large corporations is not considered a relevant factor.

Canadians want high wages. Yet they also seem to want low-priced food imported from the United States. Currently, U.S. costs are lower than those in Canada, and wages are an important factor. We can't have it both ways.

There is also the fact that the Canadian climate inevitably puts Canadian producers at a disadvantage in the production of food. There is almost no food that cannot be produced cheaper in some other country. Should we then carry this policy to its logical conclusion and stop growing food?

In a narrow, short run view, importing food can provide some immediate savings to consumers—provided some of the price differentials are passed on to the consumers by the corporations. But there are also heavy costs which should not be ignored, though they are often difficult to put in terms of real dollars.

Farmers are driven off the land, leading to the destruction of rural communities. We are experiencing the loss of farm land in commercial production. As long as we are prepared to rely on imports, then there is no need to preserve our limited, good agricultural land. Furthermore, when farmers and rural communities disappear, this contributes to the increased overpopulation of the few very large metropolitan centres in Canada. All of us are familiar with the problems of living in these huge sprawling areas.

We know that there is a steady rise in unemployment and a drop in the number of workers in the food industry (relative to population growth and food consumption). Because of the pressure of cheap imports, we have lower wages on the farm and in our food industries. Canadians are threatened by the large corporations; if we don't accept the prices offered for farm food, or the wages offered, then the plant will shut down and the goods will be imported from abroad.

The general public pays for all this through higher taxes. Our unemployment is higher than any of the other advanced capitalist countries. We have the costs of unemployment insurance plus welfare, not to mention the loss in productive capacities of the underemployment of the population.

The cheap food policy also contributes to the growing balance of payments deficit that Canada faces. The Agricultural Economics Research Council of Canada pointed out to the 1978 symposium on Canada and World Food that two-thirds of the commodities that are imported are also grown commercially in Canada, and that Canadian farmers could easily meet the production challenge. Bananas and plantation crops are only a small part of food imports.

Our trade in food reflects the "hewers of wood, drawers of water" economic strategy now in force in Canada. Our major exports are in the cereal grains; wheat and barley account for well over half of the value of Canada's exports of food, feed, beverages, and tobacco. These are unprocessed raw materials. In 1977, Canada ran a $1 billion deficit in agricultural trade outside of grains, and a growing percentage of these imports is in manufactured goods.

We also pay heavily for foreign ownership of the food industry through the annual outflow of interest, dividends, fees and service charges paid out by the Canadian branch plants to their parent corporations. Between 1973 and 1977, our net foreign indebtedness rose from $4.2 billion to $32.4 billion. This meant that it took only four years to equal the volume of foreign debt of the first ninety-eight years of Confederation.

While the dramatic devaluation of the Canadian dollar has improved Canada's merchandise trade balance, we face the prospect of increasingly borrowing abroad just to repay the interest on our past borrowings. For 1977, economists were predicting a deficit on balances of services at $7.6 billion. In interest alone, Canada would send $1.26 billion more out of the country than foreigners would send here in interest on money they have borrowed in the Canadian capital markets. The present cheap food policy not only undermines Canadian industry and jobs, it promotes further foreign domination of the industry.

Finally, we must recognize that the cheap food policy mainly benefits the large multinational corporations. They are free to shift food production around the world to maximize profits. The "open door" to importing into Canada gives them a significant cost advantage over the smaller Canadian firms which are more likely to purchase their basic foods from Canadian farmers. Thus, we see the rather strange alliance between the Consumers Association of Canada and the large corporations, both seeking to strike down tariffs and quota protections for Canadian producers, manufacturers, and food industry workers.

What then are the possible and probable alternatives for Canada? Briefly, we should look at the solutions advocated and try to judge whether they are real alternatives.

The Liberal Option: Competition Policy and Government Regulation

Most economists trained in the universities of the advanced capitalist countries firmly believe in the competitive market economy.

269

They often admit, however, that "imperfect competition" can occur. Eventually though, they tell us this will sort itself out through the natural balancing of the market.

However, in an era which is marked by a steady move towards concentration and monopoly power, this ivory tower theory seems wanting. As a result, some of the more "progressive" liberal economists have argued that we need a government anti-combines policy to preserve the market economy. It simply takes too long for the market to sort itself out, and in the meantime consumers are victims of monopolistic practices.

A second major argument in support of a government anti-combines policy was set out by the Economic Council of Canada in their *Interim Report on Competition Policy*. They argue that if the competitive market system does not work, then there will be public pressure for other forms of control. There could be regulatory commissions, as there now are for public utilities. This however, would require greater government involvement in the economy, which is deemed undesirable.

Furthermore, the Economic Council of Canada believes that if there is an increase in monopolies and centralized economic power there will be greater public demand for social ownership of industry. This also is viewed as undesirable.

There is a very weak tradition for anti-combines policy in Canada. The first act was passed in 1888, mainly at the instigation of small businesses which were being swallowed up by the large, growing corporations. As the merger movement expanded in the first part of the twentieth century, public pressure for some action increased.

As a result Mackenzie King brought in the Combines Investigation Act of 1910. It was based on King's theory that public disclosure of monopolistic practices would be adequate; the general public, through their "free market buying," would penalize the offending corporations. During its nine years of operation the Act was invoked only once; at the same time, there were more than 200 major mergers.

Over the years, there were minor changes made in the legislation. But the central feature of the Combines Investigation Act was that it simply was not enforced. The total ineffectiveness of the act was dramatized in 1948 when the Combines Commissioner, F.A. McGregor, resigned when the King Government refused to take any action on the flour milling combine.

Further legislation appeared after the report of the Committee to Study Combines Legislation, headed by Mr. Justice J.H. MacQuarrie. Monopolies were now an offence only if they operated "to the detriment or against the interest of the public." Combines were illegal only if they "unduly" lessened competition. There was still little

270

CONCLUSION

enforcement.

On the few occasions when the federal government took action, the courts supported the interests of the large corporations. Following the decisions of the courts in the B.C. Sugar Refineries Case (1960) and the Canadian Breweries Case (1960), the Combines Commissioner decided it wasn't even worth the effort to try to block the takeover of Wilsil and Calgary Packers by Canada Packers.

In 1971, the Trudeau Government introduced the first of its many Competition Bills into the House of Commons. During the first ten years of the Trudeau Government there have been seven different Ministers of Consumer and Corporate Affairs, six Deputy Ministers, and the bill has not yet been completely adopted.

W.T. Stanbury, who has made a study of how business interests influenced this piece of legislation, concluded that it failed because "there does not exist in Canada any fundamental belief in the virtues of competition as the method of allocating scarce resources and of diffusing economic and political power."

But the lack of an anti-combines policy in Canada should not come as a surprise. Such a policy would be entirely foreign to the Canadian pattern of capitalist development. From the beginning, Canadian governments have been the partners of business, not their controllers. We have only to recall the building of the canals, the creation of the great land companies, the building of the railroads, the settlement of the West, and the "bonuses" offered to industry.

Today there exists a myriad of federal, provincial and municipal systems of subsidies for private enterprise. Through tariff and taxation policies, the federal government has played a major role in the formation of capital in Canada—for private interests.

For those who think the Trudeau Government has been changing course, the facts belie such a supposition. In 1971 the firms in Canada with assets of over $100 million paid the lowest effective rate of corporation taxes. The tax structure, which provides benefits in the form of capital costs allowances, depletion allowances, investment credits, exploration and development credits, all favour the large corporations. The Trudeau Government's policy of allowing corporations to defer taxes (in reality, long-term interest-free loans) has been a subsidy to the largest corporations: 68% of the deferrals in 1971 went to the eighty-three largest corporations.

A final example here will again illustrate the problem. In 1975 Prime Minister Trudeau appointed the Royal Commission on Corporate Concentration. All three of the commissioners had strong connections with big business. To no one's surprise, their report issued in 1978 found that there was nothing wrong with the merger movement and the rise of the conglomerate firm. Indeed, they argued

271

that concentration should be accepted, and even encouraged, in order to make Canadian corporations more capable of competing in the international market against the foreign-based multinationals.

The other major problem facing the food and beverage industry is the steady growth of ownership and control by large foreign-owned corporations. The liberal regulation approach is represented by the Foreign Investment Review Agency, created by the Trudeau Government in 1973. First, FIRA made no attempt to control expansion of foreign ownership in Canada by existing corporations (they are simply re-investing profits that they have extracted from Canadian consumers and workers). Thus, FIRA has eliminated from regulation the source of over 80% of all new foreign investment in Canada. In 1976, re-invested earnings by U.S. subsidiaries alone topped $2.5 billion.

It is widely recognized that FIRA is a bad joke on the Canadian public. In 1977, at the height of the problem caused by the outflow of capital from Canada, FIRA was approving 90% of all takeover proposals. The Minister of Industry Trade and Commerce, who is responsible for FIRA, told a meeting of Chicago businessmen that "FIRA is first and foremost a service agency . . . and I intend to reduce the popular notion that it is a restricting agency rather than a consulting agency."

Barron's, one of the best known American financial magazines, stated that "it is difficult to imagine a legitimate business venture which would be impeded by the Foreign Investment Review Act." It concluded that "the only U.S. business which wouldn't be cordially welcomed to Canada is Murder Inc."

Thus, I would argue that those who hope for competition policy, or government regulation of monopoly and foreign-ownership, are at best naive. Such an approach is out of character with Canada's long tradition. Furthermore, it ignores the fact of economic and political power.

This is what is wrong with the approach of John F. Bulloch and the Canadian Federation of Independent Business. Without a doubt it is possible to put forth a series of alternate economic policies for Canada which would benefit the small and medium-sized enterprises. CFIB has been pushing such policies for years. But when their proposals run contrary to the interests of the large corporations, they are ignored. It is about time the CFIB and other groups recognize that influence over government policy by the large corporations is not just an accident; it is, in fact, a characteristic of the advanced capitalist system, and it is inherent in the system itself. Even an NDP Government would be unlikely to introduce significant changes in the laws governing business practices in Canada.

The Alternative of Capitalist Self-Sufficiency

There exists in the world at this time a clear alternative to the Canadian and American general policy of "free trade." The European Economic Community (to which Great Britain now belongs) maintains common high tariffs on the importation of all agricultural commodities, both fresh and processed.

Some of the revenues collected in this scheme go to subsidize depressed areas. But 75% of them go to direct support of farmers. In 1977, $2 billion was distributed as bonus money to farmers, to raise their incomes so that they roughly approximated those of urban workers. Another $750 million was provided in other general assistance programmes.

The EEC example stands in direct contrast to Canada's agriculture and food policy. In Europe, economists and government officials have rejected the North American policy of "free enterprise and free trade" for the food and agriculture industry.

Instead, as a social policy, they have decided that it is valuable to have a highly populated, economically viable rural community, with farmers enjoying a standard of living roughly equivalent to other members of society. This cuts down on unwanted urban sprawl, unemployment, welfare, and other government costs. It encourages farming and food processing and enables the European Common Market to be a major exporter of food.

Readers who are familiar with the Ten Days for World Development programme know that food self-reliance is increasingly being advocated for the underdeveloped countries. These views have been popularized in North America by Frances Moore Lappe and Joseph Collins through their widely read book, *Food First: Beyond the Myth of Scarcity*.

It is their contention that almost every country in the world is capable of feeding its own people with the proper re-organization of the social system of food production and distribution. The food self-reliance policy, they note, "strikes at the heart of the Global Supermarket phenomenon," whereby the multinational food corporations and the political elites in both the advanced and underdeveloped countries determine what is grown in the poorer countries and who benefits. However, Lappe and Collins do not see any major conflict with the people of the advanced countries if they adopt a policy of self-reliance.

What chance is there for such a policy in Canada? It stands in direct conflict with the tradition of continental integration. It would mean that Canada would have to more or less close the borders in food and agriculture trade with the United States. The Canadian government would have to end control of the food economy by the large foreign-owned corporations.

Again, we can show that such a policy would be economically advantageous to Canada. It would increase production at the farm level and provide more employment and economic activity at the processing level. One thing Canada needs now rather desperately is jobs in the manufacturing sector.

But such a policy has been regularly rejected by our federal political parties as well as by our influential economists and government advisers. Furthermore, it would be a fundamental contradiction to try to isolate one sector of the economy from American domination while the other major sectors remained in their present state. The largest and most powerful business organizations in Canada, like the Canadian Manufacturers Association, the Canadian Chamber of Commerce, and the Canadian Bankers Association, have strongly opposed any move away from continentalism. We must recognize that these are the interests which are most powerful in our society, and which have the major influence on government policy.

But beyond the policy level, we should also recognize that for a long time Canada has been an advanced resource dependency of the United States. This historic fact cannot be reversed simply by electing a new federal government. A change would involve a major redirection for the whole destiny of Canada.

Food as a Public Utility

Don Mitchell, in his book *The Politics of Food*, puts forth another alternate consideration: food as a public utility. This concept was firmly rejected by the Liberal Government's Federal Task Force on Agriculture which reported in 1969. Its recommendations, based on the further expansion of corporate farming and corporate food production, was in line with Canada's trends and traditions.

The alternative by Mitchell is logical. Food is essential for human survival. High quality food is essential for good health. Advanced capitalist societies have accepted the principle that education and health are public utilities, available to all, in high quality, regardless of ability to pay. Food is obviously even more basic.

There is, of course, a major difference. Health and education was not dominated by the corporate sector of the economy. The food industry, though, is central to the economic and social structure of this country.

Nothing is more representative of the style of life of a country than the way it produces, distributes and eats food. When Mitchell calls for a drastic change in the structure of the food industry, he is, in reality, calling for a virtual social revolution.

In our country food is produced at every level according to the profit motive. The concept of providing food as a service, or on the basis of quality first, is in fundamental contradiction to the present system. Food is distributed according to ability to pay. If such a policy harms a large segment of our society, well, that is considered to be the price we pay for "freedom of choice."

I know that many people are concerned about the food industry in Canada. I am also. This conclusion is not meant to encourage Canadians to throw up their arms in despair and to sit back and get fat on junk food. But it must be recognized that power is reality. Any fundamental change in our socio-economic system will be brought about only after a long struggle, which must entail an unending commitment.

Canadian history is the story of many struggles by farmers, workers, and others to protect their interests against exploitation both by forces in Canada and external imperial forces. We should all be encouraged by the growing interest in Canada in the question of the quality of food we consume and the quality of life we now have. The indications are that the time is right for popular action.

SOURCES

Adams, Ian *et al. The Real Poverty Report*. Edmonton: M.G. Hurtig, 1971.

Anderson, Marvin S. "Income Tax Data and Farm Financial Statistics," *Canadian Journal of Agricultural Economics*, XXIII, No. 1, February 1975, pp. 41-51.

Canadian Agriculture in the Seventies. Report of the Federal Task Force on Agriculture. Ottawa: The Queen's Printer, 1970.

Davey, Brian H., and Zubair A. Hassan. "Farm and Off-Farm Incomes of Farm Families in Canada," *Canadian Farm Economics*, IX, No. 6, December 1974, pp. 16-23.

Dumont, Rene, and Bernard Rosier. *The Hungry Future*. London: Methuen & Co., 1969.

"Food, Poverty and Kids: The Human Cost of Living on 17 Cents a Meal," *This Magazine,* VII, No. 3, November 1975, pp. 9-11.

Furniss, I.F. "The Importance of Agriculture in the Canadian Economy," *Canadian Farm Economics,* IV, No. 4, October 1969, pp. 1-8.

Geno, Barbara J., and Larry M. Geno. *Food Production in the Canadian Environment*. Perceptions 3. Science Council of Canada. December 1976.

Gillespie, W. Irwin. *In Search of Robin Hood*. Toronto: C.D. Howe Institute, 1978.

Hightower, Jim. *Eat Your Heart Out: How Food Profiteers Victimize the Consumer*. N.Y.: Crown Publishers, 1975.

Karamchandani, D.T. "Trends in Food Consumption, Prices & Expenditures, 1961-1973," *Canadian Farm Economics,* XI, No. 1, February 1976, pp. 17-26.

Karamchandani, D.T. "Changes in Food Expenditures Patterns, 1969-1974," *Canadian Farm Economics,* XI, No. 5, October 1976, pp. 16-29.

Langman, A.H. "Farm Food Marketing Costs," *Canadian Farm Economics*, X, No. 5, October 1975, pp. 1-11.

Mitchell, Don. *The Politics of Food.* Toronto: James Lorimer & Co., 1975.

Moore, Pat. "Farm-Food Marketing Costs," *Canadian Farm Economics.* VII, No. 4, August 1973, pp. 26-32.

National Farmers Union. "Submission to the Tariff Board on the Subject of Reference No. 152, Fresh and Processed Fruits and Vegetables." Saskatoon: National Farmers Union, January 29, 1974.

Productivity in the Food Industry. Report of the U.S. National Commission on Productivity. Washington, D.C.: U.S. Government Printing Office, August 1973.

Special Senate Committee on Poverty. *Poverty in Canada.* Ottawa: Information Canada, 1971.

Spencer, Byron G. *A Preliminary Paper on Family Food Expenditure in Canada.* Ottawa: Food Prices Review Board, February 1976.

Stanbury, W.T. *Business Interests and the Reform of Canadian Competition Policy, 1971-1975.* Toronto: Carswell Methuen, 1977.

Statistics Canada. *Perspective Canada.* Ottawa: Information Canada, July 1974.

Statistics Canada. *Urban Family Food Expenditure, 1974.* Ottawa: Information Canada, 1974, Catalogue Number 63-543.

Warnock, John. "The Farm Crisis," in Laurier La Pierre *et al.* eds., *Essays on the Left: Essays in Honour to T.C. Douglas.* Toronto: McClelland & Stewart, 1971, pp. 121-133.